In the Names of

An Dagda, the All-Father, the First Priest,
King of the Tuatha Dé Danaan,
and of Bride, the Queen of All Arts,
and Mother of Bards, Healers, and Smiths,
and of All Other Divinities of Wisdom, Art,
& Science;

A Druidic Spell

is Hereby Placed upon All who Read these Words!

If

You should Steal this Book
or Borrow it and Return it Not
to its Rightful Owner,
Who is:

_____

Or If

You should Use this Book for any Rite or Spell
that would Injure or Enslave any Innocent Person
or Cause Harm to Our Holy Mother Earth,

Then Shall

All your Tools and Weapons Turn against you,
All Beauty and Joy Depart from your Life,
and All your Cunning Avail you Naught
Save Sorrow and Despair,
Till you have Made Full Restitution
for your Crime.

Ainbheartaigh fainicí!

BOOKS BY ISAAC BONEWITS

Real Magic

Authentic Thaumaturgy

Rites of Worship

The Pagan Man

Bonewits's Essential Guide to Witchcraft and Wicca

Isaac Bonewits, 2005

Photo by Ava Francesca

BONEWITS'S
Essential Guide
to Druidism

ISAAC BONEWITS

CITADEL PRESS
Kensington Publishing Corp.
www.kensingtonbooks.com

To Robert Larson, DAL, Be.
It's all your fault!

CITADEL PRESS BOOKS are published by

Kensington Publishing Corp.
850 Third Avenue
New York, NY 10022

Earlier versions of portions of this text have appeared in *The Druid Chronicles (Evolved)*, "The Druid Chronicler," "Pentalpha Journal & Druid Chronicler," "The Druids' Progress," and/or on the web site of *Ár nDraíocht Féin:* A Druid Fellowship at www.adf.org, or the author's own web site at www.neopagan.net.

All Kensington titles, imprints, and distributed lines are available at special quantity discounts for bulk purchases for sales promotions, premiums, fund-raising, educational, or institutional use. Special book excerpts or customized printings can also be created to fit specific needs. For details, write or phone the office of the Kensington special sales manager: Kensington Publishing Corp., 850 Third Avenue, New York, NY 10022, attn: Special Sales Department; phone: 1-800-221-2647.

CITADEL PRESS and the Citadel logo are Reg. U.S. Pat. & TM Off.

First printing: August 2006

10 9 8 7 6 5 4 3 2 1

Printed in the United States of America

Library of Congress Control Number: 2005938611

ISBN 0-8065-2710-2

Contents

Foreword

Some kinda druid dudes lifting the veil.
Doing the mind guerrilla,
Some call it magic—the search for the grail.
                              —John Lennon, *Mind Games*

I f you want a Druid dude to lift the veil on Druidism, you've
come to the right place. Isaac is like an eccentric and dedicated botanist who has decided in this book to recount his
view of the exotic jungle that is modern Druidism. He's well
placed to do this because he's been in the thick of it for some
time. In fact he's played a crucial role in its development in the
modern era.

Most people think that Druidism is an ancient religion—a
relic of the distant past. Others think it's a Victorian invention,
based on a few lines found in classical texts. They're both right,
but also wrong, because although Druidism did indeed origi-
nate way back in the past, and although it was "re-invented" in
the eighteenth and nineteenth centuries, much of Druidism as
it is practiced today really owes its origins to the very recent past
of the 1960s and 1980s.

Something very powerful happened in the sixties. A wave of
spiritual energy washed over the planet and influenced thousands, perhaps millions of people. One of its most important
effects was to inspire the hippies who rebelled against establishment values. The hippies believed that governments were often

corrupt, that war was inhumane, and that rampant consumerism and corporate greed were destroying the world. At the same time they had a vision of how the world could be and became fascinated by alternative approaches to the spiritual quest. Although most turned to India for inspiration, some turned to the lands of Eire and Albion—with their mysterious stone circles and ley lines—and their Druids.

John Michell wrote a cult classic, *The View over Atlantis,* which popularized these mysteries, and John Lennon sang about "druid dudes." Slap bang in the middle of the sixties while this spiritual wave was at its height, Druidism took on a new lease of life in both Britain and America. Up until then it had been an affair of fraternal associations or of Welsh, Cornish, or Breton cultural groups. But from the sixties onward a whole new kind of Druidry was born. It was environmentally aware, it focused on spiritual practice, and it appealed to young people.

In 1963, a new Druid movement, the RDNA, was born in America; it would act as the catalyst out of which future American Druidism would grow. A few months later, in 1964, Ross Nichols founded a new Druid group in Britain, the OBOD, which would become the largest Druid group in the world by the end of the century. Isaac was a member of the RDNA, and across the pond, I was a member of the OBOD.

Twenty years after the forming of these two very different groups Isaac and I both found ourselves becoming leaders of Druid movements that were to prove seminal in the creation of the new Druidry that has emerged over the last few decades. Isaac describes how he started the ADF in 1983 in the pages of this book. The way I got to be a Druid Chief was rather more protracted, but it began at about the same time. In 1984 I had an experience that changed my life. My old Druid teacher, Ross Nichols, who had died nine years previously, suddenly appeared to me one day and asked me to lead the order he had founded twenty years earlier. He told me many things that proceeded to come true, and asked me to prepare his teachings in the form of a distance learning course. I spent four years doing this until, in 1988, I was asked to become Chief, not by a being in the Otherworld this time, but by three beings from this solid mundane world.

For another twenty years the two streams of Druidism developed on either side of the Atlantic largely ignoring each other (although ADF and OBOD exchanged their publications with each other). ADF, and the groups and individuals who were influenced by it, treated Druidism as a Neopagan religion, and were particularly keen to shake off the influences of the Druidic Revival period of the eighteenth and nineteenth centuries. They were looking for roots, and like the related movement of Celtic Reconstructionism, they sought evidence of authentic ancient practices that could be revived. Meanwhile OBOD, and the groups and individuals it inspired, saw Druidry as a path of spiritual and personal development that could be followed by people of any religious persuasion or none. They had a more relaxed attitude to the Druidism of the Revival Period and to questions of historical authenticity—if they liked something and found it worked, it was in; if it didn't, it was out.

This state of affairs continued for about two decades until a couple of Americans defected. Gordon Cooper, co-founder of the Celtic Reconstruction movement, visited an OBOD summer camp, found he liked it, and started to change his understanding of modern Druid practice. The author John Michael Greer visited Britain too, then became Chief of the Ancient Druid Order in America. He has been busy ever since rehabilitating Revival Druidry—in particular with his latest book, *The Druidry Handbook*. In 2004 Gordon and John presented research papers in Oxford for OBOD's Mount Haemus Award, and you can read these on the OBOD website.

And now here comes Isaac's book, which talks about both kinds of Druidism—and the many other varieties too—with frankness and humor. It feels like we've come of age. Modern Druidry was seeded in those old hippy days, it got a boost twenty years later in the '80s, then another boost twenty years later as the two sides of the pond have started talking to each other. Events are moving fast! As fast, as the ADF motto goes, "as a speeding oak!" All good things take their time to develop organically, and that's what's occurring in Druidry.

What of the future? Isaac talks about his vision in the closing chapter of this book. He says, "Many people who grew up in the 1960s and '70s are discovering us at about the same time that they are realizing both the desperate state of our planet and the eternal relevance of our youthful ideals." Something magical happened when those youthful ideals, inspired to a great extent by the hippies, met Druidism during those de-

Photo by Glenn Capers

cades. With the benefit of hindsight, we can see that the hippies were right—they weren't just naive and doped up. The evidence is all around us. Forty years ago they warned us of the dangers of corporate greed, political corruption, rampant militarism, and the destruction of the environment. Now we can see that they were prophets in the true sense of the term. And I believe that part of Druidry's purpose in the world now could well be to redeem and develop their vision—as fast as a speeding oak!

—Philip Carr-Gomm
CHOSEN CHIEF, ORDER OF BARDS
OVATES & DRUIDS

Preface

So I'm sitting here looking at my library. It includes scores of Druidic, Celtic, and other Indo-European books and journals, back issues of Druidic publications, hundreds of letters and e-mails, all the essays I've written on these topics, and my interviews about them. It's all a little bit, shall we say, *intimidating.*

I've been trying to write this book since 1980, having gone through a variety of tentative titles: *A Druidic Handbook; Druidism Ancient and Modern; Everything You Always Wanted to Know About Druidism but Were Afraid to Ask; Druidism: A Concise Guide,* and finally this one, *Bonewits's Essential Guide to Druidism.* This last title, suggested by my first editor at Citadel Press, offers me a way out of my feelings of being overwhelmed with too much to say and not enough years in which to say it all, just as a similar one did with my witchcraft writings.

At the beginning, I wanted to write a book that would give readers the basics of what was known and conjectured about the Paleopagan Druids, screening out the nonsense and the hyperbole. I wanted to tell everyone everything they needed to know about this ancient path and its modern revivals so they could begin solitary or group practice with a solid grounding. Now, as I gaze upon a flood of Druidic, semi-Druidic, and completely pseudo-Druidic books on the market, including a few really good ones by my colleagues, I find myself quailing at the task.

I have long said that when I next updated my first book,

Real Magic, all I would need to illustrate the magical Law of Infinite Data (that there is an infinite amount of information in the multiverse) was one word: "Internet." Between the ocean of (good, bad, and just plain silly) information out there about ancient Indo-European cultures, the Celts, and the many varieties of Druids past and present, and the gigantic piles of current research by scholarly authors and mystical tomes by earth religionists, the task I set for myself in the 1970s is revealed as simply impossible.

I had a similar problem with my writings about witchcraft and Wicca. There, too, infinite data made it hard to focus on producing a book that would not be redundant. I began with an effort to be *concise* and wound up with *Bonewits's Essential Guide to Witchcraft and Wicca,* by concentrating on what were the most essential things for people to know. I didn't have to worry about trying to include everything that I could possibly say on the topic.

I was cheered by the knowledge that I could always do a second or even a third volume someday (or a really big update), and, in the meantime, I would have a work that people would find useful.

This same approach shaped my efforts in writing the book you now hold in your hands. It isn't everything I know about the history, beliefs, and practices of the Paleo-, Meso-, and Neopagan Druids. It's the most important *essentials* and the interesting insights (and hunches) that have occurred to me over the last forty years. This text will give anyone interested in studying druidism, druidry, or *draíocht* (see the Introduction for my working definitions of those terms), a good *start* and will offer experienced sickle-slingers new insights for making their druidic practice more fulfilling and effective.

So I'll save the really obsessive-compulsive details for future books and keep this one down to a size that the average reader can lift. Rather than repeat information that readers can find in a hundred other texts, I will refer them to books by authors whose work I have found trustworthy (and will warn them away from really awful ones). Instead of repeating the usual materials, I'll spend a great deal more time talking about the ancient Indo-European peoples than about their Celtic subset—even though it is the Celts whom most people instinctively associate with the Paleopagan Druids. Studying the Indo-Europeans is critical to understanding the Celts and the role of the clergy in both. As Jean Markale says in *The Druids: Celtic Priests of Nature*, "Any study of the druids must begin with a process of demystification." But don't worry, we'll get mystical again, sooner or later!

I will also include information about the history of Neopagan Druidism in the United States that has not been widely published, including my own career as an unindicted coconspirator in its evolution, embarrassing as that sometimes was. As I mentioned in *The Pagan Man*, illness wiped out many of my personal memories, but a lifelong habit of paper hoarding has enabled me to reconstruct many of the most important events.

Within these pages you will find a discussion of the beliefs and practices of the Order of Bards Ovates & Druids, the Reformed Druids of North America, *Ár nDraíocht Féin: A Druid Fellowship* (ADF), and the Henge of Keltria, as well as rituals from each of these major druid organizations. I also include a discussion of druidic divination and magic, a few druidical spells, and some hymns and chants to various, mostly Celtic, deities.

Acknowledgments

This book would have been impossible (or at least a great deal more implausible) without the writings of many scholars, including: Georges Dumézil, Proinsias MacCana, Nora Chadwick, Peter Berresford Ellis, Ronald Hutton, C. Scott Littleton, Alwyn and Brinley Rees, Brian Smith, Bruce Lincoln, Patricia Monaghan, Miranda Green, and others, none of whom should be blamed for the conclusions I have drawn from their works— especially since the still-living ones will probably be shocked and/or amused by them.

Also important were the writings and personal communications of many modern Druids and Pagan Reconstructionists, including: Ian Corrigan, Philip Carr-Gomm, Skip Ellison, John Michael Greer, Bob Larson, Searles O'Dubhain, Michael Scharding, Cel Sesith and others too numerous to mention.

My Biases*

Most authors never tell their readers what their personal religious, scholarly, philosophical, or political biases are, but I think it's something readers should know. My religious background as a Neopagan writer, teacher, and priest is rooted in my studies of Druidism, Wicca/Witchcraft, and Asatru (or Norse Paganism), as well as my experiences in Voodoo and Santeria. My opinions have been heavily influenced by folkloric and anthropological studies in world religions, modern occult and parapsychological research, and my participation in the evolution of the American Neopagan movement.† Unlike many other Pagan authors, I've been an opponent of imperial neogarmentism from the beginning of my career, so I have no problem calling things as I see them. I also feel no obligation to justify Paganism or my opinions about it in terms that will please members of hostile belief systems, so some readers may decide that I am biased against those hostile belief systems.

For those wondering about my Druidic biases, I will mention that I am a Third Order Druid priest in the Reformed Druids of North America, a Third Degree Druid in the United Ancient Order of Druids, an ordained Druid priest (and the founder) of *Ár nDraíocht Féin:* A Druid Fellowship, and a subscribing member of the Henge of Keltria and the Order of Bards Ovates & Druids. From the RDNA's "Zen Unitarian-

---

*Those who previously read this section and the following one in *Bonewits's Essential Guide to Witchcraft and Wicca* are free to skip them here.
†See Margot Adler's *Drawing Down the Moon* and Rosemary Ellen Guiley's entry on me in her *Encyclopedia of Witches and Witchcraft* for details.

ism" to UAOD's Mesopagan/fraternal style to ADF's assert-ively Neopagan approach, I feel that I am familiar enough with all the currently existing varieties of Druidism to be able to dis-cuss them fairly. I also can distinguish between their legitimate differences about realizing the druidic ideals that inspire us all and those rare pseudo-druidic groups that seem to exist only to bamboozle people into believing utter nonsense and/or cough-ing up money and power to unaccountable leaders.

My scholarly and philosophical biases are those of an *ama-teur* scholar who respects the basic principles of Western science and scholarship and the ideals of the Enlightenment, while rec-ognizing their dualistic and scientistic biases and limitations. Painful as it may sometimes be, when new information comes into the world of academia from legitimate research, I can and will change my mind and what I teach to match the new data. Fortunately, as Neopagans we are not bound to fossilized words of ancient scriptures nor the writings of old dead men. We are free to adapt and evolve our religions to match what we learn from science and scholarship, a freedom that modern druids of most varieties are seemingly happy to exercise.

As for my political biases, I'm a capital "L" Liberal and a card-carrying member of both the American Civil Liberties Union and the Green Party. So now the reader can filter what I have to say through particular screens, based on her or his own biases!

Unusual Word Usages in This Book

I try to avoid offending anyone accidentally and I dislike lan-guage customs that oversimplify matters that are complex or that conceal hidden or unverified assumptions. So I've gotten in the habit over the years of using terms such as "and/or" and "his/her." These read somewhat clumsily to most current En-glish speakers, as do various nonsexist terms such as "chairper-son" or "clergyperson," yet these usages are actually more precise than the older ones, since they don't carry the excess baggage of hidden implications (to many people, a word like "clergyman," for example, implies that only men can be clergy).

Those slash marks, as well as parentheses, come in quite handy when discussing ambiguous topics (a frequent need in books that deal with magic and religion). For example, "god/dess" means a deity who can be thought of in terms of either or both genders, "priest/ess" can mean a priest and/or a priestess, depending on the situation, and so on. Once you've seen a few of these, the rest will be easy to figure out from their context.

Perhaps more annoying to English language purists is my occasional use of "they," "them," and "their" when discussing individuals of deliberately unspecified gender. Sometimes we also need the plural/singular distinction kept vague, and parentheses work well with ambiguous pronouns for this, as in the sentence, "You should practice with your working partner(s), otherwise they may not understand what they are supposed to do." Such usages are now quite common in idiomatic American English precisely because the common people (if not the grammarians) have learned that ambiguous terms are often useful. The context should make clear which of several meanings are appropriate for the reader to understand.

Since this book was written simultaneously with several others, I've had to divide related materials between them. These books and earlier ones will therefore be frequently referenced in each other's pages, though I try to make each work capable of standing on its own.

Most of the time, I use italic text the first time I define a term and quote marks when referring to the word as a word later. I also use italics for foreign words, emphasis, the names of books and periodicals, and so on. See Appendix D for suggestions on how to pronounce the various Irish Gaelic names and terms I'll be using from time to time.

For those who might not be familiar with them, I should point out some calendrical abbreviations. "YA" means "years ago," which is roughly equivalent to "BP" or "before the pres-

ent time,"* used by some scholars. "CE" and "BCE" mean
"Common Era" and "Before the Common Era," respectively,
which the world's five billion non-Christians prefer to the AD
and BC with which most Westerners are familiar. I'll be using
SMALL CAPS for all those abbreviations throughout the book.

Those of you who have spent a lot of time at my Web site,
www.neopagan.net, will no doubt recognize many paragraphs
here and there. I've spent decades writing and polishing some
of this material. Now that it is finally appearing in book form, I
haven't seen much of a need to inflate materials that I've previously made clear and succinct just so everything will sound new.
I have tried hard to make it all flow smoothly. I've also included
a number of new bits of interest even to longtime fans, so please
bear with me and enjoy the tour.

*"BP" really means before 1950 CE.

Introduction

"We will worship with the druids.
They drink strange, fermented fluids,
Then run naked through the wuids,
*So they're good enough for me!"**

Were the people originally called "druids" Celtic shamans traveling to the Otherworld on behalf of their tribes? Were they con artists exploiting the ignorance of the masses for their own profit? Were they wise philosophers who pretended to believe in magic and many deities? Did they do this for the sake of those unable to attain the sublime heights of monotheism? Were they mystics, poets, and artists wandering in the wildernesses of northwestern Europe? Were they a whole class of intellectuals and artists, serving their communities by preserving knowledge from one generation to the next? Did they build Stonehenge, other stone circles, even the pyramids of Egypt? Did they come from Atlantis or India or the shores of the Black Sea? Were the druids unique or did they have colleagues in other cultures performing similar tasks?

Who are they now? Are they neo-shamanic, crystal waving, soul travelers? Bloodthirsty fanatics sacrificing virgins in stone circles? Aging Freemasons standing around in Egyptian head-

*From the Pagan version of "Old Time Religion." The author of this particular one of the 12,357 verses is not known.

gear giving speeches to one another? Environmental activists and tree huggers? Artists, poets, and musicians? Magicians, healers, and counselors? Or are they priests and priestesses of new old religions?

A primary purpose of this book is to help the reader understand who all these people were, or weren't, or might have been, or are, or are not right now, or might be someday. Before we begin, however, let me define a few terms that the average reader may not already know.

Druidism, Druidry, and *Draíocht*

The three terms "druidism," "druidry," and *draíocht* are often used interchangeably by modern Druids (and druids), with overlapping definitions. As I will use them in this book, however, "druidism" refers to the original activities of the people called "druids" (with a small "d") way back when they were an entire social class of intellectuals among the Celtic peoples (with direct analogues in the other Indo-European cultures). It is also applicable to modern people and groups who call themselves Druids—mostly Neopagans who, as a religion, get that big "D" when referred to as such*—and who prefer to focus on the religious aspects of serving a community. Many Meso- and some Neopagan Druids use it to refer to philosophical systems ("isms") held to by ancient or modern Druids.

"Druidry" can be thought of as "what druids do," in the sense that artistry is what artists do and carpentry is what carpenters do, and so on. To these folks, being a druid is more a matter of creative arts, nature mysticism, and/or fraternal activities than a religion of any sort. Confusingly, the Irish term *draíocht* (or sometimes *draoidheacht*) is used by Celtic Pagans today to refer to a distinct style of magical and psychic activity

---

*Yes, the decision to put a lowercase "d" or a capital one can get tricky. Mostly I'll use "D" to refer to the categories of Paleo-, Meso-, and Neopagan Druids, as well as to individuals who consider themselves to be members of a religion or philosophy called "Druidism" and "d" for everyone else. When quoting others, I'll honor their preferences.

infused with poetry, song, and other performance arts—yet, in Modern Irish, the *-ocht* or *-eacht* endings are used to translate the English "-ry" ending!

In Irish the term *draoi* or *draoidh* originally referred to the members of the intellectual class, as we will see. In Modern Irish it can mean a druid, wizard, magician, diviner, or trickster. *Druid* was originally the plural form of *draoi*, but in Modern Irish *druid* refers to a small bird (starling or wren), and is also a verb-root meaning "to close" or "draw near"—a suitable concept to associate with people who were capable of opening or closing the "Gates Between the Worlds" (see Chapter 17).

Draíocht in Modern Irish can mean druidic arts, druidism, or (both stage and real) magic in general, and *draíochta* means magical spells and charms.

Those who consider themselves "purists" (and a few racists here and there) will insist that the word "druid" can only be applied to people in religious, magical, or social leadership roles within ancient Celtic cultures, usually tightly defined to mean people who speak or spoke languages called "Celtic" by linguists (see Chapter 4). Many of these purists will also insist that only people with Celtic ancestry can become druids today. All the other modern druids just laugh at them, or simply ignore them, for reasons which should become clear to the reader by the time she or he is finished with this work.

Throughout this book we will be exploring druidism, druidry, and *draíocht*—three branches of a single great tree (an oak, naturally). In Parts One through Three we will look at the various sorts of people who have been called (or who called themselves) "druids" over the last 2,500 years, in a more or less historical order. Part Four will give a description of some disreputable sorts who have claimed the name of "druid" in recent years. Parts Five through Seven will discuss the beliefs, practices, and rituals of modern Mesopagan and Neopagan Druids, with occasional looks back to the ancient ones. Part Eight will provide some conclusions and a glimpse into the possible future of druidism, druidry, and *draíocht* in the twenty-first century.

By the way, if you are unfamiliar with the terms "Paleo-,

Meso-, Neo-, or Reconstructionist Paganism," you might want to skip to the back of the book to read Appendix 2. Go ahead, I'll wait for you . . .

The single most quoted classical reference to the Paleopagan Druids comes from Pliny's *Natural History,* published in 77 CE. I'll stray once here from my determination not to repeat information found in most other druid books by presenting Philip Freeman's translation* of it, because it will connect to several discussions throughout this book:

> I can't forget to mention the admiration the Gauls have for mistletoe. The Druids (which is the name of their holy men) hold nothing more sacred than this plant and the tree on which it grows—as if it grew only on oaks. They worship only in oak groves and will perform no sacred rites unless a branch of that tree is present. It seems the Druids even get their name from *drus* (the Greek word for oak). And indeed they think that anything which grows on an oak tree is sent from above and is a sign that the tree was selected by the god himself. The problem is that in fact mistletoe rarely grows on oak trees. Still they search it out with great diligence and then will cut it only on the sixth day of the moon's cycle, because the moon is then growing in power but is not yet halfway through its course (they use the moon to measure not only months but years and their grand cycle of thirty years). In their language they call mistletoe a name meaning "all-healing." They hold sacrifices and sacred meals under oak trees, first leading forward two white bulls with horns bound for the first time. A priest dressed in white then climbs the tree and cuts the mistletoe with a golden sickle, with the plant dropping onto a white cloak. They then sacrifice the bulls while praying that the god will favorably grant his own gift to those to whom he has given it. They believe a drink made with mistletoe will restore fertility to barren live-

*In *War, Women, and Druids,* University of Texas Press, 2002.

stock and act as a remedy to all poisons. Such is the devotion to frivolous affairs shown by many peoples.

As one who has devoted his life to such "frivolous affairs," I
find this passage alternately fascinating and amusing. By the
time this book is over, the reader will be able to determine for
him or herself just how much of Pliny's text can be believed and
why.

But before we get to the druids themselves, we will have to
look at some of their very, *very* distant ancestors. All of the following history and prehistory will set the stage for the eventual
arrival of the ancient druids.

PART ONE

◎

The Paleopagan
Druids

I

A Long, Long Time Ago

The Evolving Picture of Human Origins

Human beings have been around for anywhere from two to several million years, depending on where you prefer to draw the species lines. In 2006, the picture of hominid (humanlike) evolution looks roughly like this (ignoring the dead ends of extinct cousins):

Thirteen million years ago (YA), in Africa, what would become our genus split off from the line that would produce orangutans, a few million years later from the one that would produce gorillas. Five million YA it split from the common ancestor to us and the chimpanzees. *Homo habilis* and *Homo rudolfensis* show up in the fossil record about 2.25 million YA, having apparently split off from *Australopithecus africanus* or some unknown offshoot 250,000 years earlier. *Homo ergaster* splits from *rudolfensis* around 1.8 million YA, giving rise to *Homo erectus* about 1.3 million YA and, separately, to *Homo something-or-otherensis** around one million YA. Around 700,000 YA, this unknown variety of hominid evolved into *Homo heidelbergensis,*† which then gave rise to *Homo neanderthalensis* about 350,000 YA and *Homo sapiens* roughly

---

*The fossils for this one haven't been discovered and/or named yet, but wait a minute and they will be. The so-called "gaps" in the fossil record for human evolution are getting fewer and smaller as time goes by.

†"Fencing Man."

150–120,000 YA. Alas, all the other hominids have disappeared, although *Homo erectus* lasted halfway through the *neanderthalensis* period and the latter two thirds of the way through our own species' adventures.

About 99.999 percent of the available genetic and archeological evidence available indicates clearly that humans evolved out of older African species, diverging from our more simian cousins and earlier models of pre-humans. It also indicates that early, middle, and modern hominids may have come out of Africa many times, each successive wave of migration prospering or faltering, depending upon each species' ability to adapt to changing climatic and other environmental conditions, until about 100–90,000 YA. At that point some members of *Homo sapiens* moved into southern Africa, while others went north to Egypt and the "Fertile Crescent" of what we now call the Middle East, and from there to the rest of the world in multiple waves of migration at widely separated intervals—southern Asia and India 80,000 YA; east Asia 60,000 YA; Europe 50,000 YA; Australia 40,000 YA; northern Asia 30–25,000 YA; and the Americas 22–12,000 YA (from several directions).

The linguistic research and reconstruction work done by Merritt Ruhlen, the author of the groundbreaking *The Origin of Language,* maps almost perfectly onto the genetic atlas created by Luigi Luca Cavalli-Sforza, author of *Genes, Peoples, and Languages,* showing clearly that all modern languages stem from one original language spoken in Africa all those tens of thousands of years ago. This split into multiple language families as people (and their genes) spread out over the earth. What does this have to do with druids? Eventually, quite a bit, but it will take us a few pages to get there.

Archeologists divide the periods of human evolution into blocks of thousands or even tens of thousands of years, which they call "ages," usually based on technological advances. *Homo habilus* started up the Paleolithic or Old Stone Age, by first using (very) primitive stone tools. *Homo erectus, ergaster, heidelbergensis, neanderthalensis,* and *sapiens* gradually improved their stone technology, bringing on the Mesolithic (Middle Stone) and Neolithic (New Stone) Ages. These were eventually followed by the Copper Age, the Bronze Age, and the Iron Age in various times and places, but usually in that order.*

Stone Circles and Megaliths

When Stone Age peoples entered what we now call Europe, whatever wasn't covered with trees was covered with ice. *Homo heidelbergensis* got there first, around 500–700,000 YA, followed by the Neanderthals around 200–250,000 YA, and the Cro-Magnons (early *Homo sapiens*), about 60,000 YA, who took over Europe below the ice line after 20,000 years or so. Whether they exterminated the Neanderthals or the latter just couldn't handle the changing temperatures as the last Ice Age came (around 25,000 YA) and went (10–12,000 YA), or a new disease wiped them out is simply unknown. Genetic researchers have shown that they did not disappear through intermarriage with the Cro-Magnons, since none of us today seem to have any specifically Neanderthal genes in our bodies.

As the ice receded, mesolithic humans moved from the shores of the Mediterranean into central, western, and northern Europe (and everywhere else they could get to). They belonged to what archeologists and anthropologists call "hunter-gatherer" cultures, since they lived by gathering what edible leaves, roots, berries, and fruit they could find, supplemented by meat when they found it already dead or they managed to kill something (or someone). Agriculture hadn't been invented yet, so their cultures and technology remained simple (if not stagnant) for thousands of years. Nonetheless, they did manage to drive almost all the giant mammals then wandering Europe, Asia, and North America into extinction.

Hunter-gatherer cultures seldom become sophisticated and complex unless they are lucky enough to live in exceptionally rich environments (such as the Pacific Northwest of the Ameri-

*These metallically named ages should not be confused with so-called "golden" ages, which generally exist only in the imagination.

cas). It is the invention of herding and/or agriculture that creates enough food for some members of the tribe to be able to stop hunting and gathering. By doing so they can become specialists in particular professions, such as clergy, blacksmiths, warriors, healers, and so on. In most hunter-gatherer cultures, almost everyone does almost everything, though there may be a gender distinction between who hunts (usually the males) and who gathers (usually the females and small children). Tribal magicians, such as the shamans among Asiatic and Native American peoples, may be recognized as having special skills, but even they usually hunt and/or gather with the others most of the time. Such cultures may also be more egalitarian between the genders and among individuals than agricultural or pastoral/herding ones are, but we have no historical evidence of any of them being matriarchal in the sense of being run by women. We also have no verification of their being particularly pacifistic, despite the efforts of feminist authors to claim such during the 1980s and '90s—which is why authors pushing those ideas had to keep redefining their terms to match the facts.*

It was neolithic peoples, practitioners of the earliest forms of agriculture (horticulture) who apparently created all of the huge stone circles and stone-covered tombs that appear along the Atlantic coast of Europe and Northern Africa. Why did they do it and how did they manage to spare the time and person-power to build them?

It seems fairly logical to us today (with all the philosophical dangers that phrase implies) that most, if not all, of the stone circles were used for rituals of some sort. Some of them may have been designed to function as huge calendars, providing sighting lines to observe such events as the sun's furthest apparent motion north or south (and thus the summer and winter solstices, respectively) and the halfway points between (the equinoxes), information that custom could relate to hunting and fishing seasons or the times to move the tribe from one part

*See my discussions of shamanism and matriarchy in *Bonewits's Essential Guide to Witchcraft and Wicca* for details on these topics.

of its territory to another. It's also possible that the examples we have of megalithic ("big rock") circles being torn down and remodeled, as at Stonehenge, represent sites where particular customary activities stopped being necessary to schedule in the old way and were replaced by new activities that required different timing.

I can hear it now: "Well, we've been going out after great ukluks every spring for many generations, but we haven't found any for the last twenty years. I guess it really doesn't matter much when the first full moon after the spring equinox happens. Dang!"

And five hundred years later, someone notices that the herds of grotz seem to pass through a nearby valley every year during the second dark moon after the summer solstice. "You know, the old folks say that people used to use them big rocks over there to plan their hunting. I wonder, if we maybe moved that brown one there over a few feet if it would line up with something useful . . . "

A thousand years later, when planting and harvesting becomes important, yet more stones get moved around to help with timing those critical activities.

Of course, this leaves the question of where all the people-power came from to move giant rocks around. I'll hazard a guess that the environment along the Atlantic coast was rich enough for long enough so that people could manage to feed and clothe themselves with time to spare. They could accomplish major long-term religious, political, or economic building projects. It would be interesting to correlate paleo-ecological and paleo-climatological data with the archeological evidence of megalithic construction periods to see if they match up in any interesting ways.

I should also point out that at least one person, a retired carpenter named W. T. Wallington, has a Web site* showing how he figured out ways to move gigantic objects, including fifteen-ton barns, three-ton concrete blocks and stones, and so on,

*At www.theforgottentechnology.com.

with extremely simple tools that neolithic farmers could have easily created and used—making megalithic construction far easier and less people-intensive than has been believed by archeologists. Says Wallington:

> I found that I, working alone, could easily move a 2,400 lb. block 300 ft. per hour with little effort, and a 10,000 lb. block at 70 ft. per hour. I also stood two 8 ft. 2,400 lb. blocks on end and placed another 2,400 lb. block on top. This took about two hours per block. I found that one man, working by himself, without the use of wheels, rollers, pulleys, or any type of hoisting equipment could perform the task. . . . I have began to build a replica of Stonehenge with eight 10-ton blocks on end and 2 ton blocks on top. One man, no wheels, no rollers, no ropes, no hoist or power equipment, using only sticks and stones. In the future, either myself, sons, or grandsons will be able to show this and other forms of "The Forgotten Technology" to the world. I believe that I have learned to use the laws of physics to my advantage.

So a few levers and a clever balancing of gravity against gravity can accomplish a great deal. Perhaps hordes of sweating men pulling gigantic stones on rollers or sleds weren't actually necessary. Small groups, obsessed with a given project, could have produced megalithic monuments over the course of only a few years. In fact, one group of obsessed (excuse me, "inspired") Neopagans has done just that, although with ropes, rollers, levers, and a little concrete.

The Stones Rising project of Four Quarters Farm has been building a megalithic stone circle on a hilltop in southeastern Pennsylvania for the last ten years, with twenty-five stones raised so far. Orren Whiddon, the Chief Coconspirator, says:

> In comparison to the Megalithic Monuments built by our ancient forebears, the Circle of Standing Stones at Four

Quarters is a small undertaking. A 200 foot by 160 foot ellipse requiring perhaps one hundred separate slabs and at least twenty years to build, the Circle seems a very large project to those of us who have taken up its completion. And it does require a very real commitment. But when we think of the level of commitment from the tribes that built the Megalithic Monuments that are our common heritage, our own commitment pales in comparison.

And here lies a lesson and perhaps the real meaning behind the Megalithic Impulse. To build these monuments requires a very real commitment that must extend over time and be communicated to others, so the work can be carried on. And it is this shared commitment that imbues these structures with meaning and magic, and causes them to speak a language all can understand, even thousands of years after their creation.

It is worth taking a moment to think of the lives and times of the Neolithic agrarian peoples of Europe who constructed the monuments that we are most familiar with. Their lives, tied as they were to the cycles of the seasons and the wheel of the year, could not have been as physically easy as are ours. And yet they were able to find the time in their lives to carry through the ceremonial commitments made by their own forbears, continuing the creation of these monuments and passing these commitments into the lives of their descendants. A continuity of ceremonial intent shared through many generations resulted in the Avebury Complex, Stonehenge, the Carnac Alignments and countless others. It is sobering to compare the spiritual dedication of our own lives and times to the people who made these gifts that have come down to us through the millennia.

In our own time the physical works of Humankind dwarf anything created by the Ancients. We have harnessed the liquid energy accumulated over millions of years within the body of the Earth, we have woven a web of quantified information that spans the planet. In fact, we in the West live as Gods returned to Earth, but have we lost their wisdom?

If the physical fact of a Circle of Stones standing upright were important, this would be child's play to achieve. It would simply be a matter of money and a few days' application of the technical magic that defines our culture.* But the physical fact is not the message here. Rather it is the context within which these monuments are created: a personal commitment of Sacrifice, Ceremony and Celebration made by many people.

So we have set upon ourselves the task of creating this Circle of Standing Stones, this Sanctuary of Earth Religion. And we do so in the old way. Realizing that the process, not the physical medium, is the message and the magic. And in so doing, we transform ourselves.†

Perhaps it should not be such a surprise that the most famous stone circle in the world, Stonehenge, was built, torn down, and rebuilt several times over a period of 2,000–3,000 years. Only the very last remodeling job was done in a way that connects it even tenuously with the druids who have long been credited with designing and building the entire monument. Archeologists, however, have found evidence of ritual activities having taken place there during the Iron Age, which would have been when the druids were there. So they could have *used* it even if they didn't build it. Nonetheless, all the (nonmodern) stone circles and other megalithic construction projects appear to predate the druids' arrival in western Europe by many centuries (not to mention the pyramids of Egypt). We will, however, visit Stonehenge a few more times before this book is done, since it has certainly played an important role in the history of Mesopagan and Neopagan Druidism.

*As was actually done by the members of Sonoran Sunrise Grove, ADF in Arizona! You can see photos of this at www.ssg-adf.org/circle.htm.
† From "The Standing Stones," © 1999 by Orren Whiddon, at www.4qf.org/_StoneCircle/_history.htm

I should note that many modern Druids, especially the Mesopagan ones, are fascinated with Stonehenge, other circles of standing stones, and the supposed "ley lines" of psychic energy they mark out upon the Earth's surface.* This is not an area of my expertise, though it is one I confess a certain skepticism over. Let's move from the Neolithic Age to the Copper Age and meet the Indo-Europeans.

Mother and Daughter Tongues

Around 10,000 YA, people living in the Fertile Crescent of what would become the Middle East and speaking an Afro-Asiatic language invented horticulture—animal husbandry and plant cultivation without the use of plows (using digging sticks and hoes instead). As their population increased, some of them stayed where they were, some moved into (probably) Anatolia, and some moved into southern Central Asia. These groups became the linguistic and genetic ancestors of what would become the Semitic, Indo-European, and Asiatic languages and cultures, respectively, which then spread out over the rest of the planet. Meantime, the other *Homo sapiens* who hadn't left Africa created scores of sub-Saharan cultures and languages, which evolved on their own and occasionally migrated across the oceans to nearby islands.

Around 7,000 YA, the folks who were farming in (probably) Anatolia began to migrate in search of fresh soil to farm. There were several waves of migration as people with stone, copper, and then bronze tools and weapons spread across much of the ancient world, conquering and/or intermarrying first with the neolithic tribes they met, then (in later waves) with the descendents of previous waves of their cousins.

---

*Terry Pratchett, author of the occultly profound (and very silly) *Discworld* novels, mentions in an interview posted at www.scifi.com, that "They say that all the pubs on the Mendip [Hills in southwest England] are connected by straight lines. What they mean is that they probably aren't officially, but you just set out across the fields and walk through the fences and things, because the [hard] cider does very strange things to your brain." I'm sure Neolithic peoples discovered cider early on . . .

Ruhlen, in *The Origin of Language: Tracing the Evolution of the Mother Tongue,* takes his readers by the hand and allows them to discover through performing linguistic exercises how the languages most westerners speak today all grew out of earlier tongues, going all the way back through the Middle East to Africa. Controversial as his theories have been among academic Indo-Europeanists, who prefer to believe that their beloved languages can't be traced any further back than 6,000 years ago—and certainly not to shared Afro-Asiatic origins!—his approaches have been duplicated by other, younger linguists, and match almost completely with the data from an academically unrelated discipline, that of human genetics. When different sciences converge on an idea from separate directions, the odds get pretty high that the idea is a good one.

But let's leave aside the older Afro-Asiatic tongues and concentrate our attention now on the *comparatively* uncontroversial topic of the Indo-European language family and its many ancient cultures. This will prove a crucial step in our efforts to understand who the Paleopagan Druids were and what they did.

On February 2, 1786, a British graduate of Oxford and supreme court judge in India named Sir William Jones (1746–1794), who had added Sanskrit to the many languages he already spoke, gave a speech to the Asiatic Society in Calcutta, in which he said:

> The Sanskrit language, whatever be its antiquity, is of a wonderful structure; more perfect than the Greek, more copious than the Latin, and more exquisitely refined than either, yet bearing to both of them a stronger affinity, both in the roots of verbs and in the forms of grammar, than could possibly have been produced by accident; so strong, indeed, that no philologer ["lover of words"] could examine them all three, without believing them to have sprung from some common source, which, perhaps, no longer exists.*

---

*Quoted in "Indo-European and the Indo-Europeans," an introductory essay by Calvert Watkins in his *The American Heritage Dictionary of Indo-European Roots, 2nd Edition.*

This insight was to inspire what would eventually become the modern science of linguistics and make etymology (the study of word origins) increasingly scholarly and scientific. Over the course of the nineteenth and twentieth centuries, linguists were able to thoroughly prove that languages come in "families" composed of "mother tongues" and the "daughter tongues" descended from them. They did this by comparing closely similar modern languages to each other as well as to known precursor languages (such as Old English or Old French) to "reconstruct" earlier or "Proto-" versions of major branches on the linguistic family tree. These families in turn proved to be parts of "super families" of even older languages. The super family that Sir William suspected stretched from India to Ireland and from Italy to Sweden is now called the "Indo-European" language family. Eventually, scholars began to reconstruct what they called "Proto-Indo-European" (PIE) as the hypothetical language at the root of all the IE tongues. Many mistakes were made by many scholars, but eventually the outlines of PIE's grammar, syntax, and vocabulary became known.

The "Indo-European" languages were called the "Indo-Aryan" ones for a while, until the Nazis made "Aryan" a dirty word in the 1930s. Originally, *Aryas* meant "shining ones" or "noble ones," the term that the eventual rulers of India called themselves in the *Vedas*. The later rulers of what became known as Celtic territories called themselves *Gaels*, which meant "shining/noble ones" as well (or possibly "upper classes"). As we shall see, such terminology is in keeping with the central role that light in general and fire in particular played in Indo-European Paleopaganism.

German scholar Friedrich Max Müller (1823–1900), who translated many, many books on Eastern religions (albeit with a creedist slant), is credited with coining the term "Aryan" in the 1850s, originally with reference to the race and language of the allegedly "barbaric" invaders of India from the west (see below). In 1870, he was using "Aryan" to refer to the "highest" race of humans. His racism and creedism are revealed far more by his private letters than his published works, but sometimes were obvious. By 1888, however, he was backpedaling furiously, insisting that it was a purely linguistic term, but the damage had been done—the term was picked by German nationalists to support their fantasies of an "Aryan master race." This tied into the incredible racism and creedism that other western scholars had shown towards India and its Paleopagan religions almost from their first "discovery" of it.

The negative reaction of non-Nazi linguists to the Nazi's "blood and soil" obsession and the atrocities generated by it, led to a well-meaning but dualist insistence that language families and genetic backgrounds had nothing to do with each other. This doctrine was dealt a fatal blow when the congruence of Ruhlen's and Cavalli-Sforza's research results showed that there was indeed a connection, even though it was a statistical rather than an absolute one. After all, people who speak the same language tend to wind up breeding with one another and producing offspring.

However, let us see what peoples, speaking what languages, wound up creating the Indo-European speaking cultures and their religions.

The Traveling Peoples

Around 8000–7500 YA (or 6000–5500 BCE), the tribes that would speak the mother tongue that linguists today call Proto-Indo-European migrated away from their former homeland in the Fertile Crescent and moved to a new one, which was *probably* in Anatolia (modern Turkey). Why do I keep saying "probably"? Because if you research the topic of geographic origins for the Indo-European languages, you will find that some researchers believe the PIE homeland was on the north shores of the Black Sea (modern Russia and the Ukraine); some that it was on the eastern shores (Armenia); some that it was on the southern shores (Turkey); and some in India!

I find Ruhlen's arguments for Anatolia the most compelling, but I suspect that the Proto-Indo-Europeans might have lived all around the shores of the comparatively small freshwater lake that was then in the center of the area now known as the Black Sea. This PIE culture could have been there for 500–1,000 years before the melting glaciers to the far north raised the world-wide sea levels high enough so that the Mediterranean broke through the thin mountain ridge that we now call the Strait of Bosporus. This occurence led to a catastrophic flood of Biblical proportions* for the locals around 7000 YA. The inhabitants would have fled to higher ground around the edges of what became a new salt sea. Centuries later further migrations began when the population density grew too high—though some might have just kept going away from the original disaster, bringing neolithic horticulture to Europe. Such a theory might reconcile the evidence that has been put forward over the years concerning the various shores of the Black Sea as having been the PIE homeland and the conflicting times offered for the various migrations. Over the millennia the population must have increased several times in this PIE homeland, so that tribes would migrate every few centuries. There may have been several successive waves of migration bringing agriculture and Copper Age technology to Europe and Asia, but we have little linguistic evidence of them.

Whether they started out in Anatolia, or had passed through it on their way to the lost lake, then migrated back south again to get away from the flood, one group of PIE speakers eventually created the "Anatolian" family of languages. These included Hittite, Luvian, and Lydian, which were spoken in the lands we call Turkey and Syria.

Around 2000 BCE, some of the PIE tribes went south and east, founding the "Indo-Iranian" language and culture, which spread over large parts of western and central Asia, eventually producing such daughter languages as Old Persian, Kurdish, Avestan, and Bactrian.

Most Indo-European linguists believe that during the sec-

---

*Literally. There are some scholars who believe that this flood was the origin of the Mesopotamian and later Canaanite myths about a "universal" flood, and hence the familiar Biblical tale of Noah.

ond millennia BCE one of the Indo-Iranian groups (probably the ones speaking Avestan, I would guess) had a big polytheological split* and divided into the Iranian speakers and those who would become the Indic language cultures (the ones who called themselves the *Aryas* and who spoke Sanskrit). The latter folk moved into what is now called the Indian Subcontinent and birthed the languages called Urdu, Hindi, and so forth.

I should point out, however, that many Indian scholars insist the Indo-European languages and their associated cultures all started in India and went west from there. I suppose that would have been possible if the Afro-Asiatic speakers of 9000 YA had gone directly across southern Asia and into India, then many years later PIE speakers (having developed in India) had gone west to Iran and Anatolia, with those staying behind developing Sanskrit. I don't think this matches very well with either current Indo-European linguistic theories or the genetic migrations research, but those may change over the next few decades. Certainly, such an Indo-centric theory does fit better with a great deal of evidence that shows PIE cultural elements in India long before the western theories can account for them,† and multiple references in the *Vedas* to the Sarasvati River flowing, even though it dried up between 3000 and 1900 BCE. This loss of a major river may have sparked migrations from the area, just about the time the Iranian culture was supposedly being established.‡

Around 1600–1700 BCE another group of PIE speakers wound up living on the land between the Black Sea and the Caspian. They became known as the Armenians. Around 1400–1500 BCE, some went west to the Balkans and became known as the Greeks; their language is called Hellenic. At sometime before 700 BCE, PIE speakers who went further west established the Italic languages and cultures, including Oscan,

---

*The Iranian deities became the Indic demons and vice-versa!

†However, that evidence might merely indicate pre-PIE migrations of the source Afro-Asiatic culture.

‡See www.gosai.com/chaitanya/saranagati/html/vedic-upanisads/aryan-invasion. html for some of the evidence and arguments about the Aryan invasion theories.

Umbrian, and others which died out, having been replaced by the best known of the Italic tongues, Latin. Latin, of course, gave rise to what are called the Romance languages: Spanish, Portuguese, Italian, French, and Romanian.

One group of PIE speakers was particularly prolific—the ones who would eventually be known as the Celts. By 500 BCE, their territory covered most of central and western Europe north of Italy and Greece and south of Scandinavia. The Celtic languages are usually divided by linguists into two major categories, those spoken on the Continent (Continental Celtic), which included Celtiberian and Gaulish, and those spoken in what are now known as the British Isles (Insular Celtic). The latter are usually divided into the Goidelic (Irish Gaelic, Scots Gaelic, and Manx) and the Brittonic (Welsh, Cornish, and Breton) tongues.

One wave of PIE speakers went to northern and northwestern Europe, becoming the Germanic peoples. During the first millennium CE, they wound up taking over much of the territory that had been Celtic, and even wound up in Northern Africa! The languages we think of as Norse (Norwegian and Icelandic) as well as Swedish and Danish, grew out of the North Germanic branch of the Germanic family tree; Old High German, Old Saxon, and Old English were parts of the West Germanic branch, and Gothic was spoken by the East Germanic speaking tribes.

Yet another bunch of PIEs migrated to northeastern Europe and northwestern Asia, becoming the Balts and the Slavs. The Baltic languages included Lithuanian, Latvian, and Old Prussian; the Slavic ones eventually were divided into East Slavic (Ukrainian, Belarusian, and Russian), South Slavic (Slovene, Serbo-Croatian, Macedonian, Bulgarian), and West Slavic (Polish, Slovak, Czech, Sorbian, and Old Church Slavonic). Obviously, these three subdivisions probably developed in that order and the Baltic ones last of all (being the furthest from the Black Sea).

There are several important factors to consider about the migrations of the Indo-European speaking peoples. To begin with, tribal movements didn't always go in one direction, there was a lot of back-and-forthing over the many centuries—one group of Celts even wound up back in Anatolia, courtesy of the Roman Empire! An early group of PIE speakers went all the way into China and their extinct language is now known as Tocharian.

Further, we simply don't *know* how peaceful or bloody most of the migrations might have been. Those who have argued in the past for a blood-drenched history to these migrations pointed out that previous inhabitants of a given piece of territory probably had to be persuaded, sometimes at sword-point, to let the newcomers in—and there went the neighborhood! The pre-Indo-European cultures in Europe were all still in the late neolithic or "New Stone Age" cultural stage of development. This means that they had only stone axes, arrowheads, spears, and knives (lots of which have been found) with which to defend themselves. The Indo-European newcomers had bronze weapons and armor with which to fight or hunt, plus bronze axes with which to clear the great forests that covered the continent, eventually bronze-edged plows to till the soil, and so on. Certainly several of the IE cultures were known to be warlike and some, such as the Persians, Greeks, Romans, and Germans traveled vast distances to conquer territory.

However, current linguistic and archeological theory is that much of the transmission of Indo-European languages and their associated genes may have been as much through the peaceful transfer of knowledge, trade, and the exchange of spouses between neighboring tribes as through warfare. The popular image of the Indo-European "barbarians" raping, looting, and pillaging their way across a continent owes much to the cultural outlook of nineteenth century archeologists and linguists (most of whom were from highly imperialist cultures), the historical records of the previous empires known to them, and the violent "folk wandering" of Germanic tribes after the fall of the western Roman Empire. These factors may outweigh both the available archeological evidence about Bronze and Iron Age migrations and the surviving Indo-European myths and sagas. This stereotype of violent Indo-European barbarians ignores the history of such perpetually migrating people as the Romany ("Gypsies"), who started out in India speaking an off-shoot of Sanskrit, and went throughout all of Europe as useful merchants of goods and services, without conquering anyone, cheerfully mixing their genes with all and sundry.

Peaceful or violent, the power of the Indo-Europeans' superior bronze (and later iron) technology can be judged by the fact that, by the time of the Roman Empire, nearly every language spoken in Europe (except Basque, Lappish, and Finnish)* was a member of the Indo-European language family. Everything west of the Ural Mountains was pretty much dominated by a loose conglomeration of related agricultural and pastoral societies, each of which was a mixture of one or more Indo-European cultures and those of the previous holders of its territory. The largest group of cultures north of the Roman borders was that of the Celts, and the second largest that of the Germans. Some scholars consider the Germans to be so closely related culturally to the Celts as to be practically a subset, at least in archeological terms (this annoys German archeologists terribly), although there are differences revealed by their myths that should not be overlooked.

At the opening of the Common Era, European Paleopaganism consisted of at least four interwoven layers: firstly, the original pre-Indo-European religions (which were of course also the results of several millennia of religious evolution and cultural blending between multiple cultures); secondly, the Proto-Indo-European belief system held by the PIE speakers before they began their migrations; thirdly, the Copper and Bronze Age variations of the PIE beliefs as adapted to different bioregions and already existing cultural complexes; and fourthly, the full scale "high religions" of the "fully developed" and more-or-less distinct Iron Age Indo-European cultures. Disentangling these various layers is going to take scholars a very long time, if indeed it will ever be actually possible. Fortunately, we don't have

*No, I didn't forget about Hungarian—it didn't exist as a language at the time.

to know every detail in order to see the broad general outlines of the common Indo-European religious and cosmological beliefs, nor to show the basic social structure beneath them—and that will provide us with our first useful information about the famous druids.

2

Indo-European Paleopaganism

The Twentieth Century's Mythological Revolution

Around the turn of the nineteenth-to-twentieth centuries, the field of comparative religion and mythology was extremely unfashionable, due in large part to the excesses of German scholar Max Müller (mentioned earlier) who is often credited with beginning the field. He developed a Darwinian view of religious evolution with so-called "primitive" religions (including all the polytheistic ones) as innately inferior to the monotheistic ones, especially Christianity. He was very schizophrenic about the *Vedas*, alternately considering them sublime and full of rubbish. While he often praised (especially in the comments to his published translation works) the "wisdom of the East" in the abstract, he frequently condemned the "tyranny" of "superstitious" Pagan priesthoods and the inferiority of polytheistic beliefs and cultures to monotheistic ones.

By the end of his career, Müller tried to prove that all mythology was really based on rationalizations of natural phenomena, especially solar ones. He thought that mythology could be thought of as a "disease of language," in that abstract concepts were turned into personifications who then became deified. Indeed, all myths were "really" solar hero myths if you just stared at them for long enough.* He was mired in what I have come to

---

*This eventually led to the 1870 publication at Trinity College, Dublin, of a satirical essay called, "The Oxford Solar Myth, a Contribution to Comparative Mythology," by R. F. Littledale, in which Müller himself was "proven" to be just another solar myth, using his own methods against him.

know as "monothesisism," the insistence on finding a single grand explanation for everything.* Many of Müller's critics suffered from the same problem, of course, as did many of his colleagues in other disciplines, due to the centuries-long influence of the Christian monotheistic university system from which all Western science has developed. Nonetheless, by the end of the nineteenth century, Müller and his followers had made comparative mythology (if not religion) an unfashionable topic in European and American academia.

It was Georges Dumézil (1898–1986) and Mircea Eliade (1907–1986) who, in the early twentieth century, revolutionized the field of folklore and mythological studies, reviving the comparative method in careful yet creative ways.† Dumézil, in particular, used sociological and anthropological research methods in addition to linguistic and traditional folkloric ones, leading to a genuine paradigm shift in both Indo-European studies and comparative mythology. Dumézil has actually been criticized for daring to change his mind about the details of his theories as he learned more throughout his career—as if a theory only has value if it is rigid and a scholar only if he or she never grows!‡

We will be looking at some of the Indo-European mythological evidence in this and the following chapters, so it's important to remember that most of the myths and sagas we know were composed to entertain the warriors at their feasting, and thus may have placed far more emphasis on violence and bloodshed than was actually experienced by their ancestors. As every bard or advertising executive knows, sex, violence, and flashy magic are popular themes for entertainment. Bawdy humor and

---

*"For every complex phenomena, there is a clear, simple explanation that is wrong."

†I am not going to fill this book with long quotes from either man, but will refer readers to their many excellent books, beginning with the ones in the Bibliography. Both men have been criticized, Dumézil falsely and Eliade with reason, as political right-wingers, but that doesn't necessarily mean that we should dualistically dump their useful ideas.

‡ As Michael Scharding said to me, "It's like surfing; stay on top or get swamped and swallowed."

erotic tales (of the sort that the farmers and servants might have told) were not approved of by the Christians who wrote down the previously oral Celtic, Norse, and Germanic literature for us, nor by the monks and imams who decided whether to make new written copies of Greek and Roman myths. Stories of blood and thunder, however, were quite acceptable, so the former were mostly forgotten while the latter were preserved for posterity. For that matter, stories which showed Paleopagan clergy and magicians in a positive light were also unlikely to be preserved by Christian or Islamic scribes, but ones that made them seem scary, weak, or foolish were occasionally included.

Dumézil noticed that the same major characters kept showing up in all the different Indo-European myths and legends of which we had records, going through very similar plotlines; furthermore, they seemed to reflect a common social structure among all the IE cultures. There were usually two deities who ruled over matters of magic and law; he called this the "first function" of "magical and judicial sovereignty." As we shall discover, "sovereignty" wasn't necessarily the best word to have chosen for the first function, since Dumézil used it to refer to rulership or authority over areas of human activity. The IE peoples used it to refer to a ruler's right to rule, based on a correct relationship to the local Earth-Mother goddess. Examples of these deity pairs include Odin and Tyr, respectively, from the Norse pantheon, and Mitra and Varuna from the Vedic. The "second function" includes the war gods such as Ares, Thor, and Indra (and I think the death gods belong here as well, for reasons that will become clear as this book progresses). Then you have the "third function" of fertility and support; this was usually handled by brother-sister pairs such as Freyr and Freya or else by twin brothers such as the Vedic Asvins, with occasional divine blacksmiths and craftsmen.

I believe that there is also a "fourth function" of dirty-workers (serfs, servants, and slaves) to be discerned in the Indo-European myths, and possibly a "fifth function" of cosmic rulers tied to Outsiders, or the forces of order and chaos, respectively (see the discussion below).* There are also a number of "multifunctional" or even "omnifunctional" deities such as the Dagda, Bridget, and the Morrigan in Irish myth, Thor and Freya in Norse myth, Agni in Vedic myth, and Hermes in Greek myth. Notice how the males are all fire/lightning gods, as is Bridget (see Appendix F).

Other common Indo-European deity roles included a Goddess of Sovereignty, whose approval was necessary for a tribal chief or king to rule properly (these were usually local Earth-mother/river goddesses), and a Gatekeeper deity in charge of borders and thresholds of all sorts (examples would include Hermes, Heimdall, and some of those omnifunctional deities). We'll discuss sovereignty and gatekeeper deities in Chapter 4. For now, let's turn to the social and political structures of the Indo-Europeans.

Indo-European Social Castes and Their Associations

Indo-European myths and legends clearly reveal Dumézil's three primary functions through the plotlines and backgrounds, including mortals who belong to different occupations: clergy (intellectuals who were responsible for magical/religious and judicial/secular functions), warriors (and possibly hunters), and producers (farmers, fishers, herders, craftspeople, and so on). People doing dirty work (my fourth function) are usually present in the myths, but very far in the background. Leading each tribe was a king who had responsibilities towards all the other functions, who was usually mated to the local earth goddess, and who had peculiar links and responsibilities to those outside the tribe (my fifth function).

I call these groups of occupations "castes," a term the reader may be familiar with from India. Caste is a modern term, from the Portuguese for "pure" or "chaste," applied by Westerners

---

*Other Dumézilians have been exploring the possibilities of additional "functions" to the first three for a few decades now, beginning (I think) with Rees and Rees, whom we'll meet in Chapter 4.

to an ancient social structure of four main social classes that the Indians themselves call *varnas*, from a Sanskrit root referring to color, especially skin color. In Hinduism a *varna* is the largest sort of *jat*, a word generally meaning group or class, especially of people. This latter is sometimes applied to tribes or other large groups of people living in India, but is most often used to refer to groups organized by occupation within the *varnas*. We could call these *jats* (or *jati*, both spellings are used) "subcastes" and even "subsubcastes." India today has over 3,000 subcastes of the four *varnas*, and over 25,000 subsubcastes!

In Vedic India and today, the four *varnas* are (from the top down) the *brahmans* (clergy/intellectuals), the *kshatrias* (warriors), the *vaisias* (producers/merchants), and the *sudras* (dirty workers). Because of Vedic obsessions with purity and cleanliness, the *sudras* became known as the "untouchables" and most "outsiders" became merged into their *varna*. One of the key concepts of the caste system there is that one is born into his or her *jat*, social mobility between the *jats* and *varnas* having vanished sometime between 500 BCE and 500 CE in various parts of India. As we will see, this entire system was originally the easternmost version (or possibly the origin) of a common Indo-European pattern.

In all the Indo-European cultures, clergy were associated with magical and spiritual power, as well as wisdom and knowledge of all sorts. They were responsible for the accurate transmission of knowledge from one generation to the next, including teaching and performing the critical religious ceremonies that would maintain cosmic order. In Europe, their special tree was the oak (various species, depending on location) or the ash where oaks were scarce, and their part of the body was the head.

The warriors were associated with force, both physical and emotional, with blood, and with death. Their job was to protect the members of their tribe, to attack the members of other tribes, and to go hunting or cattle-raiding (both of which could involve lots of bloodshed) when there was no war on. The tree most associated with them was the yew (or other evergreens), possibly because of the use of yews as a source of weapons (bows and spears shafts) and/or the immortality symbolism of evergreen trees in general. The part of the body associated with them as a group was the heart.

The producers were associated with fertility, strength, and physical support for the rest of their tribes. Their special tree was the birch that, as the first tree to put forth new foliage in the spring, was symbolic of fertility (hence its use for Maypoles), and their body part was the hands. These various body-part associations are the source of the many cultural references in Indo-European languages to "head and heart and hand" as expressing the totality of being or effort.

As usual, the serfs/servants/slaves were left out of this triad, as they were from most things considered important, since they just did all the work that nobody else wanted to do—skinning animals, digging latrines, cleaning stables, serving as concubines, and so forth. They were usually prisoners of war or the descendants of such, but were sometimes purchased from other tribes. I'm not sure they had a tree of their own, but it might have been the beech. The percentage of these fourth function people in most Indo-European cultures varied widely, depending upon local economic, military, and political circumstances.

As for my fifth function, the ruler of each tribe was associated with the spirit of the tribe as a whole, and thus its relationships with the mortals and spirits both within (the four functions) and without. I'm not sure that he (it was usually a he) had a particular tree associated with his rulership, but the holly tree or even the mistletoe plant might have served that purpose. "Outsiders," both mortal and immortal, didn't have special trees that I know of, but witches (one kind of outsider we'll discuss in Chapter 4), were associated with willows and thus with rivers and all their archetypal connections to women's magic and chaotic spirits. The mistletoe could work as a plant for the outsiders/outdwellers as well, as it is outside most primitive taxonomic categories.

As we shall see in the next two chapters, these functions with their associated castes and subcastes can be listed simply enough, but when we combine their connections to the structures of Indo-European cosmology, we wind up needing at least four dimensions to make sense of them!

More on the Clergy

Let's focus for now on the "first function" Indo-European clergy, who basically included the entire intelligentsia of their cultures: poets, musicians, historians, astronomers, genealogists, judges, diviners, and, of course, leaders and supervisors of religious rituals. Officially, they ranked immediately below the local tribal chieftains or "kings" and above the warriors. However, since the kings were quasi-religious figures, usually inaugurated by the clergy, and often dominated by them, it may have been a toss-up as to who was in charge in any given tribe.

The Indo-European clergy seem to have been responsible for all public religious rituals (private ones were run by the heads of each household). Various members of the priestly caste would be responsible for music, recitation of prayers, sacrificing of animals (or occasionally human criminals or prisoners of war), divination from the flames of the ritual fire or the entrails of the sacrificial victim, and other minor ritual duties. Senior members of the caste—the druids, *brahmans* (India), or *flamens/sacerdotii* (Rome) and such—would be responsible for making sure that the rites were done exactly according to tradition. Without such supervision, public rituals were generally impossible, because their re-creation of the cosmos might be erroneous, which would bring enormous danger to the tribe. Hence perhaps Caesar's comment* that all public Gaulish sacrifices required a druid to be present.

There are definite indications that the Indo-European clergy held certain polytheological and mystical opinions in common, although only the vaguest outlines are known at this point. There was a belief in reincarnation and/or survival after death

---

*In *The Gallic Wars*, a valuable though slanted source of information.

in one or more "otherworlds" similar to the earthly one, in the sacredness of particular trees, in the continuing relationship between mortals, ancestors and deities, and naturally in the standard laws of magic (see my book *Real Magic*). There was an ascetic tradition of the sort that developed into the various types of yoga in India, complete with the Pagan equivalent of monasteries and convents. There was also, I believe, a European "tantric" tradition of sex and drug magic, although it's possible that this was mostly surviving pre-IE shamanic methods or borrowings from the Central Asian and Finnish territories (which were still in the hunter-gatherer style of culture necessary to shamanism) being absorbed and transmuted.

Only the western Celtic clergy (the druids) seem to have had any sort of organized inter-tribal communications network, via traveling bards and *brehons* (judges/mediators). Most of the rest of the Indo-European clergy seem to have kept to their own local tribes. Among the Germanic peoples, the priestly class had weakened by the early centuries of the Common Era to the point where the majority of ritual work was done by the heads of households (see the "Geeks Against the Jocks" below).

We don't know whether or not any but the highest ranking clergy were full-time priests and priestesses. At the height of the Celtic cultures, training for the clergy was said to take up to twenty years of hard work (although this may have simply reflected growing up in druidic families), which would not have left much time or energy for developing other careers. Among the Scandinavians, there seem to have been priests and priestesses *(godar, gydjur)* who lived in small temples and occasionally toured the countryside with statues of their patron/matron deities, to whom they were considered to be "married" (as happens with clergy in some African American Mesopaganisms such as Voodoo). In the rest of the Germanic, Slavic, and Baltic cultures, however, many of the clergy may have worked part-time, a common custom in many tribal societies.

The Geeks Against the Jocks

Indo-European myth and history are filled with references to social and political conflict between members of the clergy and the warrior castes. From 3000 BCE to 500–1000 CE, depending on what Indo-European territory you are looking at, we can trace the war between the geeks and the jocks that goes on even today (and that you no doubt remember from your own school days). Different Indo-European cultures worked it out in different ways. As I put it in *The Pagan Man:*

In Ancient Rome, the warriors became more important than the clergy and made most of them governmental functionaries or political appointees. This seems to have gone along with the "historization" of Roman myths, whereby various deities became described as mortals in the stories.*

In the Celtic cultures, the clergy and the warriors seemed to have been in a state of balance (in that neither side was depicted in the myths as more important than the other), at least until the Romans arrived in the first century BCE, which is when we first begin to have detailed knowledge of them.

Over the next century or so, the Romans slaughtered members of the druidic class (throughout Gaul and the parts of Britain that they conquered) by the hundreds, wiping out the native intelligentsia before conquering the tribes. Later, the Roman Church was to wage a centuries-long battle against the Irish and Welsh druids, finally converting, killing, or banishing them by 600 CE or so.

The Romans weren't able to conquer the Germanic tribes, but the job of suppressing the clergy class was done by the Germans themselves. That is to say, the competition between the clergy and the warrior classes in the Germanic/Norse cultures was "won" by the warriors. By the

---

*See *Archaic Roman Religion*, by Dumézil.

early medieval period, Germanic Paleopagan clergy spent most of their time attending to local shrines dedicated to specific deities. The majority of religious activities were led by the male or female heads of households, or tribal chieftains acting as clergy. There were *skalds* (equivalent to the Celtic bards or poets) attached to the households of tribal leaders, much as the *fili* (poets) later were in medieval Ireland. There were some traveling soothsayers/prophets, usually women, called *volvas* who practiced a form of divination and oracular trance possession called *seidh*. This eventually became associated predominantly with women and effeminate men, because the magical techniques usually involved passivity and receptivity rather than assertive magical action.

In Vedic India it would appear that the Brahmin caste "won" the conflict and made itself the supreme social class and dominant arbiter of values in Indian society and culture. Interestingly, if one goes with the Indo-centric theories of all the Indo-European languages and cultures having come out of India, it could explain the millennia of conflict between the geeks and the jocks. Perhaps the departing warriors repeatedly tried to prevent the clergy from ever getting "out of hand" again.

Most of the time, however, the two top castes made it a point to cooperate in leading/dominating/enslaving (pick a verb based on your biases) the other castes. Even their divine counterparts, however, found that this wasn't always easy.

The Wars in Heaven

According to Dumézil and his followers, the Indo-European cultures all had stories of two major "Wars in Heaven." The first was between the "current" deities and a previous generation of (often monstrous) deities, such as the Formorians (in Irish myth), the giants or Jotuns (Norse), the Titans (Greek), the Devas (Iranian), or the Asuras (Vedic). The second was a war between deities representing the first two functions on one side against those representing the third function (and fourth?) on the other, such as that between the Norse Aesir and Vanir. The current deities, of course, always beat the previous ones (though often taking some of them into their ranks), and the deities of the first two functions always either conquered or established a truce with the third function deities, resulting in the divine status quo of the myths. There's a third conflict as well, between the deities of the first and second functions, though this doesn't usually rise to the level of all-out war (see "The Geeks Against the Jocks" above).

In the Irish mythology that has come down to us in *Lebor Gabála Érenn (LGÉ)* or *The Book of the Taking of Ireland* (also called the *Book of Invasions)*, the first war happens more than once, with the victorious deities of some of the invasions becoming defeated representatives of chaos in the later ones. The repetition may be due to the fact that *LGÉ*, as we know it today, is a blending of multiple medieval manuscripts. Such a contortion was done in an effort to make Pagan myth fit into the structural template of the Old Testament history the Church was teaching. Or it may be due, as Alwyn and Brinley Rees argue in *Celtic Heritage,* to the five "invasions" representing five functions that they derive from Dumézil's three by splitting what I've called the fourth into two parts and giving the fifth to the outsiders (see Chapter 3).

Dumézilians speculate that the "war between the functions" stories represent memories of Indo-European conquests of local (non-IE or earlier-IE) peoples by invading clergy and warriors. This fits well with the usual theories of bloodthirsty patriarchal Indo-Europeans raping, pillaging, and looting their way across Europe and Asia, though not so well with more recent studies (such as those by Colin Renfrew) indicating that IE cultural diffusion may have been rather more peaceful than that, albeit stressful to the changed cultures.

3

Indo-European Cosmology and Worlds-View

Worlds, Realms, and the Otherworld

Now, let's take a look at common Indo-European concepts of cosmology, or the way that their universes were structured. This information is vital to understanding their spiritual beliefs and practices, from the sublime to the ridiculous. We'll begin with what I call the "Three Worlds" (of the Land, the Waters, and the Sky); the "Three Realms" (of the Cythonic/Underworld, the Middle, and the Celestial); and the place known as "Faerie" or the "Otherworld" and its distinction from our normal waking world. Be aware that some modern Druids use the terms "worlds" and "realms" interchangeably or opposite from the way that I do—it doesn't matter, the principle is the same, but this is the vocabulary I will use in this book.

Indo-European tales make constant references to land, sky, and various sorts of waters (lakes, rivers, springs, the sea, and so on) as comprising all of normal physical reality. For example, there was one famous Celtic chieftain who reportedly said that he had only three fears: that the sky would fall down upon him, that the sea would overwhelm him, and that the earth might open up under him. I believe references to these three events occurring as punishments for oath-breaking can also be found. Parallels often existed between the functions and these natural places—clergy were associated with the Sky, warriors with the Waters, and producers with the Land. Certainly, these are what we could consider three places where physical animals can be observed: birds in the sky, animals on the land, and fish in the waters, for example.

We could classify the Land, the Waters, and the Sky as being the three worlds of organic beings as understood by the Indo-European cultures. However, while they are certainly present, they don't work quite properly for Lithuanian mythology and cosmology, despite the myths and language there being thoroughly Indo-European. Instead, the Lithuanian myths are more likely to use terms that are usually translated as "Sky," "Land," and "the Underworld." The Vedic peoples are said (in English) to have used "Sky," "Middle Air," and "Land" as their big three places. The Norse have a total of nine worlds instead of three. During a "cosmological lunch" at the Wellspring Gathering (my Druid organization's annual festival) in 1991, a Lithuanian Pagan, a Norse Pagan, a Celtic Pagan, myself, and several other participants came to some tentative conclusions of how one cosmology can reconcile all these seemingly different systems. These conclusions have worked well for artistic, magical, and mythological purposes since then. Here was our reasoning:

Mircea Eliade, one of the most brilliant folklorists and historians in the twentieth century, pointed out in several of his books the nearly universal tendency for tribal peoples to have a cosmology with a vertical axis (a "World Tree," a shamanic pole, a magic mountain, and so forth) in the sacred center of their tribes' territories. In Indo-European terms, that vertical axis may have originally reached from a "Celestial Realm" in the far heavens (home of the stars, sun, moon, and planets, where dwell the distant creator deity and sometimes the major tribal deities), through a "Middle Realm" (of ordinary mortal activity), and down to an Underworld or "Chthonic Realm" (where demons, dead people, old deities, and other chaotic beings dwell—i.e., a lot of the "Outsiders" we'll be looking at soon). This would give us three realms on the vertical axis. I do not believe that it is a coincidence that the focus on the vertical realms in Lithuanian mythology occurred in a geographical region of extreme verticality!

In more horizontal territories, the three worlds of the Land, the Waters, and the Sky may all be seen on a horizontal axis filling the Middle Realm, and reflected into the Celestial and Chthonic Realms as well. The ancient Irish, for example, had "lands" in the Celestial Realm and underneath the ocean (which was equated with what I'm calling the Chthonic Realm). There were also Celestial and Chthonic "Waters," and possibly types of "Sky" as well. This sort of multiplication could be done in various ways by the different Indo-European cultures, including dark/light variations (see "The Light and the Dark" below), leading to different numbers of what are usually translated as "worlds."

Some of the confusion in Indo-European cosmological studies may have been caused by the early translators. Remember that none of these ancient peoples used English or any other modern language. So the words we see in translations may not be precise matches from culture to culture. As one example, the term in Sanskrit that often gets translated as the "middle atmosphere" or "middle air" may really mean the local or nearby world of the Sky, while the word usually translated as "sky" in Vedic cosmological studies may translate better as what I've called the Celestial Realm.

But wait—there's more. Try to remember your high-school geometry classes and add in another axis at right angles to the others. This is because Indo-European cultures also had the near-universal concept of an "Otherworld" / "This World" polarity. The Otherworld is a concept that shows up in most religions as the "place" where spirits live. Usually it's perceived as interpenetrating mundane reality or "This World" in which most people live their lives, but with particular locations where it is easiest to contact. The Otherworld isn't the same as the Chthonic or Celestial Realms,* but it is connected to them, as it

---

*Although in Christian mythology, heaven is associated with the Celestial and Hell with the Cythonic. Departed souls who haven't gone to either place yet are said in modern Christian folklore to roam about the Middle Realm as ghosts, slipping from the Otherworld to this World on special occasions.

is to the Three Worlds. This would explain why there are so many ways to get into Faerie—the version of it best known to English speakers—such as via the *Sidhe* hills ("fairy mounds"), ocean voyages, diving into lakes, becoming a bird and flying there, and so on. The supernatural Outsiders might have been viewed as living mostly in the Otherworld and using its connections to travel throughout the realms and worlds. Each Indo-European culture would have associated various sorts of beings, from the demonic to the divine, with each of the "places" we've defined. Among the Irish, for example, the Outsiders were usually chthonic/deep-oceanic, but were sometimes associated with very distant lands, waters, or skies.

Gateways Beyond: The Fire, the Well, and the Tree

How does one get from one of these places to another? In the Middle Realm, one can go physically into water or walk about on land. You can even throw spears or arrows up into the sky. Sometimes this can get you into Faerie, as just mentioned, but it's usually by accident. If you want to deliberately walk between worlds, you need a psychic/magical/spiritual/artistic "Gateway" of some sort. The Indo-Europeans seem to have three major Gateways, usually referred to as the "Sacred Fire," the "Sacred Well," and the "Sacred Tree."

Fire, as a primeval divine force, was seen by the Paleopagan Indo-Europeans as existing in, and communicating between, all three realms, all three worlds, and across the Otherworld/this world divide. The stars, sun, and moon were celestial fire; underground coal, peat, or volcanic fires were chthonic. In the Middle Realm, Fire existed in the Sky (lightning, smoke), on the Land (camp-, hearth, and forest fires), and even in the Waters (alcoholic beverages, soma). Will-o-the-wisps (swamp gas) were seen as Otherworld Fire visible in this world, and were especially dangerous because following them could take you across the invisible line to a place from whence you might never

return.* Although it is most associated with the Celestial
Realm, the world of the Sky (via lightning), order, maleness,
and knowledge, Sacred Fire burns in and through all the categories of reality and can be used symbolically to tie them all together.

This universality of Fire may be why Fire deities (Dagda,
Agni, Thor, Hermes, etc.) so often become omnifunctional
ones (see Appendix F) or otherwise exceptionally important.
Agni, for example, is said in some of the *Vedas* to be the only
deva (deity) who will survive the end of every cosmic age (except for the highly abstract Isvara figure who functions more or
less as a supreme being behind all reality). Perhaps Fire's primal
priority is behind some of the emphasis that Müller put on solar references in myths.

While Fire was very important to the Indo-Europeans, Water
could also be a primary Gateway. The Water found in the Sacred
Well, like the Sacred Fire, exists in all the physical and spiritual places. However, it is most strongly associated with the
Cythonic Realm, the world of the Waters (naturally), chaos, fe-
maleness, and inspiration. Often found in the Indo-European
myths is a sacred "fire-in-the-water" symbolism. This can sometimes refer to alcoholic or hallucinogenic beverages, but also to
what Hindus and Buddhists would consider a Tantric concept—
the results of a union of sacred male and female forces. For example, the Irish Fire God, the Dagda, makes love with the River
Goddess Boanne in the middle of her river. Their offspring is
Angus Og, the God of love and passion. (River Goddesses are
also usually local Earth/Fertility/Sovereignty Goddesses, so
there are serious reasons why the Dagda does what he does with
them—see the next section for details.) Some Neopagan Druids
invoke this symbolism of Celestial Fire and Cythonic Waters as
the "Two Powers" united within themselves in ritual.

---

*Considering the similarities between tales of those abducted by the faeries and by
UFOs, it is especially amusing that the U.S. Air Force tried so hard, for so many years,
to explain away UFO sightings as "swamp gas"—making right-angle turns at hundreds of miles per hour, but never mind . . .

The third common kind of gateway for the Indo-Europeans is a sacred pole or tree, called the "axis mundi" or "axis of the world" by folklorists. It is used to mark sacred centers and borderlines, as well as to connect all the worlds and realms. To the Norse, this "World Tree" is called Yggdrasil. To the Irish the World Tree was called a *Bilé*, a term applied to trees of particular interest, especially at boundaries. Bile was also the name of a deity associated with the dead. As we'll see in the next section, the dead are usually thought of as able to travel everywhere, so associating a God of the dead with borderlines made good sense. For the Greeks, Mount Olympus served some of this purpose. Their Gateway deity Hermes has a name based on "herms," the phallic rocks used to mark the borders of fields. For all the Indo-European peoples, many species of trees were considered holy for different purposes and associated with different social castes, as we have discussed. Perhaps individual examples of each type could serve as a sacred tree/axis mundi for different sorts of ritual. We do know that many public ceremonies among the Balts, Slavs, Celts, and Germans were held in fenced groves of sacred trees. These were usually of birch, yew, and oak (or ash where oaks were rare), depending upon the spirits, ancestors, or deities being addressed, as well as the specific occasion.

Many Indo-European peoples believed that there were particular deities who were in charge of opening and/or guarding the gates between the worlds. The Norse God Heimdall is the guardian of the rainbow bridge leading to the world(s) of the Gods. The two-faced Roman deity Janus is the guardian of every threshold. The Greek God Hermes is the messenger of the other Gods and the psychopomp (guide) of the dead to the afterlife. Among the Irish, I think it is most likely Manannon Mac Lir, the God of the Ocean, who opens the Gates. However, the omnifunctional goddess Morrigan may also play this role (at least as psychopomp). There is also an unnamed "gatekeeper" who guards the door of the Irish Gods' hall at Tara (the ritual center of Ireland). If we are going to be annoying with my postulated

African offshoot of IE influence (see Appendix F), we could mention Ellegua/Esu/Exu, the Yoruba/Voodoo guardian of the Gates. Like Hermes, he is also a trickster figure.

The Three Kindreds, Sovereignty, and the Outdwellers

Indo-European peoples divided the spirits with whom they lived into three major, overlapping categories, which modern Druids know as the "Three Kindreds"—the deities (often called some variation of "the Shining Ones"), "the Ancestors" (a.k.a. the "Mighty Dead"), and the "Nature Spirits" (a.k.a. the "Noble Ones"). Standing aside from the other deities were the local river/earth/fertility goddesses who were considered to represent the "Sovereignty" of the land for every tribe. Indo-European kings (chieftains, really, for most of them) were required to mate with the local sovereignty goddess (or her representative) and to maintain a good relationship with Her (hence, the Dagda's mating with the river goddesses). Bad weather or harvests were considered signs that the relationship was getting rocky and required magical intervention on the king's behalf by the tribe's clergy.

The category of "Outdwellers" included the spiritual equivalents to mortal outsiders such as foreigners, aboriginal peoples, sorceresses, madmen, criminals, and so on. These were the faeries, elves, giants, formorians, banshees, and so forth. In short, when we talk about the outdwellers, we mean spirits associated with aboriginal mysteries, female power, danger, magic, and chaos in general—frightening concepts to the patriarchal IE cultures who were obsessed with maintaining the cosmic order. There is also a hint (via the aboriginal and female power concepts) that this part of the cosmology is intimately associated with the local sovereignty goddesses.

The Outdwellers are usually associated with the Cythonic Realm, just as rulers are with the Celestial Realm. The clergy/deities, warriors/ancestors, and producers/Nature-Spirits are linked symbolically to the Three Worlds of the Sky, the Waters, and the Land, respectively.

The Light and the Dark

Remember those three axes we used earlier to try to visualize the structure of Indo-European cosmology? Well, in keeping with matters mystical, we need to add another axis going through the centers of the others! This fourth dimension has had powerful effects, not all of them positive, on all Indo-European cultures, including those of the modern world.

Indo-European metaphysics seem obsessed with the alternation of polarities (things that come in connected pairs), usually described as dark and light and usually associated with chaos and order (Eliade's "profane" and "sacred"), respectively. There's a dark half to every Celtic day (sunset to sunrise) and year (Samhain or Halloween to Beltaine or May Day), for example. Applying this to Dumézilian theories could be quite enlightening. The dual first function (magical vs. judicial) of the clergy, the confusion over the roles of berserkers (fighters who go violently insane in battle) vs. heroes in the second (warrior) function, and the roles of the third (producer) function's twin (or sister-brother) deities, would be much clearer if we assumed that each function has a dark (= dangerous) side and a light (= safe) side.

That would give us a pattern where the first function would consist of the dangerous magician and the safe judge; the second function would be the dangerous werewolf/berserker and the safe hero; the third function would give us the reluctant (and, therefore, dangerous) and the enthusiastic (safe) producer; and the fourth function would have the rebellious or sneaky (dangerous) and the obedient and honest (safe) slave. The fifth or Outside/Center function then consists of the dangerous Outsiders and the safe king. What the mythologies make clear, of course, is that these "dangerous" and "safe" categories do not equate with "evil" and "good." This is because you can have, for example, good Outsiders and evil kings. However, the conservatism of most tribal societies would lead to prejudices for and against the safe/dangerous polarities in fairly obvious ways.

The Outdwellers, who can be seen as the ultimate outsiders, as the spirits who live in the Otherworld, are often going to be seen as dark, even if some of them are otherwise bright or attractive. This dark/light split might also throw some light (you should pardon the expression) on the "good demons" and "evil gods" in different Indo-European myths, many of whom are said to be descended from both dark and light spirits. Note that this dark/light polarity goes through all the worlds and realms, all the gateways,* all the Kindreds, all the castes, the Outdwellers themselves, and anything else people might have observed.

The Zoroastrian insistence that light = good and dark = evil was the source of the black vs. white dualism that plagues Western cultures even to this day, thanks to Zoroastrianism's influence on Gnosticism, and the latter's influence on Judaism, Christianity, and Islam.

For now, let's turn to the people most readers probably thought this book was going to start with, the Celtic Paleopagans, but with an awareness of their historical and spiritual place as just one branch of the amazing Indo-European peoples.

---

*There is even "dark fire," in the case of Balor of the Evil Eye, a character in Irish myth who is slain by his grandson Lugh of the Long Arm, who is considered by many to be a "light fire" deity. Certainly much of the iconography of Kali Durga in Hindu myth involves dark fire, but in Her case on the side of "good."

4

Celtic Paleopaganism and the Druids

The Celtic Peoples

Archaeologists and linguists use the word "Celtic" in different ways.

Archaeologically speaking, the first "Celtic" peoples were the ones living in central Europe around 750–500 BCE. This early Iron Age culture, the first north of the Alps, is named after a burial ground in Hallstatt, Austria, to the southeast of their archeological territory, though the culture seems to have had a range from the western edge of modern Russia on the east, through Austria, Switzerland, and southern Germany, to eastern France and Belgium in the west.

The second phase of Celtic culture is called the "La Tene," named after a lake in Switzerland. It lasted from around 500 BCE through 50 CE or so. It is primarily this latter phase that we have the most historical material about. The gigantic geographical distribution of the Celts during this time covered most of Europe north of the Roman Empire. It extended from Thrace in the east (north of Greece) to Spain in the southwest and to the British Isles in the northwest—indeed, all but northern Germany and Scandinavia! We have references in Greek and Roman literature to the *Keltoi, Galli,* and *Galatae,* all used quite loosely. So anyone who has western, central, or eastern European ancestry probably has a few of these Iron Age Celts among their ancestors.

Linguistically, when we talk about Celts we mean, as mentioned earlier, the speakers of the tongues in the Celtic branch of the Indo-European language family. Unfortunately, we have very little information about any but the westernmost members of this branch (the Gaulish, Celtiberian, and Insular ones). Since the overwhelming majority of modern people who are interested in the ancient or modern druids are, or are descended from, the people in just these parts of Europe, the lack of information about the central and eastern Celtic languages is mostly annoying to linguists.

Miranda J. Green, in *The World of the Druids*, warns us:

> We need to pose the (ultimately unanswerable) question as to whether the European Celts possessed any degree of ethnic consciousness or whether the term "Celts" was merely a convenient but somewhat vague label used by Mediterranean chroniclers to identify essentially heterogeneous groups of people living north of the "civilized" world of Greece and Rome. The precision with which the term "Celts" was used by Classical writers may, of course, have varied widely.

As we shall see, however, the cultures most associated with druids all match the basic patterns of the other Indo-European cultures we have discussed in previous chapters, so whether the people the archaeologists like to call Celts called themselves such is really irrelevant. We can just think of them as temperate Europe's Iron Age Indo-Europeans and we will already know a great deal about them.

Celtic Provinces as Cosmology

In Alwyn and Brinley Rees's classic *Celtic Heritage: Ancient Tradition in Ireland and Wales*, they discuss the ancient Irish and Welsh cosmology and social systems from a Dumézilian approach. Most of their discussion focuses on the Irish, so I'll concentrate on them for now. The Irish caste system had the king on top, then the druids, then the warriors. So far, so good; this is the same IE social structure I just reviewed. But their third "producer" caste was split into an upper and a lower class. The upper producer class consisted of the wealthy farmers and advanced artisans, the lower producer class of the folks who got stuck with the society's dirty work—agricultural serfs, satirists, clowns and jugglers, kitchen help, etc. In other words, what I have called a "fourth function."

Each of the castes traditionally had a province of Ireland (a similar pattern arose in ancient Wales) symbolically connected to it: Connacht for the druids, Ulster for the warriors, Leinster for the free farmers, Munster for the serfs. But in some of the old tales, Munster was split in two: East Munster for the regular serfs and West Munster for the Outsiders. There was a "fifth province" of Meath, which was considered the ritual center of Ireland and the place of the "high kings" who supposedly ruled the entire island. I think this fifth province and the fourth-in-a-half province of West Munster together account for my "fifth function."

Leaving aside the fifth function for a moment, note the geometric relationship of the four main provinces in Ireland and Wales: clergy in the west opposite the farmers in the east; warriors in the north opposite the serfs in the south. Rotate this pattern 90 degrees clockwise and you get the caste associations common to the Norse peoples: clergy in the north opposite the farmers in the south; warriors in the east opposite the serfs in the west. Rotate this pattern 90 degrees more and you get the directional associations used by the Vedic peoples in laying out the multiple fire altars used in their main fire sacrifices: clergy in the east opposite the farmers in the west; warriors in the south opposite the serfs in the north (who didn't get a fire). In all these cases, the king or queen is placed in the center. It would be interesting to see if directional associations in the other Indo-European cultures can be shown to reflect this same pattern.

Castes and Subcastes: What Druids Did

Naturally every physical province had all kinds of people living in it, and indeed these cosmological/social patterns were apparently repeated within each province and within each caste. Among the members of the clergy caste, for example, the druids per se, who presided over sacrifices or were judges (the magical and judicial roles), corresponded to themselves. The diviners and poets corresponded to the warrior caste, because of their connections to death and the ancestors (for divination) and the creation of epic poetry celebrating the accomplishments of the warriors (among the Paleopagan Greeks, the poets were considered a type of diviner, using their powers to look into the past rather than the present or future, which *might* have been true for the Celts as well). The bards corresponded to the farmers and craftspeople (as providers of musical nourishment and support), and the servants who helped with various druidic activities to the serfs. Perhaps the highest ranking local or national druid (or "Archdruid") corresponded to the local king or national "high king" and also had a spiritual connection to the outdwellers. The following charts give one way to think about these subcastes of druids, and possible subcastes of warriors and producers, divided by whether they were likely to be perceived as "safe" or "dangerous" most of the time:

DRUIDS

Function	Light	Dark
First (wisdom and magic)	judge, mediator, counselor, teacher, philosopher	ritualist, magician
Second (war and the dead)	poet, historian, genealogist	diviner, sacrificer, satirist?
Third (support and wealth)	bard, storyteller, musician	invoker, healer

Function	Light	Dark
Fourth (service)	secular servant	ritual servant
Fifth (order and chaos)	Archdruid	sorcerer, witch

WARRIORS

Function	Light	Dark
First (wisdom and magic)	Trainer	War magician?
Second (war and the dead)	Hero	Berserker
Third (support and wealth)	Weapons smith, charioteer	Cattle thief, hunter
Fourth (service)	Scout?	Corpse fetcher, burier
Fifth (order and chaos)	War chief (usually the king)	Enemy, outsider

PRODUCERS

Function	Light	Dark
First (wisdom and magic)	Animal breeder, plant expert	Horse whisperer
Second (war and the dead)	Fisher, healer	Hunter
Third (support and wealth)	Farmer, craftsperson, gold or silversmith	Blacksmith
Fourth (service)	Plowman, cook	Shepherd, cowboy
Fifth (order and chaos)	Oldest?	Tinker, trader

As shown, there might have been what amounted to an out-sider subcaste within the druids, including such "low class" in-tellectuals as sorcerers, or these occupations might have been reflections of the druid caste within an outsider caste (I can't figure out what would have been the fourth and fifth subfunc-tions).

It's entirely possible that the warrior caste didn't have as many subcastes as the other major castes did, although I suspect that a careful review of the Irish and Welsh literature might tease them out. The warriors might have simply drafted the services of the lower castes when they needed them, especially in smaller tribes. However some roles, such as charioteer, can be seen as a reflection of the bardic subcaste (third of the first) within the warrior caste (making it third of the second).* Being a hunter, on the other paw, can be seen as third of the second or second of the third, in both cases on the dark or dangerous side.

As for the producers, we know that some of them were con-sidered *Aeos Dana*, "people of art," which included black-smiths, gold and silversmiths, woodworkers, supervisors of large farms, herbalists, etc., and in some tribes these folks might have been considered members of the druid caste.

So please don't get the idea that all these categories were necessarily clear-cut, present in every Celtic tribe, or that peo-ple always belonged to just one subcaste. A satirist, for example, could be someone who created satires (scathing poems which were said to be able to actually make people ill to the point of death) on a regular basis, in which case he or she was probably an outsider (third of the fifth). But they might have been any poet at all whom someone had been unlucky enough to seri-ously annoy (second of the first).

If we look at just the reflections of the first function within the fifth, we can see that outsiders wind up on both the dark and light side, while rulers of any sort are missing:

---

*See "Brothers, Friends, and Charioteers: Parallel Episodes in the Irish and Indian Epics," by Alf Hiltebeitel, in *Homage to Georges Dumézil (JIES Monograph No. 3)*, edited by E. C. Polomé.

DRUIDIC OUTSIDERS

Function	Light	Dark
First (wisdom and magic)	Storyteller	Sorcerer, witch
Second (war and the dead)	Soothsayer	Necromancer
Third (support and wealth)	Juggler	Satirist
Fourth (service)	?	?
Fifth (order and chaos)	?	?

If every major caste had subcastes within it reflecting the larger pattern, then you could very quickly get many subcastes. If the larger pattern had then been reflected into each of the subcastes to produce sub-subcastes, perhaps you would have *eventually* gotten thousands of castes as happened in India. The Celtic druid caste existed only for a couple of millennia as such, whereas the Brahmin caste is more than twice as old and wasn't conquered by a hostile culture until the Muslims showed up— so it had a lot more time to get really complex and fossilize.

So anyone in the Celtic (or other Indo-European) cultures who worked primarily with their mind could be considered a druid of sorts, even if he or she officially belonged to one of the other castes. Perhaps rather than using nice neat grids to try and understand them, we should be using Celtic interlace to show how they looped back upon themselves, or a kaleidoscope image to show multiple reflections of reflections.

Sacred Trees and Sacred Groves

If there's one topic the modern world still universally associates with druids (other than Stonehenge), it's trees, especially oak trees. This is not surprising, given the linguistic connections between the Latin *druids,* Irish *draoi,* Welsh *derrwid,* and various words for "oak," "strong," "firm," and so forth (see appendix E). So whether druid means "oak-man," "strong-seer," "truth-knower," or some blend of all of these, oaks and other trees are clearly part of the picture, culturally and symbolically.

One of the few words we know in Gaulish is *nemeton* (*nemed* in Irish), which appears to have meant "sacred place." This was, we are told, usually in a grove of trees, although it could be in a temple instead of, or in addition to, a grove. Although a few temple foundations have been dug up in Celtic territories, sacred groves without any buildings would have left little or nothing for archeologists to excavate. So we must take the Classical writers and Celtic folklore at their words. The oak grove is the type most frequently mentioned, though ash trees appear to have been used as symbolic equivalents in places, such as Ireland, where oaks didn't grow as well. Oak and ash might even have been dark and light trees for druids.

Yew groves are also mentioned in connection with the druids, especially for bloody sacrifices or the hanging of dead bodies. Since yew and other evergreen trees were associated with the warrior caste, as mentioned earlier, it is no great stretch to postulate that rites involving death and the dead might take place in such groves. To this very day, the one tree most likely to be planted around cemeteries by Western Europeans, and their offshoot cultures, is the yew. Perhaps some of those "bloody druid groves" were actually just cemeteries. Or they might have been places where the seers and the poets went to converse with the dead for inspiration. We know that the Celts had long-lasting headhunting cults. The worship of skulls was also practiced to connect with the mighty dead. So yew groves might easily have been decorated with skulls. Bodies might have been left in the open air long enough for the birds to pick clean as was done in ancient Persia. That would have made a lovely sight for a Roman or Greek tourist!

I'll point out here that all the Indo-European peoples practiced human sacrifice at one time or another in their histories, as have most non-Indo-European ones. The pious denunciations of the druids by some of the Greek and Roman writers, or the later Christian ones, ignore the Greek and Roman records in this area. Both actually did the same (and far worse in the Roman "games"). They also fail to mention the atrocities committed by Christians against non-Christians almost from the beginning of their faith. What were the murders of Paleopagan clergy in their temples, or of Hypatia at the library of Alexandria or the inquisitions, or the crusades, if not human sacrifices? Any time people believe that they have a religious right to kill other people, trouble is not far behind (witness the past, present, and future of the Middle East).

So, yes, there is evidence, both literary and archeological, that members of the druid caste performed human sacrifices (along with a lot of animal ones). The human victims seem to have been mostly convicted criminals (that is, capital punishment), prisoners of war (perhaps when there were too many to feed as slaves), and the occasional volunteer.* This isn't the place for a discussion of the magical and spiritual principles of sacrifice—see my *Rites of Worship* for that—but for now, let's just accept it as yet another quaint Celtic custom that we don't want to revive in the twenty-first century!

Birch trees and their groves may have been the locations for fertility rituals (or "wild parties" as they are known to modern researchers) held by the producers. Birches play a prominent role in fertility symbolism among the Indo-Europeans in general, so there's no reason to think this wasn't also true for the Celts. The "maypole" traditions, which usually involve birch trees, may have been brought into England by the Germanic invaders known to us as the Angles, Saxons, and Jutes (famous for making such good rope). Hazel was a tree strongly associated with druids, especially in Ireland, and hazelnuts were symbolic of wisdom. Whitethorn may have been a tree connected to the druids as well (as in the song, "Oak and Ash and Thorn").

Of course the most famous image connecting druids to trees

---

*See *The Death of a Druid Prince* by Anne Rossard and Don Robbins for one possible case of a volunteer.

is the mistletoe harvesting ritual described by Pliny and quoted earlier. Let me tell you, climbing up an oak tree while wearing a long white robe isn't easy—I know, I've done it! Short, white tunics would have been much easier (and I actually switched to white jeans and a turtleneck). Golden sickles are highly unlikely to have been used by the ancient Druids, however, despite what Pliny says. This is because their cutting edges would have been too soft for harvesting mistletoe, which is an exceptionally tough plant. Gold-plated ones, on the other hand, would have been possible. If the ancient Incas could figure out a way to make gold/bronze alloys that, when heated properly, brought their gold to the surface, then the Celts *might* have too, though I doubt golden sickles would have been common.

Mistletoe was supposedly used by the Paleopagan Druids for herbal healing, though it would have had to be used most carefully, since it can be highly poisonous. I suspect its value was far more spiritual than herbal. As a green plant growing up in the air even in the dead of winter, it would have symbolized survival and immortality more than other evergreen plants did, even without dragging James Fraser's *Golden Bough* theories into the discussion.

In our modern world we often forget just how important trees were to our ancestors. Trees provided food, shelter, medicine, dyes, and more to the Celts and the other Indo-Europeans. As intellectuals, at least some of the druid caste would have been expected to understand the botanical properties of the trees that surrounded them. See Ellen Evert Hopman's book *Tree Medicine Tree Magic* for an excellent introduction to what most such druids would have been expected to know.* For a discussion of the religious and spiritual value of trees, see *Sacred Trees*, by Nathaniel Altman.

For now, let's move on to some well-known and completely bogus facts about the Paleopagan Druids.

---

*But skip her Appendix on "Calendars and Alphabets," for reasons which will become apparent in Chapter 19's discussion of ogham.

Things the Druids *Didn't* Do

There is zero historical evidence, despite New Age claims, that the Paleopagan Druids had anything to do with the mythical continents of Atlantis or Mu, even without the evidence from plate tectonics that there never were any such continents.* As we have seen, they were *not* the architects of Stonehenge or of the megalithic circles and lines of Northwestern Europe, which were created by neolithic peoples long before the Celts arrived on the scene.

They did not construct the pyramids of Egypt or the pyramids of the Americas, though they have been credited with both. In fact, there is no evidence that they ever designed anything other than wooden barns, stone houses, and an occasional hill fort, though they may well have been responsible for wooden temple buildings.

There is no proof that any of the ancient druids were monotheists, or "Pre-Christian Christians" (see the discussion in Chapter 5), or that they understood or invented either Pythagorean or Gnostic or Cabalistic mysticism, although much of Druidic mysticism may have come from the same common Indo-European roots as had Pythagorean and (parts of) Gnostic mysticism.

Neither did the druids all wear long beards, as the preceding chapters should have made clear. The idea that *all* the ancient druids were men is, in large part, the result of Christian censorship of Classical, Irish, and Welsh references to the female half of the druidic caste. While there are dozens of such references remaining, they are usually negative (often calling them "witches" or "hags") and are vastly outnumbered by the ones referring to male druids. This is in keeping with both Greek and Roman sexism. It also supports the historical Christian preference that women be excluded from positions of spiritual power and respect, even retroactively in "false religions." The Christian and

---

*I tend to think of Atlantis having more archetypal than physical reality, though either the Black Sea flood or the volcanic explosion of Thera might have provided a physical peg to hang the myths on.

Islamic screening of Roman and Greek literature, and the Christian monopoly on the replication of Irish and Welsh literature is simply not discussed among most scholars, who seem to blithely assume that the documents as we have them are trustworthy reflections of ancient Celtic cultures. It's *possible* that the druidic caste system was as sexist as its bramanic counterparts eventually became (under the influence of Islam?). Nonetheless, you can't have a hereditary caste without children, which generally requires the cooperation of women to bear and raise the next generation of caste members.*

There is some indication that the Paleopagan Celts had social mobility, based on demonstrated talent. They also were less sexist than the Romans, so at the very least *some* Celtic women, whether born to the caste or not, would have become practicing druids of some sort. In cultures with many goddesses, it would be hard to get away with totally suppressing female spirituality and there are enough remaining references to female druids, seers, poets, healers, and so on to make it clear that they were not unusual. Certainly all the other Indo-European cultures had women in positions of power in their clergy castes and Celtic women were renowned for not being shy, retiring sorts.

As for white robes, those and the golden sickles seem, as discussed, to date from the famous mistletoe-harvesting passage in Pliny. White was, however, a color associated with the clergy caste in most of the Indo-European cultures. Red was connected with warriors, blue or green with producers, brown with servants, and black with outsiders—this is why so many IE-influenced cultures have flags that are red, white, and blue or red, white, and black.† The Irish flag is currently orange, white, and green. Orange is the color now associated with the province of Ulster, which was originally the province of the warriors, whose color was red. The traditional color associated with Leinster and the producers was *glas* (which could be blue or

---

*Shakespeare and other Elizabethan dramatists ran into this same problem.

†Red, white, and black were used to great (if evil) effect by the Nazis, and are also the colors used in decorating folkdance and other ritual garb by Balts and Slavs even today.

green, depending on how long the woad leaves were boiled). I'd say that's close enough! In each case, it's the major castes that are getting the attention, though other explanations are usually offered. White is indeed a color associated with druids, but speckled clothing and feathered cloaks are also mentioned. The modern Order of Bards Ovates & Druids associates white, green, and blue with those three steps of their training system.

Druids and Witches and Shamans, Oh My

Were the female druids the people who later became called "witches"? Certainly there are a few references to Celtic priestesses and seeresses. There were even entire communities of them living on islands, providing healing, spiritual, and magical services that later generations of Europeans associated with village wise women. Modern people (especially Neopagan Witches) often want to consider these later women witches. Yet, as I make clear in *Bonewits's Essential Guide to Witchcraft and Wicca,* the word "witch" was apparently a neutral-to-negative term to the Anglo-Saxons for as far back as we can trace it. If the witches *had* been the "priestesses of the Old Religion," they would have been former members of the druid caste. But they weren't. There is no historical or linguistic evidence that witches were ever considered clergy of any sort until the Catholic Church invented "Diabolic Witchcraft" in the late Middle Ages. On the contrary, the linguistic sources of *wicce* (female witch) and *wicca* (male one) are found in roots relating to invoking, necromancy, magic, bending, weaving, and wakefulness. The willow was the tree most associated with them, and a tree with symbolism further removed from oak would be hard to find in Europe.

Now it *is* possible that the people I used to call "Classic Witches," but who are probably better referred to as the "cunning folk," might have been members of the druid caste, or its reflection within the producer caste. These were the men and women who provided herbal, medical, and magical services to their communities. But we have no historical record of them leading group rituals, nor of being thought of as religious workers. Calling one of them a witch would have been a deadly insult, at least within historical times.

I should point out that a number of Wiccans and Neopagan Druids (including myself) practice both types of magical and religious activities, and that the two modern movements have entwined histories. The Chosen Chief of the Order of Bards Ovates & Druids, Philip Carr-Gomm, has even published a fascinating book on blending the two, called *Druidcraft*. Such blendings, however, are a modern phenomenon, not an ancient one.

Were the Paleopagan Druids perhaps shamans? No, even though some druids are described as occasionally doing some of the same things that shamans did (and do). Druidic cultures were agricultural and pastoral. There were usually multiple druids in any Celtic tribe because, as I've said repeatedly, they were a social caste. People were born druids and/or trained to become such, and/or married into a druidic family. Shamans, on the other paw, come from hunter-gatherer cultures, are usually few in number, are usually reluctantly recruited to the role, and don't pass their occupation on to their kids (many are gay, lesbian, or transgendered, so this would have been awkward to arrange). The fact that druids, like magical and religious workers in many other places and times, sometimes practiced soul travel (or astral projection) doesn't make them (or the others) shamans. This is why I tend to look very suspiciously at all the books and classes about "Celtic Shamanism," because they are rather like teaching Inca Asatru, or African Hinduism, or Chinese Voodoo. Such syncretistic paths can be created today (and probably have been), but it's simply less than honest to project them back into the distant past. It's hard enough reconstructing what really happened in Paleopagan times without dressing up New Age nonsense with Celtic décor. Real shamanism was and is a wonderful and distinct type of magical technique and religious worldview. Please don't do both it and druidism (not to mention witchcraft) an injustice by mixing them up, with or without dragging in the faeries.

Let's get to the unpleasant part of our story and go over the facts quickly.

The Word Is "Genocide"

According to the 1948 United Nations Convention on the Prevention and Punishment of Genocide,

> Genocide means any of the following acts committed with intent to destroy, in whole or in part, a national, ethnical, racial, or religious group, such as:
>
> - Killing members of the group
> - Causing serious bodily or mental harm to members of the group
> - Deliberately inflicting on the group conditions of life calculated to bring about its physical destruction in whole or in part
> - Imposing measures intended to prevent births within the group
> - Forcibly transferring children of the group to another group

Genocide was a common practice in the Roman Empire, as it was among many other empires before and afterward. Accusing the "noble" Julius Caesar of religious genocide is generally not done by respectable historians and certainly few until the late twentieth century ever applied it to his successors and heirs. Yet a close look at what was done makes it quickly clear in the twenty-first century that genocide is indeed the correct term to use.

When conquering Gaul the Romans discovered that the druids were a major source of trouble. Their traveling members kept warning tribes who hadn't yet been subjugated what to expect from the Latin tourists. As previously mentioned, Julius Caesar made it a point in his conquest of Gaul to kill every druid his troops could get their hands on, except for a few traitors willing to be his "native guides." This military and political agenda has to be kept in mind when reading his many comments about the druids in *The Gallic Wars* and the comments made by later Roman authors anxious to please later Roman emperors, who also killed druids when they could.

When the Roman Empire changed hands and continued under new management, the Church perpetuated this policy of killing or banishing every druid (or other Paleopagan clergyperson) who would not convert. Thus, by the end of the eighth century CE, those druids who had specifically religious or magical/psychic functions, as well as most of the historians and political advisors, had been either murdered, converted, or banished throughout the Western Celtic lands. Yes, I know there have been plenty of books published that claim the druids all happily converted when presented with a "superior" religion. But the evidence to support this claim comes from the Christian victors or those anxious to curry favor with the Church, not from the vanquished.

In parts of Wales and Ireland, and possibly in the Scottish Highlands, fragments of Paleopagan Druidism seem to have survived in heavy disguise through the institutions of the Celtic Church, the bards and poets, and the brehons, as well as in peasant folk customs (especially the seasonal celebrations). The argument has been made that the druid priests and priestesses comprised a socially lower class after the conversion of Ireland, while the poets and the brehons within the former druid caste took on many of the powers formerly associated with the other druids. The conversion of Ireland was one of merging Christianity with the native Paganism by expressing the former in terms congruent with the latter—"infiltrating and subverting," in other words. The Church did this rather than slaughter heathens who refused to convert. Christianity in Ireland was rather odd by continental standards for a few centuries until the Pope crushed the independence of the Irish Church in the twelfth century with the help of England. Even after this, the poets and brehons remained semi-pagan for centuries.

Some of the survivals of druidic belief and practice in Ireland

and Wales, along with a great deal of speculation and a few out-right forgeries, later inspired the creation of the Mesopagan Druid fraternities we shall meet in the next chapter. These groups have passed on these fragments (and speculations and forgeries) to this very day, augmenting them with a great deal of folkloric and cultural research.

Other Indo-European Paleopagans in Europe didn't fare as well. The march of Christianity was relentless, crushing all organized opposition (or even just alternate opinions) among the Paleopagan Greeks, Romans, Slavs, and Germans over the course of several centuries. The consolidation began in the towns and slowly moved out into the rural areas (as discussed in Appendix C).

However, Baltic Paleopagans, living amid swamps, thick forests, and rough mountains, were the last Europeans to be conquered by the Church and seemed to have fared better. Work done by Russian and Eastern European folklorists, anthropologists, and musicologists during the mid-twentieth century among the Baltic peoples of Latvia and Lithuania indicated that Paleopagan traditions among the peoples there *may* have survived in small villages even into the twentieth century! Some of these villages still had people dressing up in white clothes (decorated with red and black designs) and going to sacred groves to do ceremonies, supposedly as recently as World War II. Soviet social scientists interviewed the local clergy, recorded the ceremonies and songs, and otherwise made a thorough study of their "quaint traditions" preparatory to beginning efforts to turn them all into good Marxists. Some of the oldest "fossils" of preserved Indo-European traditions (along with bits of vocabulary from Proto-German and other early Indo-European tongues) seem to have been kept by Finno-Ugric peoples such as the Cheremis in Estonia. Most of this research was published in a variety of Soviet academic books and journals, and has never been translated into English.

Modern Baltic Reconstructionist Pagans in the *Romuva* movement have been working on collecting and reviving these customs for almost two hundred years. They claim that they have an unbroken tradition going back many centuries, but they may actually be no older than the Mesopagan Druids we shall meet in Part Two. Even so, revivalists would have only had a century or three gap between them and their predecessors, so some legitimate survivals may have occurred. Time will tell.

PART TWO

The Mesopagan
Druids

5

Druidic "Survivals" and Revivals

The Lesson of the Marranos

Before looking at supposed druidic survivals, let's glance at the people known as the "Marranos," the secret underground Jews of Spain and Portugal. From 1391 CE through 1992 CE, when being a Jew was first incredibly dangerous, then illegal, brave people who wanted to cling to their Jewish heritage were forced to do so in secret. The infamous Spanish Inquisition was established in 1478 by Pope Sixtus IV to examine the sincerity of *conversos* (converts) from Judaism and Islam (and was extended in 1536 in Portugal). Called *marranos* (pigs) or *escondidos* (hidden) by the Inquisition when they were discovered (and usually executed, at least for the first few centuries), they lost more and more of their faith as the decades rolled by.* During the Protestant Reformation, many of them left for Holland and France. In the seventeenth century, many of them left for the Americas and their descendants can be found today in Portuguese- and Spanish-speaking communities from Brazil to Texas (Jews were still being burned to death by the Catholic Church in Portugal and Spain into the middle of the eighteenth century).

In the second half of the twentieth century, members of this underground community around the world invoked the Israeli

*See *The Mezuzah in the Madonna's Foot* and *The Marrano Legacy*, by Trudi Alexy.

Law of Return and demanded the right to immigrate to Israel and be accepted as Jews there. Upon investigation by Israeli scholars and rabbis, it was discovered that these people had lost 99 percent of their heritage over the five hundred years and knew next to nothing about Judaism.* Some of them might light candles on Friday nights (but hide them in jugs), clean the house of leavened bread before Easter, or hide a mezuzah or two, remember a handful of Hebrew words, and courageously observe some of the Jewish holy days with fragmentary rituals, but that was about it.†

As I said in *Bonewits's Essential Guide to Witchcraft and Wicca*, the marranos started out with written literature that was kept available (albeit only in part—the Old Testament—and in lousy translations) by their conquerors, yet still lost almost everything that makes their faith unique in only five centuries. This doesn't bode well for nonliterate religions trying to survive without any public support for two or three times that long.‡

True, the Irish and the Welsh cultures had (censored) versions of their old oral religious literature written down by Christian monks, but it didn't do would-be Pagans much good moldering away in monastery libraries. It's also true that customs of Celtic storytelling, poetry, music, and law lived on well into modern times, and that folk memory can preserve nuggets of myth. But none of this is enough to keep an intact religious system alive, whether for the nonexistent "Old Religion" of Paleopagan witch-priestesses, or for the thoroughly attested religions of the Paleopagan Druids.

---

*After education by rabbis, most were allowed to immigrate to Israel, where they became known as the *anusim*.

†Visit the Web site of Casa Shalom, the Institute for Marrano-Anusim Studies, at www.casa-shalom.com/for more on this fascinating topic.

‡Michael Scharding pointed out to me that the secret Christians of seventeenth-twentieth century Japan also lost almost all their beliefs and practices.

Druid "Fam-Trads"

But what about people who were descended from ancient druidic families? Couldn't they have kept the religion alive for centuries? Probably not. Everything in Celtic culture, as in all cultures, was connected to everything else. Unlike in the modern world, where it is reasonably safe to be a secularist or to have minority religious views (at least if you live in a big city), those living in Paleopagan cultures were in fishbowls, where everyone around them knew what religious, economic, political, or social activities they engaged in. Remember, being a Paleopagan Druid meant belonging to a social caste, an economic class, and having particular duties a person was expected to perform. When most of that caste, class, and set of duties were absorbed by the Church, there wasn't much left for the druid priests, seers, and ritualists to do—not if they wanted to stay alive. The poets, bards, storytellers, and judges kept their traditions and institutions going for several centuries under Christian rule, but the religious specialists were very thoroughly silenced, or reduced to the role of village clever folk.

Over the last few centuries, as we shall see, there have been people who claimed to be descended from druid families. They supposedly kept Paleopagan Druidism as a religion alive through secret family teachings and customs, down through the centuries. Since the early 1970s, thanks to my accursed coinage of the term "Family Traditions" or "Fam-Trads" for supposed underground families of occultists who now call themselves "witches," more and more people have been popping up in the Neopagan scene claiming to be "Fam-Trad" druids and expecting other druids (of all varieties) to accept them as authority figures.

Unfortunately for their arguments, *everyone with Celtic ancestry is descended from the druids*—because social classes interbreed, whether officially or unofficially. With my Irish, Scots, Welsh, Breton, British, and French ancestry, I can claim with 100 percent reliability that I am descended from druids via two-thirds of my ancestors. So what? While I might get an occasional intuitive nudge from one of my ancestors, having them in my family tree doesn't, all by itself, prove *anything* about the authenticity of any druidic teachings I might care to "pass along." Furthermore, although some supposed "Fam-Trad" druids may speak a modern Celtic language, not one of them that I've met so far has been fluent in Old Irish, able to recite their ancestry for twenty generations, willing to compose alliterative Old Welsh poems on request, prescribe twenty-seven uses for oak bark, oak leaves, and acorns, etc. Knowing a few poems, a spell or two from the *Carmina Gadaelica* (see Chapter 20), or a half-a-dozen healing herbs, or how to astral project—all of which can be learned from books these days—does not make one a holder of a secret underground tradition of religious Druidism.

The Culdees and Celtic Christianity

The druids are often associated with a movement within the Irish church that is usually called the Culdees. Generally these folks are said to have been early druid converts, deeply mystical, and to have only believed in those parts of Christian theology of which the speakers or writers themselves approve.

*The Catholic Encyclopedia** gives a less romantic view, saying that "Culdee" is

> a word so frequently met with in histories of the medieval Churches of Ireland and Scotland, and so variously understood and applied, that a well-informed writer (Reeves) describes it as the best-abused word in Scotic church-history. The etymology of the term, the persons designated by it, their origin, their doctrines, the rule or rules under which they lived, the limits of their authority and privileges have all been matters of controversy; and on these questions much learning and ability has been shown, and not a little partisan zeal. In the Irish language the

---

*See www.newadvent.org/cathen/04563b.htm for the full entry.

word was written *Ceile-De,* meaning companion, or even spouse, of God, with the Latin equivalent in the plural, *Colidei,* anglicized into Culdees; in Scotland it was often written *Kelidei.* All admit that, in the beginning at all events, the *Culdees* were separated from the mass of the faithful, that their lives were devoted to religion, and that they lived in community . . .

Appearing, then, first in Ireland, they subsequently appeared in Scotland, and in both countries their history and fate are almost identical. Attached to cathedral or collegiate churches, living in monastic fashion, though not taking monastic vows, the Scotch, like the Irish Culdees, were originally men of piety and zeal. The turbulence of the times and the acquisition of wealth sowed the seeds of decay, zeal gave way to indolence and neglect, a celibate community to married men, church property was squandered or alienated, even the altar offerings, grasped by avarice, were diverted to personal uses, and by the end of the thirteenth century the Scotch Culdee houses had in almost every case disappeared.

We can see here a certain amount of bias on the part of the encyclopedia's editors, who assume that clergy having spouses was a terrible sin (it was normal among the Paleopagans), and that interfering with the flow of money to Rome was even worse, but the overview is probably close to correct. A great deal of effort has been expended over the last few centuries to claim that the wisdom of the ancient druids (who weren't "really" Pagans according to these folk) was passed along through this church within the Church. It has been said that the Culdees represented an esoteric or occult tradition within Christianity going back to St. John the Disciple (via the Gnostics), and that the Culdees were early New Agers whom you wouldn't mind having over for tea. For example, the Web site of *An Ceile De, the Living Celtic Spiritual Tradition,** says:

---

*At www.ceilede.co.uk.

The Order of the Ceile De—or Culdee (the servants, or Spouses of God)—carries the oldest continuous spiritual tradition of the Celtic countries. The path of the Ceile De is and always has been toward a search for the Ultimate Reality—Union with the Divine. Rooted in Druidism, it has a deep reverence for our Mother Earth and all Her children . . . Branching into Christ-consciousness, it fulfills itself in Unconditional love.

The spiritual life of the Ceile De is largely contemplative and nurtures a deep and devotional relationship with that Great Mystery we call God—the Invisible Beloved Whose Face is Everywhere . . . It holds Christ-consciousness as the highest human aspiration. It also involves a development of the imaginal faculties through creative study of Celtic mythology and the Gods and Goddesses of the Gaelic pantheon.

It encourages an integration of all of the above with everyday life. Through this work, we kindle within ourselves a sincere and passionate desire to awaken from the unconsciousness and powerlessness that causes, at best, our gnawing discontent; at worst, the gradual destruction of our world.

All of which sounds wonderful but is very much a projection of modern concerns onto the distant past. Here we have a form of Mesopaganism where liberal Christianity and Celtic myth meet and mingle (I suspect with severe damage to the latter).

The original Culdees *may* have originally been descendants of Christian converts from the druid caste, but they seem to have been puritanical fanatics rather than dewy-eyed mystics wandering (like their imaginary druidic predecessors) in a Celtic fog. Their history contains much ugliness and little that would make them appealing to modern minds. So how did they become so spiritually correct?

The answers lie with the ideas of the British Antiquarians, whom we'll meet soon, about the ancient druids and the various Liberal Catholic movements of the last three centuries.

These latter groups contained various "heretics," mystics, occultists, and opponents (often, though not always, gay) of the Roman Church. Essentially they started up their own denominations of Catholicism by getting their leaders ordained as bishops by "official" bishops (usually from the Dutch Orthodox Church) recognized by the other forty Catholic Churches. Therefore, they could have the precious "apostolic succession" supposedly going back to Jesus. But they tended to be insecure about their status, so there was a lot of "cross-ordination" between the clergy, just to "make sure." A bunch of them who were English and Irish decided that they would start their own Celtic Churches and started looking for groups they could lay claim to. This was during the Celtic renaissance period of the late nineteenth and early twentieth centuries, when all the British Isles were awash in nostalgia for an imaginary Celtic past led by wise, patriarchal, monotheistic druids. The would-be Celtic Catholics discovered the Culdees, ignored the parts they didn't like, then labeled themselves modern Culdees.

Poof! Yet another new old religion was born, one that has now moved away from the exclusively Celtic Catholic idea to become far broader, feminist, environmental, and semi-Pagan. This is not to say that there weren't Irish, Scots, and Welsh mystics who were Christian, because there were (there have been and are Christian mystics all over the world—they usually get sainted and/or burned). Most of the Celtic Christian movement doesn't seem to have much to do with these folks, however, as far as I can see, preferring to think and talk about the imaginary druidic "sources" of their teachings. If you are interested in learning more about the Celtic Christian movement as a whole, there is a large Celtic Christian Web ring of around one hundred Web sites.* You may want to check their references that "the ancient druids believed that . . . " with what we've discussed so far in this book, or with any book written about the druids by a trained scholar during the last thirty years, rather than by one of . . .

*Search for it at www.webring.com.

The British Antiquarians

In 1659 CE, the scholar John Aubrey, having done some quasi-archeological (the science hadn't been invented yet) fieldwork at Stonehenge, made the suggestion that Stonehenge *might* have been a temple of the (Paleopagan) Druids. He developed this suggestion cautiously over the next few decades in his correspondence with his fellow scholars and in the notes for his never fully published work, *Templa Druidim* (Temple of the Druids). In 1694, a fiery young Deist* named John Toland discussed the theory with him and became very enthusiastic about it. In 1695, excerpts from Aubrey's book were published, including his theory about druids at Stonehenge, which thus saw wide distribution for the first time.

In 1717 CE, a young "antiquary" (that's what such folk were called before the term "archeologist" was coined) named William Stukeley obtained a copy of Aubrey's complete manuscript of *Templa Druidim,* including the portions never published. Stuckeley thought the theory about Stonehenge being a druid temple was a terrific idea and began to develop it far beyond Aubrey's original concepts.

In 1723 CE, the Druid stone altar was invented by Rev. Henry Rowlands in his "monumental" work, *Mona Antiqua Restaurata.* His druids are patriarchs right out of the Bible, and the altars they use are cairns (piles of stones) and the capstones of cromlechs (roofs of passage graves). He does at least allow the druids to remain in their groves, rather than forcing them to build huge stone temples. These druid stone altars quickly became part of the rapidly growing folklore of druidism. Prior to 1723, druids were required to use altars made of sod or tree stumps—adequate, perhaps, but hardly as glamorous.

In 1726, John Toland published his *History of the Druids,* in

---

*Deists were ultraliberal Christians or Jews who believed in a "Supreme Being" as a cosmic "first cause" of existence, who had then gone away to let His "clockwork universe" run by itself. Deism frequently served as a barely acceptable social cover for atheism. See most of the founding fathers of the United States.

which he pictured the druids as unscrupulous con artists and theocratic tyrants. This was a rather surprising act for the man who supposedly had, nine years earlier, helped to found a druid order and been its first chosen chief (see below). He did, however, put further forward the theory that Stonehenge had been built for druidic worship.

Scholarship of equal value was, of course, being produced in France as well. In 1727, Jean Martin presented patriarchal druids (Christian style) in his *Religion des Gaulois.* Throughout this century, on both sides of the Channel, ancient druids were being invented, though in France these Pre-Christian Christians tended to be patriotic heroes resisting invasion, while their English counterparts were the greatest mystics in history.

By 1796 CE, all megalithic monuments in Northwestern Europe were firmly defined as druidic, especially if they were in the form of circles or lines of standing stones. In that year, yet another element was added in La Tour d'Auvergne's book, *Origines Gauloises.* He thought he had discovered a word in the Breton language for megalithic tombs, *dolmin,* and by both this spelling and that of *dolmen* the term became part of archeological jargon and of the growing druid folklore. Of course, none of these people knew that the megalithic monuments, cromlechs, and dolmens all predated the Celtic peoples by many centuries.

By the end of the eighteenth century, the folklore, also called Celtomania, went roughly like this:

The Celts are the oldest people in the world; their language is preserved practically intact in Bas-Breton; they were profound philosophers whose inspired doctrines have been handed down by the Welsh Bardic Schools; dolmens are their altars where their priests, the Druids, offered human sacrifice; stone alignments were their astronomical observatories.*

*Salomon Reinach, quoted by Stuart Piggott in the latter's *The Druids.*

Much of this Celtomania was promoted by authors such as Godfrey Higgins *(Celtic Druids)* and Lewis Spence *(The History and Origins of Druidism, The Mysteries of Britain)*, who are quoted by credulous occultists, would-be druids, and Christian fundamentalists even today.

The Fraternal Druid Orders

Explaining the tangled skein of Mesopagan Druid history is more than this brief work can manage. From the 1700s onward, there have been many druidic revivalist groups in the British Isles and elsewhere, most of them with similar sounding names and harking back to the same dozen or so (real or alleged) founders. Add in overlapping memberships and the kind of small group politics that plague all esoteric organizations, and you have a very confused picture for historians to straighten out. Here is where I'll try to account for the major groups.

It is said by some Mesopagan Druids that in 1245 CE a gathering was held of underground Druids and Bards from several parts of the British Isles, and that they managed to agree upon some sort of theological unity. This miracle accomplished, they founded a special group called the Mount Haemus Grove, which is said to still be in existence, with an "unbroken" line leading back to its origins. Such claims, like those made for Witchcraft groups, need to be treated most carefully. There does indeed seem to be something calling itself the Mount Haemus Grove operating today, which is recognized by *some* of the Mesopagan Druids in England. The fact of its current existence cannot, unfortunately, be taken as proof of either its legendary history or its alleged continuity. It may be possible to show a continued existence back to the 1700s, but going back any further will require much more research than seems to have been done so far.

In 1717 CE, it is claimed, John Toland held a meeting at which druidic and bardic "representatives" (elected by whom?) from Wales, Cornwall, Britanny, Ireland, Scotland, Anglesey, the Isle of Mann, York, Oxford, and London supposedly appeared and formed the Order of the Universal Bond, also known as the Ancient Druid Order (ADO) and the British Circle of the Universal Bond (BCUB). The ADO has supposedly continued to this very day (or rather, at least one current group claiming to be part of a Universal Druid Bond says that it goes back this far). The present name of this group's governing body is The Mother Grove, *An Tigh Geata Gairdeachas* (of the Gatehouse of Joy).* Some scholars believe that the ADO was founded in the late 1800s and that the 1717 story is a myth connecting their members to the Masons, who founded their grand lodge in London in 1717 from four local lodges, one of which met at the same Apple Tree Tavern where Toland was said to have started the ADO.

In 1781 CE, Henry Hurle set up the Ancient Order of Druids (AOD), which is sometimes called "the" Druid Order, as were a few other groups, leading to no end of historical confusion. Hurle's group, which may have claimed descent from the supposed founding of the ADO in 1717, was a secret society based on Masonic organizational and ritual patterns—not surprising, since Hurle was a carpenter and house builder, and thus would have been familiar with Masonry. The AOD, like most of the similar mystical societies formed at the time, was heavily influenced by Jacob Boehme (1675–1724 CE), a Protestant Christian mystic, greatly involved with alchemy, hermeticism, and Christian Cabala. He was also a student of the famous Meister Eckhart. Boehme's mystical writings attempted to reconcile all these influences and had a tremendous impact upon later generations of mystical Christians, Rosicrucians, Freemasons, and Theosophists. Mixing his idea into the druidic stew, of course, made matters even more confused for those attempting to discover what the ancient druids really believed and practiced.

In London, Druid groups appeared along with Rosicrucian

---

*This name is a reference to a "first degree" initiation script used by this and/or other druidic groups, which involves a symbolic gatehouse to the druidic path.

and Freemasonic organizations. As the ADO/BCUB put it in their introductory booklet, *The Ancient Druid Order*, "The seventeenth century saw the emergence of the Order into its more modern shape. In the seventeenth and eighteenth centuries there was a complex of mystical societies, Hermetics, Rosicrucians, Freemasons, and Druids, who often had members in common."

Overseas, the link between Deism, Masonry and Druidism also appeared in the small town of Newburgh, New York. G. Adolf Koch has an entire chapter on "The Society of Druids" in his book *Religion of the American Enlightenment*. Deism and downright atheism were popular during the 1780s and '90s among the American intelligentsia, especially those who had supported the American and French revolutions. In fact, a rather large number of the key political figures involved in both revolutions were Deistic Masons and Rosicrucians (see *The Illuminoids*, by Neal Wilgus), which rather dampens claims by the Religious Reich* to America having been founded as a Christian nation. Koch tells the story of the Newburgh Druids thusly:

> Some influential citizens of Newburgh had organized themselves into an interesting radical religious body called the Druid Society. Like its sister organization, the Deistic Society in New York, it was a radical offshoot of an earlier and more conservative society. A Masonic lodge had been established in Newburgh in 1788, and it seems, as one attempts to piece together the fragmentary facts, that as the brothers, or at least a number of them, became more and more radical in the feverish days of the French Revolution, the metamorphosis from Mason to Druid resulted. The Druids held their meetings in the room formerly occupied by the Masons and continued to use a ceremony similar to the Masonic. It is interesting to note, too, that as the

---

*See my essay on Understanding the Religious Reich at www.neopagan.net/ReligiousReich.html

Druid Society died out contemporaneously with the end of [famous Deist of the time] Palmer's activities in New York City, a new Masonic lodge was instituted in New-burgh in 1806.

The question naturally arises as to why those apostate Masons chose the name of Druids. It seems that when they abandoned Christianity, with which Masonry in America had not been incompatible, they went back to the religion [as they conceived of it] of the ancient druids who were sun worshippers. It was commonly believed at that time, by the radicals of course, that both Christianity and Masonry were derived from the worship of the sun . . . The Druids thus went back to the pure worship of the great luminary, the visible agent of a great invisible first cause, and regarded Christianity as a later accretion and subversion of the true faith, a superstition, in short, developed by a designing and unscrupulous priesthood, to put it mildly in the language of the day.

It appears that the famous American revolutionary Thomas Paine, among other radicals of the time, was convinced that Masonry was descended from Druidism. Koch refers us to an essay by Paine, *The Origin of Freemasonry,* written in New York City in 1805. In this essay he mentions a society of Masons in Dublin who called themselves Druids. The spectacular fantasies and conjectures that have been offered over the centuries to explain the origins of Masonry, Rosicrucianism, and Druidism are beyond the scope of this book. Suffice it to say, that the sorts of Druidism with which Paine and his friends might have been familiar were far more likely to have been offshoots of Masonry than vice versa.

Iolo Morganwyg

Following the successful *Eisteddfod* (bardic gathering) organized by Thomas Jones in Corwen in 1789 CE, a huge variety of Welsh cultural and literary societies mushroomed and flourished. In 1792, a stone mason named Edward Williams, who was also an early agitator for Unitarianism (back when it merely meant non-Trinitarianism), and a member of several of these groups in London, was drinking with some friends in a London pub.

"You know," he said to them, "I've never mentioned thish before, but my family have been druidsh for generationsh . . . "

"Really?" they replied. "Tell ush more!"

And so he did.* He told them about his childhood in the Glamorganshire hills, of the Welsh bardic traditions and the rich oral folklore of the local storytellers there, and what he knew about the ancient druids.

"Great idea," they said. "Lesh do it!"

So later he held an Autumn Equinox ceremony for his friends on top of Primrose Hill (in London). Along with some other Welsh bards, he set up a small circle of pebbles and an altar, which he called the *Mean Gorsedd*. There was a naked sword on this altar because part of the ritual involved the sheathing of this sword. At the time, no one paid very much attention to the ceremony or its obvious sexual symbolism (which, if noticed, might legitimately have been called Pagan), at least not outside of the London bardic community.

Williams, however, was not daunted. He declared that the Glamorganshire bards had an unbroken line of bardic and druidic tradition going back to the ancient druids, and that his ceremony was part of it. He began to use the religious/pen name of Iolo Morganwg (Iolo of Glamorganshire). He said that the ancient druids had been monotheists and, by an amazing coincidence, Unitarians! He then proceeded (almost all scholars agree) to translate, mistranslate, and occasionally forge various documents and "ancient" manuscripts, in order to prove these and his subsequent claims. Many people feel that he muddled genuine Welsh scholarship for over a hundred years. It was Iolo who promoted the use of the *awen* symbol (see Chapter

---

*This conversation, and others like it to be retold later, was found by me in the bottom of a pint of Guiness . . . but it's a reasonable reconstruction based on the few known facts.

13), even though it would have been far more appropriate for Trinitarian than Unitarian druids to use.

The effects of Iolo's work did not stop there, however, for later writers such as Lewis Spence, Robert Graves (in *The White Goddess),* and Gerald Gardner (father of Wicca) apparently took Iolo's dubious scholarship at face value and proceeded to put forward theories that have launched dozens of occult and mystical organizations (most of them having little if anything to do with authentic Paleopagan Druidism).

In 1819, Iolo managed to get his stone circle and its ceremony, now called, as a whole, the *Gorsedd,* inserted into the genuine *Eisteddfod* in Carmarthen, Wales. It was a success with the bards and the tourists and has been a part of the *Eisteddfod* tradition ever since, with greater and greater elaborations.

Throughout the nineteenth century, art, music, drama, and poetry were using these fanciful druids as characters and sources of inspiration. Various eccentrics, many of them devout (if unorthodox) Christians, claimed to be druids and made colorful headlines. Wealthy people built miniature Stonehenges in their gardens and hired fake druids to entertain (or scare) their guests. Mystically oriented individuals drifted from Masonic groups to Rosicrucian lodges to Druid groves, and hardly anyone, then or now, could tell the difference. Ecumenicalism was the order of the day and in 1878, at the *Pontypridd Eisteddfod,* the Archdruid presiding over the *Gorsedd* ceremony inserted a prayer to Mother Kali of India! This might have been magically quite sensible, and was certainly in keeping with traditional Pagan attitudes of religious eclecticism, except for the fact that the British attitude towards Indian culture and religion was not exactly the most cordial at the time. Of course, maybe they were anticipating ADF's Pan-Indo-European approach to Druidism (see chapter 7).

Evolution and Branchings

But before this, in 1833, the secret society founded by Hurle, the AOD, apparently split up over the question of whether it should be mainly a benefit (charitable) society or a mystical one. The group that voted for being a charitable society called itself the United Ancient Order of Druids (UAOD). With branches all over the world, it still exists as a charitable and fraternal organization rather like the Elks or Shriners, with both their membership and their rituals overlapping heavily with those of mainstream Masonry. Meanwhile, the other group, still apparently calling itself by the old name (AOD), also continues to exist, as a mystical organization.

In 1858, a group in England calling itself the Order of Druids seceded from the UAOD, and may still exist today. Meanwhile, in the 1840s the UAOD of the United States had been founded after an American succession from the AOD. In the 1870s German lodges of the UAOD-US were founded, as well as the UAOD of Australia.

In 1862, the Welsh Mss. Society published a work by Iolo Morganwg's son, Rev. John Williams (ab Ithel), also known as Taliesin ab Iolo. This was volume one of *Barddas; or, a Collection of Original Documents, Illustrative of the Theology, Wisdom, and Usages of the Bardo-Druidic System of the Isle of Britain, with Translations and Notes*. Not surprisingly, this book is usually referred to as the *Barddas*. The work was composed almost entirely of his father's manuscripts, scraps of writing, and various notes—that is, of Iolo's translations, paraphrases, edits, and sheer inventions of supposedly ancient Welsh bardic materials. Thus, though the work was put together by his son, it is usually referred to as "Iolo's *Barddas*."

This may have been the single most influential book in the Mesopagan Druid revival, despite being filled with enough historical and logical errors to sink a fleet of ships. Most of these errors were due to the father's and the son's efforts to reconcile what was known of Paleopagan Druidism with a Masonically influenced form of liberal Christian theology. The two men built on the previous efforts of medieval Welsh monks to make Welsh history match the Bible, just as Irish monks tried to match their history with it.

In 1874, the Ancient and Archaeological Order of Druids (AAOD) was founded by Robert Wentworth Little, an English Mason and Rosicrucian, who was also responsible for the founding of the Societas Rosicruciana in Anglia (SRIA), the mystical organization from which the Hermetic Order of the Golden Dawn sprang. In 1886, the name of the AAOD was changed to the Ancient Masonic Order of Druids (AMOD) and most of the members who weren't Masons left. These refugees kept the previous name and continued going on. There are still Druid groups in England using both of these names.

In 1912, an American Freemason named James Manchester received a charter from the AMOD in England to start the AMOD in America (AMODA), with a membership restricted to male Masons. Near the end of World War II, women began to be admitted to membership, a fact which kept the organization from being recognized by mainstream Masonic authorities. Its first female Archdruid, Juliet Ashley, took office in 1952, which apparently caused internal dissension. In 1976, the order changed its name to the Ancient Order of Druids in America (AODA). Manchester, Ashley, and other members of the order were active in Masonic, Rosicrucian, Hermetic, and other occult organizations, leading to ideas and rituals from those other sources influencing those of the order. The current head of the organization is John Michael Greer, a Mason, author of *The Druidry Handbook,* and a member of both OBOD and ADF! He tells me:

When the Hermetic Order of the Golden Dawn [the most famous ceremonial magical order in England] blew itself apart in 1900–1903, a lot of members who got sick of the politics bailed out, and a significant number of them ended up in the Druid scene. That happened again when Christina Stoddard, the head of the Stella Matutina, went wacko in the early 1920s and started insisting that there

were hordes of Black Rosicrucians stalking her. So between the two world wars you had a whole series of hy-
brid Druid-Hermetic groups like the Cabbalistic Order of
Druids and the Ancient Order of Druid Hermetists, and a
lot of their practices ended up as part of the general Druid
scene in Britain.

Over the twentieth century, events of a Druidic nature were
occurring outside of England and the USA, of course. In Wales,
the National Eisteddfod Court runs an *Esteddfod* every year, al-
ternating between northern and southern Wales, and has the
"Gorsedd of Bards" arrange the rituals for each occasion. Bardic
and Mesopagan Druidic groups have also arisen in France, Britanny, Cornwall (where they were responsible for rescuing the
Cornish language from the very brink of extinction), the Isle of
Man, Scotland, Ireland, various parts of England, Australia, and
elsewhere. Oddly enough, Mesopagan Druidism proved to be
popular in Germanic and Scandinavian countries, despite these
regions not thinking of themselves as Celtic.

In 1964, the head of the Ancient Druid Order, Robert Reid
(son of the founder, MacGregor Reid), passed away and an
election was held for his successor. A British college professor,
occultist, mystic, and poet named Ross Nichols (1902–1975)
had been a member of the group for ten years and its secretary,
but split from it, in part over the results of this election. He also
wanted to steer a druid group more towards Celtic and British
resources, rather than the Asian and Middle Eastern-influenced
practices (via Theosophy and Rosicrucianism) of the ADO. To
this end he founded the Order of Bards Ovates & Druids*
(OBOD) and was elected its first Chief.

He was very Mesopagan, mixing liberal Christianity, Buddhism, Sufism, and other mystical systems with Celtic myth and
folklore. He decided that eight holidays would be better than

*This has been punctuated different ways over the subsequent years. For this book
I've chosen to use the style (no commas and an ampersand) used in the group's Web
site at www.druidry.org.

three, using the same pattern he and his friend Gerald Gardner had worked out for what was to become Wicca (see the calendar discussion in Chapter 12). He encouraged young people to join, one of whom, Philip Carr-Gomm (1952–), would become his apprentice, editor,* and eventual successor. As Ronald Hutton puts it,

> All through his life he continued to annex fresh concepts to his scheme of mysticism. In his last ten years [1965–1975], the latter absorbed the modern Pagan cycle of eight seasonal festivals, the new interest in megalithic astronomy and geometry, and the new belief in energy-bearing ley-lines, which joined sacred sites in the landscape. He contributed to the development of Glastonbury as a major center of modern mysticism. In this fashion, he anticipated and assisted the assimilation of the image of the Druid to a modern counterculture.†

For years I had wondered why OBOD believed that bardhood and ovatehood had been steps in the ancient druidic training system towards full druidhood (the historical evidence is slim for this belief). When we look at the founder's professorship, the answer became clear. What he created with OBOD was primarily a semiacademic training system, with bards, ovates, and druids being the equivalent of what Americans would call bachelor's, master's, and doctoral degrees.

In the 1970s, an architect and artist named Colin Murray founded the Golden Section Order Society for the Preservation of Celtic Lore. For many years he published *The New Celtic Review* with beautiful hand-lettered articles and essays about ley-lines, Celtic mythology, holiday customs, megalithic monuments, ogham, tree-lore, and so forth. He died much too early

---

*See Nichols' posthumous *Book of Druidry*, edited by Philip Carr-Gomm and John Matthews, and *In the Grove of the Druids*, by Carr-Gomm.
†"The New Druidry," in *Witches, Druids and King Arthur*, by Ronald Hutton.

in 1986. His widow, Elizabeth Murray, was one of the prime movers behind the formation of the Council of British Druid Orders (see below).

When Ross Nichols died in 1975, his fresh experiment in Mesopagan Druidry died with him, or so it seemed. Then Philip Carr-Gomm stepped up to (cricket) bat. Though he had a vision of Nichols asking him to revive the Order in 1984, he was reluctant to do so until he was officially asked by the other members in 1988. Finally consenting, he continued Nichols's policies, developing and expanding the original OBOD teachings into home learning courses, which attracted many young people in the 1980s and 1990s, which led to the Order's spectacular growth. Carr-Gomm is a professional psychologist who applies his knowledge of human nature to his Druidic activities, as well as a deeply committed environmentalist who shares my opinion that druids should be ecological activists.

Today OBOD is the largest Meso/Neopagan Druid organization in the world (not counting the strictly fraternal men's groups such as the UAOD), with over 8,000 members. Under Carr-Gomm's leadership it has moved slowly away from Mesopaganism towards Neopaganism and been actively involved with both environmental activities (including planting thousands of trees) and protest campaigns to preserve ancient holy sites.

The British Druid Order (BDO), was started by Philip Shallcrass (author of *Druidry*) and Emma Restall Orr (author of *Spirit of the Sacred Grove*) in 1979, apparently with some of the same promptings that led to the founding of ADF a few years later. Like OBOD, the BDO is a bridge between Mesopagan and Neopagan Druidry. According to their Web site,*

> The Order seeks to pass on the Druid tradition through hands-on teaching and direct personal experience. This is done through our affiliated *Gorseddau,* through camps, talks, workshops, sacred walks, sweat lodges, howling un-

---

*At www.druidry.co.uk.

der the full moon nights, singing on high hilltop days, wading in the waters of life, forest gatherings, fire-dancing, spirit-weaving, soul-healing, eisteddfod and re-creation sessions. Through these events we simultaneously present and recreate the spirit of the Bardic/Druidic tradition. Events are provided at minimal cost, being primarily for people not profit.

Other recently founded Meso/Neopagan groups include the Secular Order of Druids (SOD), founded by Tim Sebastian in the late 1980s to fight for the rights of everyone who wanted to worship and celebrate at Stonehenge; the Glastonbury Order of Druids, founded by Rollo Maughfling also in the late 1980s; the Druid Clan of Dana (DCD), founded in 1992 by Olivia and Lawrence Durdin-Robinson as a branch of their global goddess network, the Fellowship of Isis (FOI); and the Loyal Arthurian Warband (LAW), founded in 1990 by a performance artist and countercultural activist named John Timothy Rothwell, who became known as Arthur Uther Pendragon (yes, he legally changed his name). All of these groups had overlapping memberships and goals, among them the opening of Stonehenge for ritual use (especially at the solstices and equinoxes), the revival of goddess worship, and the preservation of ancient holy sites and the environment in general.

In 1989, an important step for the Druid revival was taken when the leaders of OBOD, SOD, GOD, and the AOD joined to create the Council of British Druid Orders (COBDO), which was quickly joined by the LAW and several other druidic orders (including ADF and Keltria as associate members). Its membership has grown and shrunk regularly as various political tiffs ruffled feathers and old groups dropped out to be replaced by new ones. At the moment, however, neither COBDO nor any other group can be said to speak for all British druids.

Counting out and pinning down the number and variety of Mesopagan Druid organizations that have existed, even just in England, may well be impossible. As I have mentioned in discussions about the history of Wicca, and as the AOD booklet quoted earlier hints, the British Isles are very small! Esoteric and fraternal organizations have always tended to have overlapping memberships, attend each other's rites, and borrow ideas and terminology from each other. Thus where Piggott or another scholar may see a dozen "different" druid orders, their members may see one or two or three, working along often parallel lines, and all holding to the same ideals of wisdom, character, and public service.

The Stonehenge Connection

Although we have little evidence that the Paleopagan Druids used Stonehenge as a meeting and ritual site—I think it plausible but unprovable—there may have been several different Mesopagan Druid orders who held ceremonies (summer solstice rites were the only ones held by anyone until recently it seems) at Stonehenge in the 1800s. In 1900 CE, another of the standing stones fell over and the owner of the land (Sir Edmund Antrobus) decided to fence the monument and charge admission, the better to (a) keep a closer watch on it and (b) earn enough money to repair the damage being committed by tourists. This caused a problem almost immediately, when a druidic group was holding the next Summer Solstice ceremonies and the Chief Druid was kicked out by the police (he supposedly laid a curse on Sir Edmund, the affects of which are unrecorded).

There is a photograph* dated August 24, 1905, showing a visit of the Grand Lodge of the Ancient Order of Druids, which apparently was the occasion of a mass initiation of several hundred people at Stonehenge. Another druidic group known to have used the monument through the years between 1905 and 1914 CE was called the Druid Hermeticists. During this time period, Summer Solstice celebrations seem to have happened regularly.

*Shown in Julian Richards's wonderful *Stonehenge: A History in Photographs*.

In 1915, Sir Edmund died and Stonehenge was sold at auction to a Cecil Chubb, who immediately gave it to the British government, at a ceremony in which druids of some sort assisted. Since 1919, when Stonehenge became a national monument, many different Mesopagan Druid groups have asked government permission to use it, while other groups (because of political and metaphysical squabbles) celebrated instead at various nearby spots. Some groups, of course, may have used Stonehenge without government permission or knowledge. In 1920, the Summer Solstice was celebrated by George McGregor Reid's Church of the Universal Bond (which was probably the British Circle of the Universal Bond).

From the 1970s to the '90s, Stonehenge was repeatedly blocked off from use by Mesopagan Druids and everyone else, at least around the Summer Solstice, in order to control the activities of the British counterculture (which had begun having festivals nearby and using the neighborhood for antinuclear and ecological protests), and to prevent damage from vandalism. On June 22, 1998, under a Labor Party Prime Minister, the Mesopagan and Neopagan Druids and their friends (at least a hundred of them) were once again allowed to exercise their civil rights by celebrating the Summer Solstice inside Stonehenge. The following year, however, conflict between the British government and protestors again kept the Druids from celebrating within the circle of stones, though things improved again in 2000 and the situation has been positive ever since.

Ironically, one of the best cultural weapons on the side of the Meso- and Neopagan Druids in these conflicts over Stonehenge is the "everybody knows the ancient druids worshipped at Stonehenge" meme that has reproduced itself for over a hundred years from British schoolbooks into the minds of young students. T.K.E. Kendrick has an excellent discussion of how this false belief became embedded in British consciousness via the educational system in his classic book *The Druids*. This should serve as a warning to those of us who write about speculative historical matters, not to be too sweeping in our statements!

6

*The Reformed Druids of North America**

Early History

The Reformed Druids of North America (RDNA) started out as a quasi-religious Mesopagan protest against coerced religion at Carleton College, in Northfield, Minnesota, back in 1963. In those dark days, the student handbook included a rule that required all students to regularly attend the church of their choice (on the traditional monotheistic grounds that coerced religion was better than none). It was in mid-April that a handful of friends were sitting in the campus cafeteria complaining about the situation. One of them, David Fisher, spoke.

"You know," he said to them, "I've never mentioned this before, but my family have been druids for generations . . . "

"Really?" they replied. "Tell us more!"

And so he did.

He shared what he knew about the ancient druids, possibly including some material from one of the fraternal druid organizations.

"Great idea," they said. "Let's do it!"

Together they conspired to found a Druid religion on campus, in order to test the freedom allowed by the college's rule. After all, it was a win-win situation for them—if the college au-

*All quotes from scripture in this chapter are taken from *The Druid Chronicles (Evolved)*, which has been deliberately copyright-free since 1976.

thorities gave the students chapel credit for attending Druid rites, then they would look very silly. But if they didn't, then the students could make a stink about religious discrimination. They decided to call themselves "reformed" because they knew they might make some historical errors and because they were going to avoid performing blood sacrifices. The story of this decision is told in Chapter the Fifth of "The Early Chronicles" in *The Druid Chronicles (Reformed):**

1. And it came to pass that the time was near at hand for the altar to be consecrated.
2. Now it was the custom that when an altar was to be consecrated, that a sacrifice should be made upon it, which sacrifice should be of a living thing, yea, a thing which doth testify to the bounty of the Earth-Mother.
3. And the purpose of this sacrifice is to consecrate the altar.
4. But behold, there did arise a dispute among the Druids concerning this sacrifice, which was to be made upon the altar.
5. For there were some among them who were in favor of a small sacrifice and some who were persuaded that the sacrifice should be a large one;
6. those being in favor of the small sacrifice having a desire that it be of the living leaves and branches of a tree;
7. those being in favor of the large sacrifice having a desire that it be of the living flesh and blood of an animal or bird.
8. Wherefore, there did ensue a dispute among them concerning the manner in which this sacrifice should be made.
9. And it came to pass that Howard, who was Preceptor, did arise and he spake unto them, saying: "Have ye not forgotten that we are reformed, yea, even do we call ourselves by the name of Reformed, wherefore, we must put

---

*This was their half-serious, half-humorous collection of self-written "scriptures."

behind those things which do bring offense to our senses;" for Howard was one of them who were in favor of the small sacrifice.

10. But another did arise, who did call himself Jan, for he was in favor of the sacrifice of an animal, and he spake unto them saying: "Have ye not forgotten the customs of old—which were the customs of our predecessors before us? Verily I say unto you, nothing will be acceptable to the Earth-Mother save it were nothing smaller than an animal or fowl, yea, even a chicken."

11. Wherefore, there was about to occur a great schism between those on the one hand who were of the first faction, and those on the other hand who were of the second faction.

12. And they were exceedingly wroth one with the other.

13. But behold, Jan did rise up and relent his position, asking neither that flesh nor blood be spilt upon the altar; for he did perceive that they were not strong enough and that such a schism would be their end; wherefore, he did relent that the schism might not take place.

14. And it came to pass that the altar was consecrated by the burning of living leaves and branches of a tree; and it came to pass that the altar was consecrated on the third Saturday after the celebration of Beltane (which is the first day of the month of May).

Yes, it does read a bit like the King James Bible. This was an esthetic (and humorous) choice by the early Reformed Druids when assembling their "scriptures," and has been followed to this very day by most of those adding materials to it.

So the Reformed Druids met on Sunday afternoons outdoors on the campus, performing rituals that gradually attracted more and more students, and turning in their chapel slips to the Deans of Women and Men. Much to the surprise of the founders, their campaign also worked! After two years of Reformed Druid rituals, the chapel attendance rule was quietly dropped by the school.

Yet even after they had won their protest, and much to the even greater surprise of the founders, many of the Druids wanted to continue the movement. The prayers they had intoned to the Earth-Mother and various Celtic divinities (real and invented), combined with Zen meditations, Christian mystical writings, and the founders' open-ended philosophy, now represented a valuable part of their spiritual lives. Of course, the fact that they consecrated a cup of the "waters of life"—*na huisce beatha* or Irish whiskey—seemed to make their rituals especially popular. The RDNA continued to exist and graduates of Carleton College spread the Reformed Druid movement wherever they went.

It was in Berkeley, California, that a former student at Carleton, Robert Larson, became the local Archdruid for a group of people, including myself, who were already thinking of ourselves as Neopagans. Under our influence (and my own not-entirely-appreciated agitation) an increasing overlap between RDNA and the Neopagan community began to form. Today, of the forty or so active RDNA groves (congregations), about a third are more Mesopagan and two-thirds more Neopagan. Many of the latter are using the name NRDNA (for New RDNA), while other Druidic movements, such as ADF and Keltria (see Chapters 7 and 8), have grown from the RDNA's trunk as specifically Neopagan branches.

The Reformed Druids are organized into congregations called "groves," each with from three to ten or more members (though dozens of others may show up for major holiday celebrations). Every grove is an independent entity, and each may operate its own "flavor" of Reformed Druidism. At times there have been groves practicing (among the Neopagans) Norse, Wiccan, Eclectic, Zen, and even Hasidic Druidism. The older RDNA groves (i.e., the ones run by original Carleton graduates) often continue to mix Christian, Taoist, Native American, and other mystical traditions with their Druidism. Individuals frequently follow more than one variety at a time, depending upon their personal interests.

Attempts to keep any sort of national structure going have

fluctuated wildly in their effectiveness, due to the strong individualism of the members and the difficulties faced by college students attempting to maintain organizational stability with a rapidly changing population.

Obviously, Reformed Druidism is a uniquely American phenomenon. Because of its lack of discrimination against women and minority groups, its sense of humor about itself, and its distrust of all organizational structures, it is different from most other philosophical and religious movements that had previously called themselves "Druidic."

And yet the Reformed Druids do have some fundamental concepts in common with the Paleopagan and Mesopagan Druids who preceded them and the Neopagan Druids who developed from them. Down through the ages, the role of the druid has always been clear—scholar and artist, poet and priest, philosopher and magician—the one who seeks, preserves, and extends the highest wisdom her or his people are capable of handling safely, and who uses that knowledge and inspiration for the benefit of the community. In their own way, the members of the RDNA tried to do some of this, especially the mystical and philosophical parts.

The Branchings of the Reform*

As of 2006, there are two overlapping Branches of Reformed Druidism: the Reformed Druids of North America (RDNA), and the New Reformed Druids of North America (NRDNA). Earlier branches such as the Schismatic Druids of North America (SDNA), the Hasidic Druids of North America (HDNA), and others (including Zen Druidism, Chaoist Druidism, Norse Druidism, etc.), all seem defunct.† This is, of course, very organic, for if we think of these different versions of Reformed

---

*Much of this section's discussion comes from my original Introduction to *The Druid Chronicles (Evolved)* in 1976.

†My favorite, from a naming standpoint, was Robert Anton Wilson's idea: the Reformed Non-Aristotelian Druids of North America, or RNA-DNA.

Druidism as seedlings rather than branches, we can expect most of them to die before producing offspring.

The RDNA is, of course, the original group and some of the "old guard" still look askance at the offshoots, which puts them into a bit of a quandary, for the RDNA itself neither categorically denies nor accepts the absolute validity of any particular faith, including its own. This is one of the most important principles of the RDNA. It means that anyone may become this kind of Druid without feeling obligated to renounce her or his present religious beliefs and without being committed to anything but the basic tenets. Many find this approach to mysticism liberating. It certainly is in keeping with the approaches of earlier Mesopagan Druid groups who, like the Freemasons they patterned themselves after, insisted that what they were doing was a philosophy, not a religion.

While the original RDNA includes Jews, Christians, Agnostics, Atheists, Marxists and members of other faiths in its ranks, in the late 1960s and early 1970s, Neopagans (including myself) began to show up. I took one look at the group and said to myself, "Self, they're worshiping the Earth-Mother, singing hymns to old gods and goddesses, and doing rituals out in the woods. Sure looks Pagan to me!"

I then attempted to convince the rest of the RDNA (in which I became an ordained priest in 1969) that they were all Pagans, they just didn't know it. They were not amused (O.K., some of them *were* amused, but many were offended). After creating the NRDNA in Berkeley with my initiator in 1974, I moved to Minneapolis, Minnesota, where, tired of fighting with the others, I decided to start the SDNA, and later (in 1976) helped to start the HDNA. Both of these were begun as specifically Neopagan versions of the original RDNA. The SDNA in particular was defined as follows:

> The SDNA is a Branch of Reformed Druidism, emphasizing its own nature as an Eclectic Reconstructionist Neopagan Priestcraft, based primarily upon Gaulish and [other] Celtic sources, but open to ideas, deities, and rituals from

many other Neopagan belief systems. We worship the Earth-Mother as the feminine personification of Manifestation, Béal as the masculine personification of Essence, and numerous Gods and Goddesses as personifications of various aspects of our experience. We offer no dogmas or final answers but only continual questions. Our goal is increased awareness and harmony within ourselves and all of Nature. We are willing to interact philosophically and ritually with members of all other belief systems, including all other Branches of the Reform, that are compatible with our own approach and Nature. We accept our duty to assist Evolution, on all levels, and to work for the survival of our Holy Mother, the Earth.

Those familiar with *Ár nDraíocht Féin:* A Druid Fellowship (see Chapter 7) will recognize some of the basic concepts that were to inform my later creation: openness to new ideas, a commitment to growth, and a commitment to excellence (as shown by the word "priestcraft").

Hasidic Druids?!

The HDNA was more or less an offshoot from the SDNA. It, too, considered itself to be a form of Neopaganism and chose to orient itself around a total Neopagan lifestyle, based upon "repaganized" patterns taken from Jewish origins. It was created at the request of some Neopagans who had been raised Jewish. "We love Jewish and Yiddish culture," they told me, "we just can't stand the theology. Isn't there some way we could create a kind of Druidism with Neopagan polytheology and Yiddish/Jewish cultural patterns?"

"Um, I suppose so," I replied cleverly. "What would we need?"

"Laws, commentaries, and customs," they responded, "in a book or three."

"Ooooookay," said I. "Let's see what we can come up with."

And so we conspired a book of laws, which we called *The Mishmash of Hasidic Druidism*. This included such entries as the following:

CHAPTER ONE: ON IDENTITY

1. Hasidic Druidism is a way of life.
2. All ordinances of the Hasidic Druids shall be based upon identity as Hasidic Druids and are binding on no others.
3. All Ordinances and customs may be modified for reasons of health, livelihood, the avoidance of incarceration, and survival.
4. The Mishmash is an oak tree, not a stone monument.

CHAPTER TWO: ON GENERAL ETHICAL PRIORITIES

1. The Multiverse is very large!
2. Lifestyle is more important than credo.
3. Intent is more important than results.
4. People are more important than property.
5. Discipline is more important than control.
6. Survival is more important than comfort . . .

CHAPTER THREE: ON FOOD AND DRINK

1. Any food or drink found to be fatal shall be declared uncouth* and may not be consumed by Hasidic Druids.
2. Followers of Hasidic Druidism may be vegetarians, carnivores, or omnivores, as they individually choose.
3. The flesh and blood of sentient beings is uncouth and may not be consumed.

---

*This became the root of the HDNA's theory of "couthness," similar to the concept of "kosher" for Jews.

CHAPTER FOUR: ON SEXUAL CONDUCT

1. Sex is a gift of the Gods and is to be enjoyed by all concerned, as often as possible and desired, but especially during Weekends and High Holy Days.
2. Any sexual act physiologically dangerous or impossible to any participant is forbidden.
3. Sexual gratification may not be used for coercion, nor coercion (physical or nonphysical) be used to obtain sexual gratification; such is a crime against the Gods.
4. No restrictions shall be placed upon the sexual acts of any participants upon the ground of age,* species, or sexual preferences; save where danger to health and/or arrest is imminent . . .

While several of the "laws" were tongue-in-cheek, others were serious statements about ethics, lifestyle, and personal responsibilities, such as:

CHAPTER EIGHT: ON ECOLOGY

1. Humans are only part of the Earth-Mother; the attempt to dominate Nature is uncouth.
2. If one must hunt or butcher animals in order to survive, the animals killed must be killed swiftly, mercifully and with proper and respectful ritual.
3. If a stray animal comes to one's door either injured or ready to give birth, it is couth to take care of it until after its injury is healed or the offspring are ready to walk after the mother.
4. For every tree cut down for survival purposes, another must be planted elsewhere beforehand, and the spirit of the doomed tree given a day and a night in which to move into the sapling newly planted, which should be of the same species.
5. When one is camping in the wilderness, the campground

*The two kids from St. Louis were in their late teens and it was the 1970s.

must be left as clean or cleaner than it was upon one's arrival; and all fires must be dead and drowned.
6. It is as couth to clean up the air and land and water as it is uncouth to dirty these things.
7. Love your Mother and your Father and your Siblings all.

Once we had a book of laws and customs, we needed commentaries upon them, and so we sent copies of the *Mishmash* to a half a dozen Pagans of Jewish extraction whom we knew, including Margot Adler, author of the classic text of Pagan journalism, *Drawing Down the Moon.* Together we argued and wrote commentaries, striving to make sure that every verse in the *Mishmash* had at least one comment. We adopted names such as Dru Margola, Dru Lew, Dru Earl, Dru Isaac, etc. These were supposed to humorously correspond to the Jewish title "Reb," short for Rabbi. Only while writing this book, thirty years later, did I discover that "Dru" may have been a Celtic term of address for Paleopagan Druids!

Unfortunately, we didn't wind up with enough comments, so I had to invent a few imaginary Druids, including Dru Iolo (Morganwyg), Dru Amerghin, Dru Karl (Marx), Dru Lao (Tzu), etc., and have them argue with each other. Those who, like myself, were not raised Jewish may find this a little confusing—I certainly did at first! The explanation for why we did it can be found in Chapter Fifteen of the *Mishmash:*

CHAPTER FIFTEEN: ON STUDY AND SCHOLARSHIP

1. When one or more laws are taken from the *Mishmash,* the accompanying commentaries read, and the matters involved debated with wit and grace, this is a *Hairpull.*
2. It is couth for Hairpull to last at least an hour on each occasion.
3. Hairpull should be done by every family at least once every Weekend.
4. It is couth for Hairpull to be done by an entire Grove after services.

5. It is also couth for a Grove to hold weekly Hairpull indoors during the "Season of Sleep," instead of outdoor services.
6. Hairpull may take place at any other time between two or more Hasidic Druids, and this is also couth.
7. Every Grove should have a library where members may meet for study and Hairpull.
8. A scholar in the house is a blessing from the Gods; how much more blessed is the house where scholars meet!
9. If one is teaching the young or ignorant, or making ready to so teach, a scholar may be excused from many household duties.
10. Metaphysical gymnastics are uncouth, save when one is teaching their power, humor, and danger.
11. It is not couth to divorce theory from action.
12. One cannot be a scholar alone.
13. Plant an oak grove about the Mishmash.

This contained both a description of the formal arguing custom (like the arguments over the Torah known as *pilpul)* that we wanted to encourage, a couple of traditional Jewish statements about scholarship and scholars, and warnings about getting too carried away with ourselves. With the commentaries and arguments gathered into a book we called *The Te-Mara,* our Hasidic Druids could begin the process of creating new generations of comments upon the comments (which we originally intended to publish on a regular basis). For example, consider the first two laws in the *Mishmash:*

(1:1) Hasidic Druidism is a way of life.

(1:2) All ordinances of the Hasidic Druids shall be based upon identity as Hasidic Druids and are binding on no others.

The commentaries on these in the *Te-Mara* read as follows:

1:1 *A Way of Life:* Here in the opening line of the *Mishmash* we have the major characteristic that distinguishes

Hasidic Druidism among most religions, including most Neopagan religions, for Hasidic Druidism is not merely a play in which one acts once a week or once a month, but an integral part of everyday life (Dru Chwerthin).

The major emphasis in this opening line of the *Mishmash* is that actions are more important than one's claimed beliefs, as it is stated in 2:2, and from the very beginning of the *Mishmash* we are reminded to put our thought and beliefs, our hopes and our faith, into action in our daily lives (Dru Amherghin).

1:2 *And Are Binding on No Others:* No moral aspersions are to be cast upon those who are not Hasidic Druids for not following our ways (the Ancients).

And yet we know that many of those who are not Hasidic Druids do very evil things, how then can the Ancients of Blessed Memory declare that "no moral aspersions are to be cast" upon them? They can say this because they are talking about calling someone evil or inferior merely because they are not Hasidic Druids, not about calling someone evil for committing acts of an evil nature (Dru Iolo).

This Law does not allow a Hasidic Druid to hire, persuade, or coerce an Outsider into violating the laws for the Druid's own profit or convenience: use of such a surrogate is as uncouth as if the Druid himself violated the law (Dru Earl).

While there are a number of the commentaries I now find embarrassing, since they were rooted in the absolute sexual freedom doctrines of the 1970s and thus ignored the serious dangers of sexual abuse, many of the others contain a great deal of wisdom and are worth study even today. Certainly, the many hairpull sessions we engaged in for a couple of years were of significant value in helping us articulate and explore what we really believed.

Naturally, we couldn't complete the process of creating Hasidic Druidism without having a prayer book, so we put together a (very short) one called *Considdur: the Alternatives.* It included items such as the following:

LITANY OF THE EARTH-MOTHER

O Earth-Mother, Thou of uncounted names and faces, Thou of the many-faceted Nature in and above All, Nature Incarnate, Love and Life fulfilled; look favorably upon this place, grace us with Your Presence, inspire and infuse us with Your powers; by all the names by which You have been known, O Earth-Mother:

Come unto us.
Thou Whom the Druids call Danu—
Come unto us.
Thou Who art Erde of the Germans—
Come unto us. *
Thou Whom the Slavs call Ziva—
Thou Who art the Nerthus of the Vanir—
Thou Whom the Poles call Marzyana—
Thou Who art Frigga of the Aesir—
Thou Whom the Romans call Terra—
Thou Who art Diana to the Etruscans—
Thou Whom the Persians call Kybele—
Thou Who are Iphimedeia, Mighty Queen of the
      Greeks—
Thou Whom the Egyptians call Nuit, Star Mother—
Thou Who art Ninmah of Sumeria—
Thou Whom the Hittites call Kubala—
Thou Who art Mami-Aruru of Babalon—
Thou Whom the Caanities call Arsai—
Thou Who art Our Lady of Biblos in far Phoenicia—
Thou Whom the children of Crete call Mountain
      Mother—
Thou who art Oddudwa of the Yoruba—
Thou Who art Shakti and Parvati of India—
Thou Whom the Tibeteans call Green Tara—
Thou Who art Kwanyen of China—

*Repeat after each name.

Thou Whom the Nipponese call Izanami—
Thou Who art Sedna and Nerivik of the Eskimos—
Thou Whom the Pawnee call Uti-Hiata—
Thou Who art Cornmother of the Plains—
Thou Whom the Navaho call Estanatlehi—
Thou Who art Ometeotl and Guadalupe in Mexico—
Thou Whom the Islanders* call Hina-alu-oka-moana—
Thou Who art the Great Mother, the Star Goddess, the
    All Creating One—
Mother of All, we call upon You—
Terra Mater, Mater Sotier, Earth-Mother—*Come unto us!*

SPECTRUM PLUS
(An Order for the Lighting of Candles)†

Black: From darkness,
White: To light,
Green: To life. First came the life of plants,
Red: Then came the life of animals,
Yellow: Then came the life of the mind.
Purple: From the mind comes passion,
Orange: From passion comes courage,
Blue: From courage comes self-awareness,
Indigo: From self-awareness we pass beyond all
         space and time,
         To touch the Most High One.

EXORCISM‡

In the name of the Earth-Mother, the Great Goddess, She
who is called Danu, Frigga, Devi, Terra, Uti-Hiata, and by
many other Names; Mother of all mortals and immortals,
source of love and life; before whom all Gods, demons, angels,

---

*Hawaiian.
†These color associations were based on those in my first book, *Real Magic,* which
in turn were based on my observations of common color beliefs. This ritual could be
done at the beginning of the Friday night meal.
‡For those rare occasions when one is needed.

demiurges, elementals, men, women and all other entities must bow:

I cleanse this place, commanding all spirits and entities of destructive, diabolical, diseased or demonic nature of any sort so ever to quit and depart from here instantly!

Leave! For it is commanded in the name of Macha, Kali, Chandika, Kybele—the wrathful Goddess who is the slayer of demons; She who soars above the battlefields; she who is drunk on the blood of evil ones.

Leave! for it is commanded in the Mother's name and ye dare not refuse, lest the Star Goddess visit Her vengeance upon ye.

Leave! For this is to be an abode of the spirits of life and of love, and such as ye have no place here, now or ever.

In the name of the Great Goddess: So be it.

PSALM OF THE STAR GODDESS*

1. The heavens declare the glory of the Goddess, the firmament shows her handiwork.
2. Day after day shouts this; night after night reveals this knowledge.
3. No language fails to contain Her praise.
4. Her praise circles the world and rises to the Sun.
5. This praise is as joyous as love and as strong as the hunt.
6. She contains all in Her hands and Her bosom.
7. Her laws work, follow them and you will be wise.
8. Her laws are just, follow karma and your eyes will see.
9. Be awed by Her mighty knowledge;
10. Knowing and doing right is better than gold and sweeter than honey.
11. By understanding Her way, your path will always be lit.
12. She will teach you the way to balance, and to avoid pitfalls.
13. Never presume to know Her all, for She is greater than any human.

---

*This is a simple praise prayer.

Obviously, these prayers are not limited to Celtic or even to Indo-European deities, but rather encompass a wide variety of goddesses from around the world. Unfortunately, the Hasidic Druids of North America only lasted for a few years before vanishing into the mists. There have been a few attempts to revive them and as long as the collection of their works, which we called *The Great Druish Books,* continues to circulate around the globe in hard copies and on-line, anyone is welcome to take them into another generation of evolution.*

The RDNA "After Isaac"

After I left in 1982, most of the RDNA groves fell out of communication despite the continued publication of newsletters like the *Druid Chronicler* and *Druid Missal-Any* until 1991. There were two other Druidic offshoots of the RDNA after I schismed, the Reformed Druidic Wicca (later renamed "Missionary Order of the Celtic Cross," or MOCC) in 1984 and the Order of the Mithril Star (OMS) that joined the RDNA briefly at the end of the twentieth century. The main Carleton Grove itself nearly died off in the 1980s, but was ironically revived by the fortuitous discovery of some of my writings by students in the attic of an off-campus house. This renaissance integrated the now flourishing Neopagan movement and current ecological interests, making the RDNA even more eclectic than ever. As student Druids graduated, they again began founding quirky "missionary" groves, a practice not seen since the mid '70s.

By 1993, a new era of Reformed Druidism was vigorously underway, much to the credit of one of their Archdruids, Michael Scharding, who began the International Druid Archives and collected much of the RDNA, ADF and Keltrian materials (among a dozen groups), re-establishing communication between the RDNA groves and other offshoot Druid

---

*Let me know if you do—someday I'd like to produce a full-sized book about this approach to Neopagan Druidism.

groups. The rising availability of the Internet, the compilation and distribution of several large RDNA books, known as *A Reformed Druid Anthology,* and free speedy e-mail allowed the few remaining RDNA groves to quickly branch out to most corners of the country—and even to places like Japan and France in recent years. As the cost and difficulty of communication decreased, this flowering was also true for the RDNA's offshoots, whom we will meet in the next chapter.

Additional Notes

It should be remembered that many of the members of the RDNA do *not* consider themselves to be Pagans of any sort, but rather followers of a way of inquiry that is applicable to any faith. They don't even like the term "Mesopagan" despite its clear historical applicability. Reformed Druids believe that among the many obstacles to spiritual growth are dogmatism and orthodoxy—the formalization of beliefs in a fashion that discourages continual spiritual inquiry, or that encourages others to adopt them without their own inquiry. Many also feel that most of the world's religions are beset by these problems and must constantly combat their ossifying influence. The Neopagan members of the Reform agree that it is necessary to keep a wary eye and a keen sense of humor about the whole problem.

The Neopagans seem to place more of an emphasis than the non-Pagans upon the following areas: magic, craft, poetry, song, dance, use of solar and lunar cycles, Neopagan ecumenical rites, civil liberties actions, and active worship of many gods not mentioned in the original RDNA literature. All Reformed Druid movements are interested in ecological activities and in the creation of new liturgies.

Thanks to the Apostolic Succession from Carleton College (maintained by using the same basic ordination ceremony, with or without additions, for the priesthood), all Third Order priests and priestesses of any branch of the Reform are equally legitimate, though personal beliefs vary widely and some groups may not allow priests of a different branch to lead some of their specialized rites.

In none of the currently existing branches of the Reform is either sex given precedence over the other, nor any race, color, nationality, or culture considered superior. The specifically Neo-pagan branches accept only Pagans for the priesthood. The priesthood of the RDNA and the NRDNA, on the other hand, are open to members of all faiths.

There are approximately 4,000 or so people who have been part of the Reformed Druid movements since the founding in 1963, and their groves (currently around 40) can be found all over the world, though most are in the United States. I think one of the best summaries of Reformed Druidism was written by Michael Scharding, Archdruid of the Washington, D.C., grove, RDNA, and grand editorial poobah of the infinitely ex-panding *Reformed Druid Anthology* Project:

Less Is More, a Summary of Reformed Druidism*

Reformed Druidism is a gentle protest against organized religion. We're not really anarchists, just simplists.

We've noticed that good Arch Druids spend a great deal of their time explaining what Druidism is not. In a Taoist sense, what is not there can make something useful (like a doorway in a wall).

You may notice that in each individual grove, you might find one or more exceptions to these rules of thumb.

1. Not Celtic-Focused. Any inspirational source is okay, 25 percent or more of the members seem to choose Celtic.

2. Not a Religion. We're rather split on this one. Some say it's a religion. Some say it's a philosophy or outlook. Some say some rather silly things. Others ignore the ques-tion as unimportant and not tending towards edification.

3. Not Neopagan. Well, actually, about 40 percent of us are Neopagans. We do resemble Neopaganism very closely (which came after our founding), but most of us don't de-

*Online at www.geocities.com/mikerdna/lessismore.html, reprinted by permission.

fine ourselves or the entire Reform as such. We generally do include Neopaganism among our many possible sources of inspiration. The New RDNA, however, is more firmly in the Neopagan camp. As a rule, Druids are mischievously difficult to pin down.

4. *No Established Dogma.* We don't take anybody too seriously, especially ourselves. We really like Nature, think a lot, and sometimes share our thoughts in writing. We do have two basic tenets and some think that's too much.

5. *No Established Ritual.* Attendance is, of course, unnecessary, in general, and perhaps undesirable. Members of some groves occasionally meet on the eight festivals and the moons, but we are split on whether ritual is more distracting to Druidism or if Druidism is more distracting to ritual. Regardless, we recognize that a lack of ritual can become a ritual, in and of itself! There are other ways to get together than liturgies.

6. *No Strong Priesthood.* Sure we've got priests (they grow like weeds) but no established common seminary program, just a period of observation and loose mentoring. Non-priests can lead services of their own devising, of course. The RDNA has generally hobbled its own priests, for their own good.

7. *No Membership Requirements.* We're not exclusive, any background can join, if they respect the other members. There is no official excommunication or defrocking; Nature knows her own. Inanimate objects are equally able to join, some even doing a better job than the mobile Druids. I can think of several groves entirely composed of trees, imagine that. Groves and branches have the right to determine who can join their local groups.

8. *No Cross-Membership Restrictions.* You can simultaneously belong to other groups or dimensions. Even if other groups don't like you to be part of us, we have no disagreement with you belonging to other groups.

9. *No National Organization.* We used to have one, but it wasn't useful, so it's thankfully defunct, except in

the sense that its continued existence prevents the establishment of a replacement.

10. No Buildings. When nature is so wonderful, why hide inside a building? Some folk may own property that they share, but few groves have had a corporate ownership of facilities or funds.

11. No Money or Fees. It's sad, but we're always in the red, relying on generosity to pay for the sacramental whiskey and such. Most fees that I have seen are quite nominal and are for feast costs, mailings, or site usage.

12. No Regular Paid Publications. No official monthly journals and such, you're on your own. There is *A Reformed Druid Anthology* of past attempts, but since there's no money in it, few publish much.

*13. No Proselytizing.** We're not secretive, but how do you effectively advertise a lack of something? People generally find us, stay for awhile, and move on when they're ready. That's cool.

14. No Uniforms. Occasionally somebody dresses up in SCA clothes, but casual clothes are cool. Homemade is impressive, though. Dress appropriately for the weather.

15. No Bad Stuff. Well, we've succeeded, so far, at least. Like the vast majority of Neopagans, we don't do blood/ animal/human sacrifice (although we occasionally offer a carrot or zucchini) because we are *Reformed* and we think that's yucky. We are however divided on whether fungi should be ritualistically categorized as animal or plant because they do possess biological characteristics of both. Likewise, we don't do such uncool things like brainwashing (who wants a clean mind?), orgies (which is obviously a fast way to get STDs), take money/property, or abuse our members (who'd want to be in such a group?). We treat our members with respect, and they freely come and go.

Sounds like there isn't much to define the group!

---

*By and large, most Pagans don't approve of proselytutes.

Yep. It does seem that way. Yet, we're still here, without all those things after forty years. Guess they aren't so
necessary for everyone? How do you know a Reformed
Druid then? I guess I know most of them when I see
them, read their works, or if they say they are one.

We'll come back to the Reformed Druids (in Chapters 11
and 16) where we'll look at their beliefs and rituals. For now,
let's move on to the other major Druid group that I know the
most about—my very own ADF!

PART THREE

✦

The Neopagan
Druids

7

Ár nDraíocht Féin:
A Druid Fellowship

The Dangers of Strong Drink

I am going to somewhat immodestly begin this part of the book by focusing on the organization I started myself, *Ár nDraíocht Féin:* A Druid Fellowship (ADF). While my efforts to subvert Reformed Druidism into becoming a Neopagan form of Druidism were somewhat effective, ADF was the first successful Neopagan Druid religion to be started in the United States (and possibly in the world). Thus it can serve as a touchstone to examine other Neopagan Druid groups, whether practicing druidism, druidry, or *draíocht*. Certainly we were able to discover lots of ways not to do things!

The story of the founding of ADF is in many ways similar to that of Iolo Morganwyg's AOD and David Fisher's RDNA. In 1983 I was living in New York City and attending Irish language classes at the Irish Arts Institute. I met a fellow Neopagan there and we began meeting at a nearby pub after class. One evening, after far too many pints, I said the fateful words and my doom was sealed.

"You know," I said to him, "I've never mentioned thish before, but I've been a druid for yearsh . . . "

"Really?" he replied. "Tell me more!"

And so I did. I told him what I had learned over my years of study about the Paleopagan Druids. I told him about my RDNA initiator Bob Larson and my years with the Berkeley and

Minneapolis Groves of the NRDNA and SDNA. I told him how much fun the invention of the HDNA had been and how I had returned to Berkeley determined to make Reformed Druidism more of a "real" Neopagan religion, only to have everything blow up in my face. I told him how my old Irish teacher, Dr. James Duran, had taught me about the writings of Dumézil, Rees, and others, and how he had informed me that between the Dumézilian materials, the *Carmina Gadelica*, and the Lithuanian Pagan survivals, it would actually be possible for a small group of dedicated researchers to reconstruct most of what Paleopagan Druidism had really been. I said wistfully that it sure would be nice if there were a Neopagan Druid group actually based on excellence in scholarship.

"Great idea," he said. "Lesh do it!"

"Noooooooooooooooooo!" I screamed in despair, remembering how my clumsy political skills had destroyed my last efforts in that direction.

"Wonnerful," he replied cheerfully. "When do we start?"

It took more than a few pints on more than a few nights to convince me to try starting another druid group.* Eventually my friend and others nudged me into the first steps. I decided to start a druidic "APA"—an "amateur press association." APAs were (and no doubt may still be) collectively written and produced magazines, usually put out by members of science fiction and fantasy fandoms. In those dark days before the Internet, people would type or print out single-spaced "zines" on a favorite topic, then mail either the originals or multiple copies to a central mailer. This person (or sometimes entire committees) would do any additional copying needed, collate everyone's separate zine into a single bundle, then mail out a copy to each contributor. Some APAs would have specific themes, such as popular or obscure movies, television shows, or authors, others would be completely non-specific. It seemed to me to be the perfect way to link up amateur scholars who had no academic

---

*On the bright side, multiple pints of Guinness are much better than having an epileptic seizure, falling off my horse, and hitting my head real hard.

institutions to pay our communication expenses, and if it started to get too intense, time consuming, or expensive, I could always back out.

Right. Uh-huh. Sure . . .

*The Druids' Progress**

And so I sent out a letter to some forty or so colleagues whom I knew to be serious about the topic of druidism. In this letter I explained who I was and what I had in mind, my lifelong attraction to druidism and my search for a Pagan organization that valued scholarship and the arts as much as ritual and costumes. I mentioned Dumézil, Eliade, and the other scholars we've met in this book and my belief that a small group of committed souls could indeed do the job of reviving or reconstructing Paleopagan Druidism in a way that made sense for our modern times—that is, as a Neopagan path. I shared my vision of Druids as being "artists and intellectuals, magicians and clergy, holders of the highest wisdom their cultures (or subcultures) have to offer. This is what they used to be, and what they could be again.

I went on to invite the recipients to participate in the creation of a new Neopagan religion:

> Ár nDraíocht Féin. The Irish words [pronounced "arn ree-ocht fane"]† mean "Our own Druidism," and that's what I have in mind—a brand-new form of Druidism, not just Pan-Celtic, but Pan-European. [By this latter term, I mean to include all of the European branches of the Indo-European culture and language tree—Celtic, Germanic, Slavic, Baltic, even the pre-Classical Greek & Roman.] Paradoxically, this would resemble the original Paleopagan

---

*This and the following sections are essentially edited updates of the historical documents mentioned, which can be found on my Web site at www.neopagan.net.
†Items in square brackets are explanatory inserts I put into the letter when it was reprinted in the first issue of *The Druids' Progress*.

Druidism far more than any efforts of the last thousand years. It would be based on the best scholarly research available, combined with what has been learned [about art, psychology, small group politics and economics] through the theory and practice of modern Neopaganism, and my own knowledge of [the polytheological and practical details of] magical and religious phenomena.

I told them that I had already started this project, through the organizing of my notes and the beginning of a new book, and explained my need for feedback, advice, and research help from others to make this project work. I mentioned that I would also need some sort of minimal financing and suggested that it might take me 10–20 hours a week for 2–3 years. I told them:

What I have in mind is this: Despite my experiences with Pagan publishing in the past, I'm willing to produce a highly irregular, nonscheduled Druid publication. This would come out four or five times per year, and would simply consist of xeroxed sheets of dot matrix type like this letter. Issues would include selections from the work in progress; research materials (advice, requests, and reports for and from the readers); scholarly, liturgical and polytheological debates; Druidic rituals and guided meditations, and anything else that looked interesting and Druidic around publication time.

This, of course, was to be the druidic APA, which I named *The Druids' Progress,* for it was to chronicle our progress towards achieving some very ambitious goals. "With a little bit of luck, the blessings of the Gods and a great deal of hard work," I said, "we can create an authentically Druidic Neopagan religion our ancestors would be proud of." That last sentence was probably what tipped the scales in my head. Even without realizing it, I had moved from thinking of this as a cooperative research project to a group creative one in which the final result (ten or twenty years down the line, I said to myself) would be a living Neopagan Druid religion.

The Druids' Progress was to become a less or more quarterly publication that would publish some excellent Pagan scholarship and link a community of kindred souls.*

What ADF Was Meant to Be

As I said in an essay in that first issue of *DP*, ADF was an idea I had been wrestling with for many years: "a Neopagan Druid Order whose members would not be ashamed to honestly compare themselves with the original Druids."

The plan was that ADF would be a Neopagan religion based on solid (but imaginative) scholarship in many scientific and historical fields. We would avoid trusting anything written by Godfrey Higgins, Iolo Morganwg, Lewis Spence, Merlin Stone, H. P. Blavatsky, or other pseudo-scholars. If we had to fill in gaps in our knowledge with our own imagination, spiritual visions and/or borrowings from non-IE sources, we would go ahead and do so, but always in full awareness of what we were doing (and with full documentation of the process).

ADF would develop a slow and thorough system of training for Druidic clergy, equivalent to that gone through by professional clergy in other religions. Although our primary focus would be on the beliefs and practices of our Indo-European ancestors, and on how these could be adapted to modern circumstances, we would not tolerate racism, anti-Semitism, sexism, or homophobia.

We planned to create a carefully structured hierarchy, based on actual skills and knowledge obtained and demonstrated, with both upward and downward mobility. It would involve the setting of specific standards in all the areas necessary for functioning at the different levels, and those standards would appear in our own publications and be widely disseminated throughout

---

*It was eventually replaced by *Oak Leaves*, the current ADF journal.

the Neopagan media, in order to prevent false claims of rank. Our primary approach would be the attainment not just of competency, but of *excellence*—in fact, our official motto became, "Why not excellence?"

We didn't expect everyone in ADF to be qualified for (or even interested in) attaining the rank of clergy. After all, the original Druids were only a small percentage of their Paleopagan communities, and not everyone has (or needs) a clerical vocation. We would not promote any one true, right, and only way of Druidism, merely whatever happened to work for us. We intended to maintain friendly relations with as many other Druid organizations as possible, and encouraged our members to investigate these alternate Druid paths. We knew it would take time to put the whole system together (our other motto became, "As fast as a speeding oak!"). Based on solid research and a knowledge of the mistakes made by other Neopagan groups in the past, we thought we could create something magnificent.

How Well Did We Do?

Actually, pretty darn well! Even I find parts of the original open letter very funny. The 10–20 hours per week turned into 40–50, the two-to-three years into over twenty, and the single *Druid Handbook* into multiple publications. Most of the plans about basing what we were doing on serious scholarship were kept, as were the nondiscriminatory ideals. Our clergy training program was indeed ambitious and was published to loud howls of outrage from other Neopagan groups—some of whom quickly copied it. Ironically, the membership of ADF scrapped the original training system after only a few years, then took its time— "As fast as a speeding oak!"—to create the current one, which is now operating smoothly. We managed to stay pluralistic and even expanded our declared boundaries (including the Indo-European Vedic and Persian cultures), annoying both the fundamentalist Celtophiles and the New Age wannabe Indians alike.

On January 1, 1996, due to very poor health, I retired as the original Archdruid of ADF and became the first Archdruid Emeritus of the organization. Under the capable hands of my successors as Archdruid, the organization has now grown and strengthened into something wonderful. Having sprouted new branches, planted many groves, reached out to other Druidic organizations, it has been a proud and vigorous member of the American Neopagan community for over two decades. Today, with over a thousand members, it is the largest Neopagan Druid organization based in the United States. No doubt it will continue to grow and evolve as time goes by, but so far (I like to say), ADF is just about where I expected it to be in my "100-year plan."

We'll come back to ADF several times in the following chapters, but I'd like to end this one by . . .

Comparing ADF and OBOD

Because they are the two largest Neopagan Druid organizations in the world today. It can be interesting and useful to compare and contrast the two organizations. As John Greer puts it,

> Those differences are substantial; in fact, of all the Druid groups active in America today, OBOD and ADF have perhaps the least in common. The two organizations differ in almost every imaginable way, and what's true of one is pretty consistently untrue of the other. The distance between them offers some sense of the extraordinary complexity and richness of the modern Druid movement.*

Perhaps the most important difference is that ADF is organized as a public Pagan "church"—that is, as an incorporated

---

*This and much of the following comes from an essay ("ADF and OBOD" on the ADF Web site in 2005) by John Greer, author of *A World Full of Gods* and a member of both organizations.

institution designed to provide religious services to a larger community, including nonmembers. OBOD is set up as an initiatory lodge-style organization, with many (if not most) of its activities both private and focused on the needs of the membership.

ADF is a collection of related religions, all of which are focused on the spirits and cultures of the Indo-European Paleopagans. OBOD, as a magical/mystical system, is not committed to a single (however complex) body of belief and practice. Rather it is an eclectic blend of magical and religious customs from around the world, both Pagan and non-Pagan, which transmits an "initiatory current" to its members. Thus ADF is explicitly Neopagan while OBOD dances along the borderline between Meso- and Neopaganism. Again as Greer puts it:

> OBOD, as an initiatory order, embraces many viewpoints that ADF specifically excludes. In OBOD there are monotheist Druids, polytheist Druids, pantheist Druids, atheist Druids, and more, participating in OBOD activities together in perfect amity. There are also OBOD Druids who are Christians, Buddhists, and observant Jews alongside those who are Pagans of various traditions. This would be problematic in ADF, as it would be in most churches, but it's entirely workable in OBOD, as it would be in most initiatory orders.

ADF is dedicated to using mostly current (within the last thirty years) scholarship about the Celtic and other Indo-European peoples. OBOD in 2006 is too, although until 2000 they were using research from the eighteenth, nineteenth, and early twentieth centuries. Most of this is now known to have been grossly incorrect, but nonetheless it was worked into OBOD's magical and mystical system—one that worked for the members, making it spiritually *valid* to many, even if it wasn't historically *authentic*. Since 2000, OBOD has made a major commitment to historical authenticity, working with professional scholars to rewrite all their training materials. In ADF, I like to think, we have created a system that is both valid and authentic (up to rational limits). The test for both OBOD and ADF will come in a few decades or centuries when new research casts doubts on what we now consider solid facts (or at least plausible conjectures). Will our successors have the courage to change working spiritual technologies to match new data? I certainly hope so.

Greer also points out that ADF rituals are specifically religious ones, directed to deities and other spirits, and including sacrifices and offerings. OBOD ones tend to be more mystical and cultural, and include nineteenth and twentieth century Western ceremonial magical and quasi-Masonic elements. As he puts it, "Where ADF rituals invoke, OBOD rituals enact."

The two organizations' study systems are very different, ADF's being optional and OBOD's mandatory. Their internal structures are different, though oddly the opposite of what some consider the usual patterns for churches and orders: ADF's is complex and has multiple checks and balances, while OBOD's is simple and is dependent upon the personal skills and character of the reigning chosen chief (fortunately, with Philip Carr-Gomm, the organization has someone with no shortage of either).

OBOD has about four times as many members in the United States as ADF has, perhaps because its focus on individual spiritual growth matches the American obsession with individualism better than ADF's focus on balancing personal growth with service to the Neopagan community. Philip Carr-Gomm believes, however, that "it is more likely due to the fact that many people drawn to Druidry are actively trying to get away from organized religion and want more of a philosophy and a way of life than a religion per se." He put it this way in *What Do Druids Believe*:

> Druids in Britain view with bemusement American attempts to construct a religion that bases itself on a church model, complete with legal registration as a church, pages of bylaws, and clergy training programmes, since part of

Druidry's appeal for them lies in its dissimilarity to the church and its avoidance of regulations and distinctions between clergy and laity. Some Americans in their turn find British Druidry oddly unstructured and laissez-faire.

For the most part each different approach to Druidry simply goes about its business without paying too much attention to the other approaches. Fraternal and cultural druids exist in separate worlds, and the Celtic Reconstructionist and American religious groups generally ignore the majority of British publications and groups, and vice versa, perhaps out of tacit disapproval of each other's approaches, perhaps because they are just busy enough as it is. An interesting project for the future would be to bring together these different viewpoints to explore their commonalities and differences.

Both OBOD and ADF encourage multiple memberships in druidic organizations. Unlike the pseudo-druids we'll meet in Chapter 10, legitimate druid groups know that none of them has a monopoly on truth, let alone "Truth!" I strongly encourage readers interested in druidism, druidry, or *draíocht* to investigate and join at least three different groups—a few more of which we'll now take a look at.

8

Other Neopagan Druid Groups

The Henge of Keltria

In 1986, when ADF was only three years old, we had our first major schism—I was so proud! After all, you're not a "serious" religion until you've had at least one. While we had had a few people drop out of the organization, no one yet had staged a revolution, or at least attempted to.

At the Pagan Spirit Gathering in Wisconsin in 1986, five people, including Tony Taylor, Pat Taylor, and Ellen Evert Hopman, decided that they were unhappy with the direction they saw ADF taking. They created a list of their concerns and taped it to the door of the camper I was sleeping in at the festival. As a humorous reference to Martin Luther (the instigator of the Protestant Reformation) and the Ninety-Five Theses that he had nailed to the Wittenberg cathedral door, the list included thirteen concerns, numbered one through twelve and ninety-five. They thought these thirteen issues were not being properly handled by ADF's then board of trustees, and they wanted them dealt with immediately. After a year of not receiving their desired response, they decided to found their own organization, the Henge of Keltria.

Their primary concerns were the following: They wanted a strictly Celtic style of Neopagan Druidism rather than ADF's Pan-Indo-European approach. They wanted to be able to do most of their rituals in private, rather than in public as required by ADF. They liked ADF's scholarship but thought it insufficiently mystical and magical. They objected vigorously to ADF's structural requirements for local groves to keep financial records, make regular reports on their activities to the board, and so forth. They were really annoyed by ADF's communications bottlenecks, caused by my increasingly frantic efforts to do everything myself with insufficient time, energy, and money.

Keltria was neither the first nor the last group to branch off from ADF because they wanted a private, closed group rather than a public, open one (although why they joined ADF in the first place, knowing our intentions, has always confused me). One thing I found amusing, some ten or twelve years after Keltria branched off from ADF, was a conversation I had with Pat Taylor in which she said, "You know all those bureaucratic rules in ADF that we objected to so much in the beginning? We've wound up having to institute most of them in Keltria!" Time, tide, and the Internal Revenue Service affect all public religious organizations, sooner or later.

In the twenty years of its existence, Keltria has grown into a healthy Neopagan Druid organization, positioned in some ways on the borders between druidism and druidry. Their metaphysical system is almost exclusively Celtic with some Native American additions. They have a large Web site,* a journal, and two hundred members.

The Sisterhood of Avalon

This organization was founded in 1995 and is led by Jhenah Telyndru, author of *Avalon Within: Inner Sovereignty and Personal Transformation Through the Avalonian Mysteries.* Although this group may have originally been based on the pseudo-druidic fantasies of Marion Zimmer Bradley's *Mists of Avalon* books, it quickly grew away from those and more

---

*At www.keltria.org, naturally.

towards the druidic mainstream as the members researched Paleopagan Celtic (especially Welsh) beliefs and practices.

The SOA is a women-only blend of Neopagan Druidry and Celtic Reconstructionism, focused on using traditional Western occult methods (such as those of Dion Fortune) and modern research about the Celts to empower its members to grow spiritually, to become wise women and, eventually, to be priestesses of the Goddesses of Avalon. They encourage the learning and use of multiple arts and sciences, as well as the experiential approach to the Otherworld and its spirits. Male deities are honored but not worshipped.

As they put it on their Web site:*

> We stress the importance of immersion in some aspect of Celtic British culture—language, art, music, folk-tradition, craft, literature, and poetry—as an integral part of working in the Avalonian Tradition. We stress fact over fantasy and discernment skills over imagination. We seek a balance between scholastic achievement and intuitive wisdom.

The SOA organizes pilgrimages to and financial support for what they perceive as Goddess-centered holy sites in the British Isles. They have "levels of attainment" but no titles referring to spiritual authority, save that of the Morgen, who is the "primary authoritative spokesperson for the thealogical direction of the Sisterhood of Avalon. She is roughly the equivalent of the Archdruid in other orders and traditions." The organization has an e-mailing list, sponsors four-day intensives on particular topics, and has established the Avalonian Thealogical Seminary (a distance learning school designed to produce trained priestesses). Students are encouraged to form "learning circles" or "hearths" in their local areas, perhaps equivalent to the groves or henges of other druidic groups.

*At www.sisterhoodofavalon.org.

Ord na Darach Gile: The Order of the White Oak

This group was begun by Ellen Evert Hopman, one of the founders of Keltria (and author of *Tree Medicine Tree Magic* and *People of the Earth*) after she decided that there was a need for a druidic order that would focus on discussions of ethical and other philosophical issues among and within the various druid organizations. According to their Web site,* their mission is:

- To discuss with our peers the lessons of ancient and recent history
- To study the Brehon Laws of Ireland, the Celtic Mythological Cycles, the Wisdom Texts, and other ancient sources
- To seek ways to apply this information to contemporary Druidic practice

  In particular, we wish to apply the ethical insights we derive from the ancient Celtic past to contemporary concerns; environmental and ecological issues, human rights and social issues, and many other national and international political issues that are of rapidly increasing importance.

Those who are interested in being initiated into the order must first join the White Oak emailing list, "a semi-private virtual grove which discusses issues related to Celtic and Druidical ethics and philosophy." White Oak is a Reconstructionist-oriented druidic group, meaning that they place a heavy emphasis on serious research into Celtic Studies, especially those matters dealing with ancient Celtic views of justice, fairness, and ethical behavior, as well as the development of skills in such fields as poetry, ritual, and philosophy. They encourage their members to support such secular organizations as Greenpeace, the Humane Society, AIDS research groups, and various liberal civil liberties and activist organizations, seeing such support as

*At www.whiteoakdruids.org.

an appropriate outcome of applying ancient Celtic attitudes to the modern world.

The Insular Order of Druids

The Insular Order of Druids (IOD) was founded on the Summer Solstice of 1993 at Stonehenge by the late Dylan Ap Thuin, a poet and tattoo artist/body piercer. Due to the Stonehenge legal situation that year, there were only two druids present at dawn, one of them being Arthur Pendragon and the other a French Druid. Dylan proclaimed the formation of a seed group* to the others and to the world's press. Members of the seed group attended several quarterly meetings of the Council of British Druid Orders and became full voting members shortly after.

IOD had their first public meeting at the Druids Arms—note that pub connection again!—in Portsmouth, England in January 1994. Meetings were held once a month at this venue, for several months, and then they were shifted to the Arch Druid's home for more privacy. The meetings were for lectures, storytelling, poetry, etc.

Membership settled and entered a period of growth—and ceremonial work began in addition to the less formal monthly meetings. Their first private ceremony was held in the "grove at home" on Imolg 1994, and was very Wiccan in format. However, the rituals soon underwent a transformation as more Druidic elements were added. The rituals got larger and tended to be worked in daylight hours, "in the eye of the sun."

In February 1995, druids from several other orders (including the Glastonbury Order of Druids, the Druid Clan of Dana, and the Loyal Arthurian Warband) assisted in a group IOD initiation at Stonehenge, this time with the cooperation of the legal authorities. As Ap Thuin said:

---

*That's what some American druids call a protogrove.

The ceremony began just before dawn. The initiates were blindfolded and bound outside the circle. They were led in and reborn to the light within the sacred bluestones. It was freezing cold and the ordeal was endured by all. When the blindfolds came off—the sun had risen and thirteen Druids left the stones with "magical" memories of a day none of us will ever forget.

The IOD hosted the first English-speaking Eisteddfod (bardic competition) since the 1920s and sent representatives to the 1998 Summer Solstice event at Stonehenge (a ticket-only affair, hosted by English Heritage; Ap Thuin was blessed with ticket number 1 out of 100). Alas, Dylan passed away much too soon, and it looked for a while like the organization would die with him. Fortunately, Arthur Pendragon and Dylan's High Priestess (and Arch Druidess of IOD), Debbie King, kept the group alive, and it is now moving forward into the future. She attended the Summer Solstice rites at Stonehenge with a new Arch Druid, Barry Brent, in 2005, and the work of the order continues.

Visit The Insular Order of Druids Web site* for more information, polytheological essays, and news, as well as an online forum for the members.

The Druid Order of the Sacred Grove

This group was started by Jaron McLlyr in Las Vegas, Nevada, in 2003 along "traditional Druid lines." In its symbolism, ritual, and training the DOSG emphasizes the sacred trees important to the Paleopagan Celts. It, too, is a Reconstructionist variety of Druidism, stressing the importance of both research and common sense, drawing inspiration from the past, but focused on the future. According to the Great Charter of the Order, it exists "to revive and rediscover the Druidic mysteries,

*At www.insular.org.uk.

further the Druidic communities, and provide a safe and nurturing environment for its members; based on the teachings and wisdom of Celtic Reconstruction." Like most druidic orders, it follows more structured lines than most other types of Pagan groups. It is administered by the founding grove council and is headed by the Keeper of the Sacred Oak Bard, Ollaire Rose Wolfbane; the Keeper of the Sacred Well Bard, Ollaire Airmid McLlyr; and the Keeper of the Sacred Flame Arch Druid, Jaron McLlyr. An ordination board oversees the training and ordination of the state-recognized clergy. The Druidic College Board directs the educational program and sets criteria for advancement.

According to their founder,*

The Druid Order of the Sacred Grove upholds the pursuit of truth, the sanctity of the self, natural virtue, self-responsibility and earth veneration. It supports civic duty, social diversity, and feminine and masculine balance. It respects the right of all people everywhere to their own spiritual paths.

The group is on friendly terms with other druidic organizations, but remains autonomous. They hold formal rituals for the Celtic fire festivals, while encouraging members to hold private ones for the solstices and equinoxes. This group should *not* be confused with the similarly named Divine Circle of the Sacred Grove (see Chapter 10).

FAQs About Neopagan Druidism†

There are a number of frequently asked questions that people have about Neopagan Druidism, which have not been touched

---

*At their Web site: www.geocities.com/jaronmcllyr/Homepage.html.
†Originally published as a pamphlet by the author in 1983.

upon yet. Here are some answers, based mostly upon the practices and beliefs of ADF and Keltria. I suspect that the other
groups mentioned in this chapter would concur:

What do Neopagan Druids actually do? We're designing and
performing powerful magical and religious ceremonies to
change ourselves and the world we live in, including regular
public worship of the Old Gods and Goddesses, as well as rites
of passage (weddings, child blessings, and so on). We're adapt-
ing the polytheologies and customs of both the Indo-European
(especially the Celtic) Paleopagans and the Neopagan traditions
that have been created over the last fifty years. We're researching and expanding sound modern scholarship (instead of romantic fantasies) about the ancient Celts, as well as (in ADF)
the Norse, Slavs, Balts, Greeks, Romans, Vedics, and other
Indo-European peoples, in order to reconstruct as much as possible what the old religions of pre-Christian Europe really were.
We're working on the development of genuine skills in compo-
sition and presentation in the musical, dramatic, graphic, tex-
tile, and other arts. We're creating nonsexist, nonracist, organic,
flexible, and publicly accessible religions to practice as ways of
life and to hand on to our grandchildren. We're integrating ecological awareness, alternate healing arts, and psychic development into our daily activities. We're holding regional festivals to
help ourselves meet, study, pray, and play with other like-
minded folks. Some of us are actively preparing for the time
when Neopagan religions will be part of the mainstream global
culture, with large congregations meeting at temples and sacred
groves throughout the Western world. Together, we're sparking
the next major phase in the evolution of Neopaganism and
planting seeds for generations to come.

Are Neopagan Druids "real" druids? Organizationally, our
groups are as real as those of any other religious or philosophical movement. ADF, Keltria, and others are legally registered as
nonprofit organizations with their respective local and national
governments, and have received recognition of their tax-exempt
status. As we have seen in this book, historically speaking, there
are no "real" Druids left. The Paleopagan Druids were wiped

out centuries ago and only fragments of their traditions survived, despite the claims of some would-be con artists. Spiritually, we believe that we are following the paths once trod by our namesakes and that no other name is nobler or more suited to our modern intentions—and that makes us real as far as we're concerned!

Are Neopagan Druid groups "cults?" Not hardly. The only three dogmas promulgated by any group so far have included the Doctrine of Archdruidic Fallibility, requiring the members of ADF to accept that their Archdruid makes mistakes—not a problem with their first one!* Members of Neopagan Druid groups are encouraged to (politely) argue with their leadership, to form their own opinions and special interest groups, and to communicate as much as possible with both "insiders" and "outsiders." People without a sense of humor and proportion are discouraged from seeking leadership positions. Nepotism is discouraged, financial records are open, everyone is accountable to everyone else, and the leadership generally winds up poorer, not richer, than the average member. So what more do you want? You might find it interesting to score the Neopagan Druid movements with my Cult Danger Evaluation Frame (described in Chapter 10).

What about other Druid groups? Neopagan Druids maintain friendly relations with the Mesopagan Druid orders in England and elsewhere, as well as with other Neopagan and Druidic groups. They encourage their members to investigate these other organizations and to learn as much as they can about alternate paths of Druidism. They will, however, expose groups and individuals they believe to be fraudulent or dangerous, even though such vigilance may be controversial.

But what if I'm not Irish or Welsh? You don't have to be. Despite their use of the Celtic term for clergy ("druids"), the members of the Neopagan Druid organizations come from a wide variety of ancestries, including European, Asian, Native

---

*The second was, "There are to be no more dogmas." The third was, "No, we really mean it: there are to be no more dogmas!"

American, and African. ADF's members honor Celtic, Germanic, Lithuanian, Polish, Greek, and other Indo-European deities, ancestors, and nature spirits, as well as local land spirits. If you're sincerely interested in any of the old Indo-European cultures and its metaphysics, arts, and customs, then you're welcome in ADF.

Similarly, though Keltria focuses their attention on Celtic traditions, they are also interested in Native American studies and welcome members of any ancestry to their ranks. OBOD, on the border between Meso- and Neopaganism, is even more open to people and cultures from around the world—you don't even have to be a Pagan! In general, Neopagan Druids have no time or sympathy for racist nonsense or cultural bigotry.

Is Neopagan Druidism Wiccan? The Wiccan (Neopagan Witchcraft) movement includes the vast majority of the hundreds of thousands (millions?) of people involved in Neopaganism in North America. Many Neopagan Druids have been or still are followers of Wicca, including a sizable proportion of the older Neopagan Druid leadership. There is no serious contradiction between the paths, especially since, as polytheists, we are free to worship many deities in many ways. The primary differences between Neopagan Druidism (in ADF and Keltria) and Wicca are these: Druidism is polytheistic, medium-to-large-group oriented, public, and inclusionary; while Wicca is duotheistic, small-group oriented, private, and exclusionary. Nonetheless, the two religions have far more in common than they have separating them. Wiccan covens can (and do) function as special interest groups within larger Druid groves, along with bardic, healing, ecological, divinatory, and other groups. It is not unusual for small gatherings of Neopagan Druids to use Wiccan liturgical techniques, nor for large public Wiccan rites to borrow Neopagan Druidic methods, though it is best to keep the cosmological and polytheological distinctions clear.*

Aren't druids all men? No. Despite the stereotypes of the an-

---

*In fact, Philip Carr-Gomm has created a specific blend of druidry and witchcraft he calls *Druid Craft* in a book by that name!

cient Druids as having been long-bearded patriarchs, and the misogynist ravings of Monroe's *21 Lessons of Hogwash* (see Chapter 10), I hope this book has made it clear you didn't have to be a man to be a Paleopagan Druid. Certainly, you don't need to be male to be a Neopagan Druid (though the emphatically fraternal branches of Mesopagan Druids still segregate their members by gender). Half of the membership of ADF, Keltria, White Oak, and other Neopagan Druid groups, as well as OBOD, are female, and women hold half of the positions of power in these organizations. Neopagan Druids have deliberately chosen to make gender and affectional preferences irrelevant to participation in their activities. As worshippers of the Earth-Mother, we can do no less.

Didn't the Paleopagan Druids do human sacrifice? Yes, it's probably true. But then, so did the clergy of almost every other religion in human history, including the monotheistic ones. Nonetheless, Neopagan Druids have never practiced human or animal sacrifice in our rituals. Instead we offer the Goddesses and Gods flowers, fruits, wine, incense, oil, music, song, drama, prayer, and—most important of all—our love and our dedication. The deities seem to find it more than sufficient.

In fact, I can probably go safely out onto a limb (how druidic!) and say that there are no Neopagan or Mesopagan Druid organizations that practice any form of blood sacrifice— no matter how much we like to make jokes on the topic. Have you ever tried to get bloodstains out of white linen? It's just not practical . . .

9

Solitary Druids and Celtic Reconstructionists

Solitary Druids?

As we have seen, the Paleopagan Druids were members of a social class, usually with spouses and children. They performed
their duties in the context of their entire cultures. The idea of
druids as such being solitary worshippers of the Gods might
have seemed a bit strange to the ancient Celts. Among the
Norse, some priestesses of Freya in the ninth century CE lived as
solitary mystics, minding small temples and riding from village
to village with statues of Freya for rituals at various times of
the year. This custom seems to have developed after the Norse
warrior caste suppressed their clergy caste. There are Irish and
Welsh stories that talk about solitary mystics living in the
woods, and these people are often called druids in modern
texts. Whether the tellers of the original stories would have
done the same, however, is impossible to say.

There do seem to have been Paleopagan religious communities of either or both genders in Celtic territories, who had separated themselves from local tribes. These were perhaps similar
to ones in India. Formed in the woods (then and now) by *san-
nyasas*, retired householders who have left their previous castes,
duties, and earthly possessions behind, they concentrate on
spiritual matters. This may be an example of a cultural equivalent to the linguistic principle called "fossilization at the ex-

tremes." Here a particular religious custom, rather than a fragment of vocabulary or syntax, survives at the furthest reaches of a language family's spread.

The communities for Celtic women have been described as being situated on islands surrounded by willow trees which, as mentioned before, were the trees most associated with chaos and witches (and most likely to be found around islands, since willows grow best near water). The Sisterhood of Avalon can be seen as a modern attempt to create such communities.

Druidic organizations like OBOD, who do their teaching primarily by mail and e-mail, or via online resources and books, tend to have a majority of solitary subscribers. 85 percent of all known RDNA members are without a grove, though only half of the "active" ones are.* Druidism/druidry is still a rare enough spiritual path that finding others living nearby can prove quite a challenge. Most of the Mesopagan groups, however, are focused primarily on a fraternal group experience, something that is hard to do online. Neopagan Druid groups like ADF and Keltria tend to have their urban members be in groves and their rural members be solitary, while Internet-based Neopagan groups (whether druidic or not) are mostly composed of solitary members.

As Robert Lee "Skip" Ellison puts it in his excellent book *The Solitary Druid: Walking the Path of Wisdom and Spirit:*

> People choose the solitary Path of Druidry for many different reasons. It may be because they live in an area where others do not feel the same. It may be because others where you live may follow a Druidic Path, but you do not like them or cannot work with them. Or they simply feel the need to worship alone. These and many others are perfectly valid reasons for choosing to follow a solitary path.

---

*Note from Michael Scharding.

In keeping with my determination not to reinvent the wheel in this book, I refer the reader to Skip's wonderful book, which is specifically focused on the needs of would-be solitary walkers of the Druid path. It will also give the reader enough information to allow him or her to join and work with a group when, if ever, that time comes.

Celtic Reconstructionists and Other Nondruidic Druids

Just as there are those people who cannot, or prefer not to, work with other druids, or within a druidic organization, there are others who may be interested in all the arts, sciences, skills, and activities studied and practiced by Neopagan Druids, but who decline to call themselves by either or both terms. Those who refuse the label "Neopagan" may do so because of disdain for the poor quality of research done by most Neopagan movements, many of whom are proud of making stuff up as they go along. Or they may simply not like labels of any sort. A few of them have delusions of being completely authentic Paleopagan Celts in the twenty-first century—I call these people "wannabe Paleo-Celts"—despite their lack of headhunting and human sacrifice, their urban lifestyle, and their cheerful willingness to use modern medicine, automobiles, and computers.

Those who don't want to call themselves druids may feel that way because they believe (and I agree) that no modern person could ever master all the skills and knowledge of a Paleopagan Druid. Or they may have had bad personal experiences with religious authority figures, whether in a mainstream or minority context, and are opposed to religious ranking systems of any sort. Or they may consider all the existing druid organizations to be insufficiently authentic for their tastes.

Ironically, early in my own druidic career I was using the term "reconstructionist" to describe the kind of druidism I was interested in creating and practicing. In 1976, in *The Book of Changes,** I quoted an open letter I had sent in 1974 to the other Reformed Druid clergy:

> Let us begin by admitting that we *are* a religion and describe ourselves to each other and the outside world roughly as follows:
> "The RDNA is an Eclectic Reconstructionist Neopagan Priestcraft, based primarily upon Gaulish and Celtic sources, but open to ideas, deities, and rituals from many other Neopagan belief systems."

Leaving aside the shock waves this incomprehensible (to them) jargon set off within the Reformed Druids, it is clear that to me, in 1974, "reconstructionist" meant that we should be trying to reconstruct what our druidic predecessors had believed and practiced, then adapt it to modern times. I am not sure whether I got this use of the term from one or more of the other culturally focused Neopagan movements of the time, or if I just applied it in a novel fashion. Either way, the idea that modern druids should be trying to use the best scholarship they could find stuck with me through all the mutations that eventually led to the creation of ADF.

The Celtic Reconstructionist (CR) movement among Pagans began in the 1980s, with discussions among amateur scholars in the pages of Pagan publications or on the computer bulletin boards of the pre-Internet days. In the early 1990s, the term began to be used for those interested in seriously researching and recreating authentic Celtic beliefs and practices for modern Pagans. Some of the early leaders were members of ADF who, like the founders of Keltria, were uncomfortable with its Pan-Indo-European approach. Others considered Keltria to be "too Wiccan." When the Nemeton-L e-mailing list†

---

*This can be found in *A Reformed Druid Anthology.*
†Still going strong and joinable at technovate.org/web/nemeton.

was started in 1994, CRs began to communicate more intensely with one another.

Here is where the irony comes in. The following is from an essay on Witchvox.com called "Celtic Reconstructionist Paganism," by the CR Essay Collective;*

> Most of the founders of CR came from Wiccan backgrounds, with influences from ADF, Keltria, and other similar groups. Together and separately, they researched texts, studied Celtic languages, did meditations and spirit journey work, wrote poetry and articles, and worked to gather enough material to create the groundwork for a modern Celtic tradition that respects the ancient sources while rejecting those components of early Celtic religions that are inappropriate for modern worshippers, such as human sacrifice, slavery, and other strongly patriarchal elements of those early societies. Ethical concepts were sought out, sorted through for relevance, and applied to daily lives.
>
> Because of the limited nature of source material on Celtic tribal Paganism, these people also took inspiration from other cultures to help try to fill in the holes for building ritual and community. Norse research, village Hinduism and *puja* [worship] practices, ecstatic traditions like Voudon and Umbanda, and animist tribal religions were examined for similarities to what appeared in the primary and secondary sources on Celtic religions. The works of Sean Ó Tuathail were instrumental for many in this building movement, rejecting a four-element model and proposing a Three Realms cosmology consisting of the triad of Land, Sea and Sky. His phrase, *An Thríbhís Mhòr* (the great triple spiral) came into common use to refer to the three realms.

*Erynn Rowan Laurie, John Machate, Kathryn Price NicDhàna, Kym Lambert ní Dhoireann, and Aedh Rua Ó Mórríghan, ed. by Erynn Rowan Laurie. The essay can be found at www.witchvox.com/va/dt_va.html?a=uswa&c=trads&id=6645.

In other words, they wound up doing pretty much what the Neopagan Druids were doing! Indeed, I've had many Celtic Recons describe what they do as "druidism without the druids." The previously quoted essay puts it this way:*

> CR is not a "Religion of Clergy" as Wicca and general Druidism tend to be. Warriors, farmers, ranchers, writers, craftspeople, and many others may follow a household or homesteading path, or worship and practice with a group that has clergy. Craftspeople, writers, and others may identify as *Aes Dána* or "people of art." Individuals may consult someone they consider clergy on their own rather than being a part of a group. All are welcome, whether they feel a pull toward service as clergy or not.

It's true that Wicca is, by and large, a religion in which everyone is considered clergy.† One could make an argument that the Mesopagan/fraternal Druid groups were (and are) also such. Groups like the RDNA, ADF, and Keltria, however, were *not* founded on the idea that everybody was or should be clergy. They just decided to call their paths by the name of the clergy most associated with them, just as Hinduism was once known by Westerners as Brahmanism. This might have been a mistake from an historical point of view, but it certainly made the organizations quicker to explain to people than if they had called themselves "Celtic/Indo-European nature religionists who philosophize and research a lot and throw great parties."

One influential CR group founded in the late 1990s is called *Imbas,* from a word in Old Irish meaning "poetic inspiration," and thus equivalent to *awen,* as used by so many British druid groups. According to their Web site,‡ "Imbas is an organization that promotes the spiritual path of *Senistrognata,* the ancestral

---

*If you are deeply interested in the topic of Celtic Reconstructionism, I strongly recommend you read this essay, as it is a consensus document that probably represents the CR approach as well as any one item could.

†See my *Bonewits's Essential Guide to Witchcraft and Wicca* for details.

‡At www.imbas.org. The articles and essays there are well worth reading.

customs of the Celtic peoples. It is a path open to Pagans, Christians, and Agnostics alike." In an entry explaining who they are and aren't, they said:

WHAT WE MEAN BY CELTIC RECONSTRUCTIONISM

- Reverence for the pre-Christian Celtic deities.
- A connection with the ancestors and the land spirits. In a modern context, this means a concern for family, in its broadest sense, and a deep environmental awareness.
- A connection with the Celtic past. We strive to be as historically (and mythologically) accurate as the state of the evidence allows. When gaps in the evidence, or the realities of modern life, make it necessary to create something new it should be:

  - As consistent as possible with what we do know about the pre-Christian Celts and their legacy.
  - Clearly presented as a recent innovation. We frown on attempts to advertise something modern and invented as ancient and historical in order to give it an authority (and marketability!) it does not deserve.

- A balanced approach to understanding Celtic religion, which relies on both sound scholarship *and* poetic inspiration without mistaking one for the other.
- Celtic Cosmology:
  - Three Realms (Sea, Land, and Sky).
  - Using the traditional Celtic calendar (Samhain, Oímealg, Bealtaine, and Lúnasa).
  - Using Celtic symbols, such as triskeles and spirals.
  - Threes and nines as ritually important.
  - The World Tree and Well as a central religious image.
  - Inclusiveness. While we have the Celtic fascination with genealogy, we do not rely on genealogy or geography to determine who is Celtic.

- Respect for women.
- A moral code which stresses truthfulness, honor, and personal responsibility.

WHAT WE ARE NOT ABOUT

- Ceremonial magick or traditions influenced by it such as Wicca.
- Romantic revival Druidism (anything inspired by Iolo Morganwg or the Druidic movements of the eighteenth and nineteenth centuries).
- Eclecticism (combining Celtic religion with other cultural traditions).

This stands, I think, as an excellent overview of the basic approach of CRs (as they call themselves). I find it odd though, that such an overtly Pagan set of principles (most of them identical to ADF's) is described on the Imbas site as welcoming Christians and Agnostics, since this openness is a characteristic of the Mesopagan "Romantic revival Druids" they say they aren't! Most of the other CR groups think of themselves as Neopagan, according to Erynn Rowan Laurie,* one of the founders of the CR movement, and aren't particularly interested in Celtic Christianity or so-called Celtic shamanism. But because the word druid is used by so many people for so many different purposes, Celtic Recons, even those who get called druids by their own communities, are reluctant to use the title for fear that others will equate them with folks they consider flakes, frauds, or fools.

In any event, the Imbas Web site, and back issues of their magazine, *An Tríbhís Mhór*, if you can find any, are filled with excellent articles and essays of value to most modern druids. I also recommend The Preserving Shrine, the Web site* of Erynn Rowan Laurie.

---

*Whose Web site is at www.seanet.com/~inisglas.

The *Ord Brighideach:* A Brigidine Order of Flamekeepers is a Mesopagan (though they don't use the term) Celtic group that isn't Reconstructionist or druidic. It is dedicated to Bridget, the triple sun and fire saint/goddess of healing, smithcraft, and bardism. The members keep fires burning in Her name, in over twenty local groups called "cells," in fifteen countries around the world. Naturally, they have a Web site* and an e-mailing list (called "Brighid's Crossing"). The fires that they tend are all magically linked to the one in Kildare, Ireland, kept by the Brigidine nuns of *Solas Bhride* ("light of Brid") there since Imbolc of 1993. I visited them myself in 1999 and took the flame home with me by lighting a candle, then blowing it out. When it is re-lit, it is the flame of Bridget. This is the same way in which the members of *Ord Brighideach* pass the flame to each other. Like the sisters in Kildare, the flamekeepers honor Bride as both goddess and saint (under several different spellings).

The Daughters of the Flame† (DOF) are another group of women dedicated to Bridget and, by a "coincidence," lit their first flame at Imbolc 1993 as well. They are very similar to the *Ord Brighideach,* except that their group is for women only; some local cells of *OB* have male members. Like *OB,* the group includes both Christians and Pagans. These similarities are due to *OB* being a spinoff group from DOF. They have a blog called Brigit's Sparkling Flame,‡ which is designed to network devotees of Bridget around the world.

The folks at *Ord na Darach Gile* have an online "virtual shrine" to Bridget§ which is

> dedicated to all people who are suffering and to their loved ones who are in need of help. It is also a place to celebrate and commemorate significant life passages.
>
> It is intended for the use of all People of Faith, here

you may offer prayers, give thanks, or write petitions within our Messages area.

We take our lead from the ancient and sacred places used by our Ancestors, those Ancient Shrines and Holy Wells that dot the landscape, allowing the traveler to give thanks and to make offering for safe journey and good fortune.

Our Blessings and Remembrance sections offer words of wisdom and prayers from many traditions, not just Celtic but also Northern Traditions, Hinduism, and Buddhism.

There are, by the way, groups of people who call themselves "Gaelic Traditionalists" who have a great deal in common with the Celtic Recons. Some of these GTs started off as CRs, but consider themselves different for some reason or another (usually political). Others are Catholics looking to restore old (but Christian) Gaelic customs. GT groups are often politically conservative, while most CRs tend to be politically liberal. The key with understanding these terms, or others such as Celtic Restorationism, Neo-Celtism, *Senistrognata, Seandagnatha, Ildiachas/Iol-Diadhachas,* etc. is to find out what each person using them intends them to mean. Many will be Meso- or Neopagan and some will be purely Christian.

Some good writers to look on the Internet for in the general field of Celtic Reconstructionism would include Erynn Rowan Laurie, John Machate, Kathryn Price NicDhàna, Kym Lambert ní Dhoireann, and Alexei Kondratiev (though his book *The Apple Branch: A Path to Celtic Ritual* is not pure CR, despite cover comments to the contrary).

Druids in Cyberspace

Almost all of the organizations we've been discussing in this book have an online presence, networking their members with those of other groups, providing online discussion forums and live chats, archiving educational materials, providing recommended reading lists and ceremonial regalia, and doing almost anything you can think of to further their causes. OBOD's forum for example, has over 2,500 members.

There is also a Web site (without an organization attached) that's called Celtic Restorationist/Reconstructionist Paganism's Journal,"* which you may find of interest, and a wonderful online forum called the Summerlands,† run by independent scholar Searles O'Dubhainn and his "kitchen witch" wife Deborah. The Summerlands is a cybercommunity of druids and others interested in Celtic spirituality, with forums, live chats, reading lists, and more. I highly recommend it!

The Druid Network‡ is a specifically interdenominational (and huge) resource for modern druids of all persuasions. As they put it, "The aim of The Druid Network is to be a source of information and inspiration about the modern Druid tradition, Druidic practice, and the history of Druidry." They have public areas open to everyone and private areas open to members only, and facilitate contacts between members.

If you really want to understand an ancient Celtic culture or its modern descendants, there's no substitute for learning its language. Fortunately, these days there are plenty of Celtic language resources on the net ready to sell you books, tapes, CDs, and DVDs to help you learn. You can also subscribe to several Celtic Language e-mailing lists by sending a message saying "subscribe LISTNAME" to "listserv@listserv.heanet.ie". Included are:

- CELTIC-L (Celtic culture)
- GAELIC-L (Gaelic language bulletin board)
- GAEILGE-A (conversation in Irish Gaelic for fluent speakers/learners)

*At www.livejournal.com/community/cr_r.
†At summerlands.com, not too surprisingly.
‡At www.druidnetwork.org.

- GAEILGE-B (Irish Gaelic for beginners)
- GAIDHLIG-A (conversation in Scottish Gaelic for fluent speakers/learners)
- GAIDHLIG-B (Scottish Gaelic for beginners)
- GAELG (conversation in Manx Gaelic and support for learners)
- OLD-IRISH-L (scholars and students of Old Irish)
- IRTRAD-L (Irish traditional music list)
- IE-FILK (Irish filkers* list)
- WELSH-L (conversation in Welsh for fluent speakers/learners)
- CYMRAEG-L (Welsh for beginners)

The Virtual Druid Order (VDO) "is a worldwide druid order which exists as an online forum for the debate of all matters druidic, bardic, ovatic, or of significant Celtic interest. The order was founded in August 1999, inspired by and marking the Kernow [Cornwall] Solar Eclipse." To join the VDO, send an empty e-mail to "insular-subscribe@yahoogroups.com"—and be prepared to receive a reply from the deceased Dylan Ap Thuin, as he was the one who started it a few years ago! This group has nearly three hundred members, so the odds are good that you'll be able to find someone to talk to about just about any druid thing.

The Avalon College of Druidry (ACD) was begun in 2005 as an online college† offering courses and degrees in Celtic and druidic philosophy, modern Celtic spiritual practices, deep ecology, alternative healing arts, history, herbology, mythology, and bardic and magical arts. They seem to be very serious about functioning as the sort of college that will someday be accredited by mainstream educational agencies.

The similarly named Avalon Mystery School was founded by

---

*"Filk" songs are new songs written to old or new tunes; the term comes from science fiction fandom, though the custom is ancient.

†At www.avaloncollege.org.

Mara Freeman, author of *Kindling the Celtic Spirit*. Their approach could be described as Celtic Reconstructionist mysticism. According to their Web site:*

> Avalon is the Inner Temple of the Celtic and British Mysteries, a landscape of the soul, a country of the heart. It is the land which the poet and mystic see in vision, where the artist and musician find inspiration; where the soul goes for healing and spiritual refreshment: a timeless land of power and mystery that offers initiation and enlightenment to all those that embark upon the inner voyage.
>
> Avalon does not exist in the dimensions of time and space. It lies within the Otherworld, a place that the Celts have always taught us exists now and always, nowhere and everywhere, in the "thin" places of the landscape, within the cracks of everyday life.

There's also the Hazelnut Mother Grove of the NRDNA, which is a cyber-grove run as an e-mailing list by my old friend Stephen Abbott. To join it, send an e-mail to him at "abbotts_inn@yahoo.com" and be prepared for high weirdness and deep waters.

See Appendix B for more online resources.

---

*At www.avalonmysteryschool.net.

PART FOUR

※

The Pseudopagan
Druids

IO

Cultists and Con Artists

A Few Words for the Unwary

Not everyone who claims to be a druid is a nice person, knowledgeable about the Paleopagan Druids, or competent to teach anything even vaguely resembling Meso- or Neopagan Druidism. The American Druidic communities have been fortunate to have only a fraction of the liars and con artists that the Wiccan and other Pagan communities have, but we've got a few. In this chapter, we'll look at the most important ones.

The Druidic Craft of the Wise

This particular Mesopagan Wicca tradition was founded by a charismatic man called Barney Taylor, also known as "Fr. Eli" and "Grandmaster Eli," back in the 1970s, by mixing Mormonism, Naturopathy, UFOlogy, Wicca, Rosicrucianism, Scientology, and possibly a bit of Mesopagan Druidry.* He was fond of discussing the Order of Melchesidek, a phrase taken from the Bible. Both the Catholic Church and the Mormons use this phrase for their priesthoods, implying continuity with the original Jewish priesthood of that name. However, he might have gotten it from the *Barddas,* which explains a reference in Pliny's

---

*As a reading of his awful *Book of Wisdom* makes clear.

writings to Gaulish druids doing a sacrifice that involved bread and wine thusly:

> This seems to have come down from Patriarchal times—from Melchizedec, who "brought forth bread and wine," type of the Blessed Eucharist, that "pure offering" which was to take place under the Gospel; and though nothing is positively said of such a rite as existing in the Bardism of the Cymry [Welsh], it is likely enough that it was practiced.

Or maybe Pliny was just referring to a common custom of Mediterranean Paleopagans, that the Gauls might have easily picked up from the Greek colonies on their coastline. As I mentioned, Rev. Williams was anxious to prove that the ancient Welsh druids had been patriarchal monotheists.

Taylor has been described by some former students as engaging in extreme exploitation of them. Like Janette Copeland (see next section), he was also investigated by local police in connection with the mysterious death of a child belonging to a member. Regardless of his character or lack of it (and he certainly was a character by all accounts), thirty years later his followers are just another Wiccan tradition, probably no better or worse than many others. Their scholarship isn't very good, still being influenced by Fr. Eli's vivid imagination.* They are, in any event, unlike any kind of druid that we have seen in this book so far.

The Divine Circle of the Sacred Grove

The Divine Circle of the Sacred Grove (DCSG), founded by Janette Copeland, is a small group that has been floating around the American Pagan scene for a couple of decades, generating such disturbing reports that at one point members of

---

*You can find out more about them at their Web site: www.thedcw.org.

ADF and other druid groups decided to investigate her. The results were even more disturbing. After 2,500 pages of legal and historical records were collected, and scores of e-mails received from former members of the DCSG,* we publicized the conclusions we had reached,† only a few of which I'll mention here (and all of which Copeland claims to be able to explain, mostly as plots against her). I believe that if there is any group in the Pagan movement that could be called a cult, the DCSG is it.

Janette Copeland has used many different names, including Janette/Jeannette Gordon, Laverna Gordon, Laura Garcia, Laurie Garcia, Gerri Garcia, Laverna Copeland, and Geraldine Gumm. Her date of birth has been variously listed by her as 2/7/40, 7/2/40, 2/7/42, and 7/2/42. She has claimed to be a registered nurse, although queries to American nursing schools were unable to verify her attendance or graduation. She claimed to be a third degree high priestess in a specific Gardnerian Wiccan initiatory lineage, and an initiate of *Y Tylwyth Teg* (another Wiccan trad), both of which claims turned out to be false. She also claims to be a pipeholder for several tribes of Native Americans—also false. She has claimed to be a childhood initiate of the British Circle of the Universal Bond, although they have no records of her or her parents (who were supposedly also members). She did, however, become an early member of ADF, as well as of Our Lady of Enchantment (a Wiccan correspondence school), the Church and School of Wicca (ditto), and other Pagan groups. She plagiarized terminology, graphics, rituals, lessons, rank titles, and more from them (I know, I've seen both the original documents and her versions of them). She and her students routinely apply to other Pagan organizations for copies of their teaching materials, which later become part of DCSG's lessons.

---

*I still receive at least one a month, each detailing new abuses endured by former members.

†It is difficult to discuss this particular organization without making the legal department of my publisher nervous, so I will refer readers who want more information about the DCSG to my Web site, where I have a long essay about them at www.neopagan.net/DCSG.html.

During her "Third Circle" initiation rites, Janette ordained candidates to the Order of Melchesidek and informed them, most of the way through the ritual and with a knife to their throat, that they would now have to give 10 percent of their income to the DCSG for the rest of their lives. This from a woman who claimed on her Web site, "We attempt to be examples of high moral and ethical standards in all our workings and with all whom we come in contact." Now, tithing is a perfectly respectable religious practice and many legitimate religious groups encourage or require it—but they don't surprise their members with it under circumstances where they would fear to refuse. Members who begin to question her authority or credentials, or who decline to work in her businesses for free, or who cease to make heavy financial donations, are simply kicked out before they can influence the other members.

None of this Olympic-class dishonesty even touches on her gross ignorance about both Paleopagan Druidism and Wicca. She claimed at her lectures, for example, that Wicca was invented by the druids—in America—for people who weren't smart enough to be druids!* Janette appears to have been a student and/or lover of Fr. Eli, discussed above, has claimed to be his "widow," and now says she was his former teaching partner. Certainly, her teaching materials include the same sort of mishmash that he taught, and bear no resemblance to any historical system of druidism, ancient or modern. Education of the Pagan communities in Seattle and Los Angeles about Janette's history resulted in her skipping town and looking for new followers. These days she appears to be living in Arizona.

Lying about one's experience and qualifications is not at all unusual in the metaphysical community, or any other unregulated and uncertified community, for that matter (including large parts of American Protestantism). Dealing with pompous spouters of nonsense and unverifiable-claim makers is just part

---

*See *Bonewits's Essential Guide to Witchcraft and Wicca* for a more accurate history of how Wicca was started.

of the work that spiritual pioneers have to do. If I exposed every single bull-thrower I encountered in the New Age or Neopagan communities, I would spend all my time doing nothing else. Thus, I do not denounce people without a great deal of solid evidence, in this case gathered over a period of several years, from many sources, of serious wrongdoing.

At best, Janette Copeland/Gordon/Garcia/Gumm/etc. is a liar, a plagiarizer, and a con artist (who may or may not be conning herself as well—I suspect she is). At worst, innocent people could be seriously hurt by her and her associates, physically, financially, or spiritually.

As the reader has seen, there are many legitimate druid organizations sincerely following many branches of the path—this isn't one of them.

21 Lessons of Hogwash

In 1993, a book was published called *21 Lessons of Merlyn: a Study in Druid Magic & Lore* by Douglas Monroe. Many people in the druidic and Celtic Reconstructionist movements, as well as historians, Celtic scholars, and botanists, have never forgiven Llewellyn Publications for this act, which was made even worse by the release of *The Lost Books of Merlyn* in 1998. It's difficult to explain why these works so offended and horrified knowledgeable scholars without descending to extremely rude language. But the reader deserves to know why Douglas Monroe is on so many modern druids' "not-wanted" lists. Unfortunately, there are so many, many mistakes in his writing that it is difficult to know where to begin.

He quotes constantly from Iolo Morganwyg, hardly ever with attribution (see below), yet denounces the Mesopagan Druid orders for being based on Christian Welsh bardic traditions. He references various Irish and Welsh manuscripts, but ignores any scholarship younger than forty years ago.

His Imaginary Sourcebook

In the first book, Monroe claims that all his material comes from *The Book of Pheryllt*, a supposed sixteenth century manuscript of secret druidic lore. As medievalist Lisa Spangenberg puts it.*

"Drivel" is the most polite way I can refer to Monroe's claims. There is no such sixteenth century manuscript. Monroe's recent "sequel" to *21 Lessons of Merlyn, The Lost Books of Merlyn* is an obvious fake from the nineteenth and twentieth centuries, full of egregious factual errors and offensive sexist and racist assumptions. At best it is a piece of poorly thought-out fiction; it has absolutely no scholarly value at all. Monroe clearly knows nothing about ancient Celtic practices, languages, druids, botany, or mythology, and his ritual practices are derived from modern Wicca and ceremonial magic rather than authentic ancient Pagan Celtic practice.

Pheryllt is the Welsh spelling for Virgil; the Latin V in *Vergilius* goes to an initial "F" in Welsh, which in medieval manuscripts may be written "Ph." You may also see "ff," as in *fferyllt*. The *Book of Pheryllt* then, is a reference to *The Book of Virgil*. Virgil is the Latin poet who wrote the *Eclogues* and *The Aeneid* and lived 70–19 BCE. During his lifetime, Virgil was famed as a poet and his works became classics soon after his death. Both Christians and Pagans would select a passage at random from Virgil's works as a method of divination. The Roman Emperor Hadrian is said to have consulted the *sortes Vergilianae* in an effort to inquire into his future. Virgil's fourth *Eclogue* (written circa 41 or 40 BCE) was thought by many, including St. Jerome, to predict the birth of Christ. . . . There are numerous medieval references to Virgil as a magician, and

---

*In "What is the Book of Pheryllt?" at www.digitalmedievalist.com/faqs/pheryllt.html.

folklore about his prowess continued to multiply until the Renaissance.

The central Welsh reference to the *Book of Pheryllt* is in the late sixteenth century Welsh prose tale the *Hanes Taliesin* in which Ceridwen is described as knowledgeable about *gelfyddyd Llyfrau Pheryllt*, or "the art of the books of Virgil," in reference to a spell intended to make her son wise. This reference . . . is not to a genuine book, but rather to the myth of Virgil the wondrous magician. The scribe, needing a suitable magical text, seized upon Virgil as the magician's magician.

On the one occasion when Monroe offered to show proof of the existence of this book, the photocopies he showed a group of (dare I say it?) "real" druids was recognized by several of us as pages from *The Bardas*. Later it was discovered that the four pages he showed us were the very ones that had been cut with a razor blade from the New York Public Library's rare book room copy!

His "ancient druidic spells" are just as fake. My favorite is the reference to the "three ancient Spells of Making, the three master triads of the Druids!" Now the name of these is stolen from the hilariously bad Arthurian movie, *Excalibur*. This spell, which goes something like *"Anal Nathrock, Uthvass Bethud, Dochiel Dienve"* in the movie, isn't Welsh of any flavor, as Michael Everson points out in an essay called "Merlin's Charm of Making."* It doesn't make a whole lot of sense in Welsh, Irish, or English! But then, the actual text of the one Spell of Making that Monroe presents (in badly transliterated form) isn't much better: *"A elfyntodd dwyr sinddyn duw cerrig yr fferllurig nwyn os syriaeth ech saffaer tu fewr echlyn mor necrombor llun."* This more or less means something like, "Elements of water which lead the God of rocks that mail hunger if knighthood your sapphire the great side of the axis as dark as the

---

*Everson is an expert on Celtic languages and creator of Celtic fonts for computer users. This essay is at www.evertype.com/misc/charm.html.

moon." Wow! What great and powerful poetry that isn't—in any language.

His Historical Errors

Let's see, where to begin. Monroe has the druids, and the *Book of Pheryllt*, coming from Atlantis, a place modern scientists know never existed (at least as it is usually described) in the middle of the Atlantic Ocean. He claims that the Paleopagan Druids were all vegetarians, though this supposed fact shows up nowhere in the Celtic heroic literature where it would be expected to be mentioned amid all the descriptions of feasts. Some or all of the druid caste *might* have been, after all most of their brother Brahmin caste are, but we have no evidence of it in Celtica.

Some of Monroe's mistakes can be forgiven as having been common "facts" thirty years ago, such as "druid" meaning "oak-man," a confusion caused by the fact that it is related to Indo-European and Proto-Celtic roots having to do with strength, firmness, and oak trees (see Appendix E). Others will be obvious by this point in this book—he uses the four classical (and Wiccan) elements of Air, Earth, Fire, and Water instead of the Three Worlds or Three Realms. He insists that the sun is masculine and the moon is feminine, despite Celtic peoples having had solar, lunar, and earth deities of both genders. He leaves the sacred birds and animals out of his descriptions of druidism, despite the important role they played in the myths and legends.

Monroe uses other bits of Western (Judeo-Christian) ceremonial magical tradition, including four elemental tools, correspondences to the astrological planets, tarot cards, Mesopotamian deities, etc., claiming them all to be druidic. He mixes up his Gaulish, Welsh, and Irish deities, and has the Germanic Goddess Eostre and the Roman God Janus described as Celtic. He claims that ogham was used only for divination, when we have plenty of Celtic grave stones with ogham writing upon them; the divinatory use of ogham is a modern invention (see Chapter 19). He uses the modern Wiccan calendar of eight holidays instead of the ancient druid one of four. It just goes on and on.*

This makes it all the more ironic that his Web site quotes the Welsh druid saying *"Y Gwir yn Erbyn y Byd:* the Truth Against the World," while describing his group as "a Gnostic Brotherhood committed to upholding the ancient Druid tradition." That's odd—the ancient gnostics weren't druids or vice versa . . . He just doesn't seem to be able to open his mouth without telling a whopper!

His Botanical Mistakes

Druids, of course, are historically renowned for being knowledgeable about plants, especially healing herbs, so we should expect Monroe's Merlyn character to be the same. So in the first book he makes references to pumpkins as having been "sacred druid trees" and lists echinacea and goldenseal (see below) as having been among their healing herbs—without mentioning the herbs which we know they really did use.† He also explains how to make a tincture of mistletoe without mentioning that the berries are deadly poisonous, or whether he is referring to European or American mistletoe, which have very different medicinal properties. Of course, he obviously doesn't know the differences between European and American plants, because goldenseal, echinacea, and pumpkins are all New World plants that the Paleopagan Druids would never have known. Apparently Monroe knows nothing about them either, because he has Merlyn telling Arthur to garnish a pumpkin soup with fresh pumpkin blossoms—in early November!

His Misogyny

Monroe's books positively drip with disdain for women, ignoring the many historical and mythic references to female

---

*For a page-by-page listing of these errors and many others, visit Ceisiwr Serith's review at www.digitalmedievalist.com/reviews/21.html.

†See *Tree Medicine Tree Magic,* by Hopman.

druids, bards, seers, healers, and warriors. Here's a typical exchange between kindly old Merlyn and cute, blond Arthur:

> "See what we have here?" Merlyn exclaimed, "Nothing
> less than a true life case-in-point, courtesy of Mother Na-
> ture! Observe closely. The larger spider is the female, and
> she is preying upon the male. Why? Because now that they
> have mated and his life-force is within her, he poses noth-
> ing but a threat to her un-born young—and so she ab-
> sorbs *him* as well. So you see, Arthur, it is not for nothing
> that the female has come to be called: ***deadliest of the
> species!***" Again Merlyn smiled, and gave me a friendly slap
> on the back. Laughing at a point well-done, we made
> across the field once more.

Oh, yeah, I'm sure druidesses such as Banbhuana, Fedelm, Nessa, and Bridget would have found that a real howler!

Monroe seems to believe that only men can be intellectual, assertive, and active, while women are supposedly "better suited" to being emotional, demure, and passive. He claims that the Paleopagan Druids were all celibate men, which unfortunately would have made it difficult to produce heirs for their caste—not to mention the many Irish and Welsh references to sons and daughters of druids.

Ellen Evert Hopman, in an open letter to Monroe,* says:

> But now let us examine your views: to be born as a man
> indicates a need to develop the qualities of intellect, as-
> sertiveness, and outer world mastery. To be born as a
> woman indicates a need to develop passive, emotional,
> inner-world qualities. As we have seen from the examples
> of Celtic deities and queens, the ancients felt that women
> were just as capable as men of being warriors, healers,
> artists, etc.
>
> [You say that] women absorb life energy, while men ra-

*You can find the entire text of this at library.druidry.org/reviews/21lom.html.

diate it. This is a fascinating concept that points to a pathological fear some men have that women will somehow steal their life force by absorbing their semen. If it were true that women absorbed the life force how on earth could they nurture a baby in their womb? Women's bodies *give* life, in the form of milk, warmth, nurturing, their very blood.

The Nonresponse

So how does Monroe answer his many, many critics? By restating his claims (this is known as "assertionism," the idea that if you just keep saying the same thing over and over again it becomes true). He insults the scholars pointing out his errors, changes the subject, and calls upon the authority of other New Age or Pagan authors who are notorious for the poor quality of their research. He skips around the sexism and misogyny by claiming that he is only talking about separate-but-equal magical systems based on the "gender polarity" of male and female psychic energy (as in Wicca). As for the reality of *The Book of Pheryllt*, he says in *The Lost Books of Merlyn*,

> Well . . . let it be stated for the records, that this author has no intention whatsoever in "disputing the experts," for the question is without value to him. Why? Because my concern is not how *authentic* my sources are; this, one may only guess at, but rather how *effective* their philosophies and methodologies. I merely state that the manuscript—forged or original, ancient or recent—exists as an absolutely fascinating collection of writings, and that the framework *works*. Here objectivity ceases, when I state what I have *come to believe* through studying the text: that most of the fragments are very old, and are remnant of genuine mystic tradition; this is my assertion wholly.

How very interesting. Mesopagan Druids sometimes make the sincere argument that the magical/psychic/spiritual *valid-*

ity of a custom or belief is not the same thing as its historical *authenticity,* and that sometimes the former is more important to them. Fair enough. Many of Monroe's readers have claimed that they found the book useful from a magical point of view (although how anyone other than an absolute beginner could believe that, I don't know). Except that, as independent Indo-European scholar and excellent Pagan author Cei Serith mentions,*

> The book itself, and the back cover, claims the book to be "authentic druidry." The back cover alone uses the word "authentic" three times, and "genuine" once. Now I know that Monroe may not have written the back cover, but I do know that almost all of the back cover [copy] of my own book came from my submission letter, so I would suspect that he at least had a hand in it, and he makes the claim in the text as well.

As another author, I can confirm that most publishers run the intended cover text past their authors before printing. Certainly in the conversation Monroe had with myself and other druids at the Starwood festival many years ago, he claimed that the *Book of Pheryllt* and the druidic teachings based upon it were absolutely genuine—until we recognized his photocopies. The real reason he doesn't care whether modern druids or scholars believe in his claims is that those claims have made him thousands of dollars. The fact that naive readers might follow his advice and poison themselves doesn't seem to bother him much. It's nice that his magical system "works" for some readers, but this doesn't change the fact that it's far more Wiccan and ceremonial magical than druidic. So I agree with Cei Serith: "Bottom line: Friends don't let friends buy the *21 Lessons of Merlyn.*"

*At www.digitalmedievalist.com/reviews/21.html.

Elementary Precautions: the ABCDEF

How can you avoid being burned by a fraudulent teacher? In 1979, I developed something I called the Advanced Bonewits Cult Danger Evaluation Frame* and included it into the second edition of my first book, *Real Magic*. There was, at the time (and still is) an obsession with the topic of "cults," usually defined as groups the people using the term didn't like very much. It occurred to me that if we defined a cult as a destructive group of any sort (religious, political, social, or so forth) it might be possible to come up with some specific behavioral factors that could be used by neutral observers to decide just how dangerous, whether to its own members and/or to outsiders, a group was likely to be. Therefore, people could ascertain whether we were justified in using the pejorative term "cult" when referencing it.

While the original fifteen factors are now eighteen, this tool seems to have been popular enough; it is the item most downloaded on my Web site since 1996. It has been quoted by the Federal Bureau of Investigation (much to the horror of the Christian doomsday cultists it was used by the FBI to describe), the Government of South Africa (in an official report on expanding the previously exclusive Christian laws on marriage),†and on scores of Web sites and blogs. So the reader may find it useful as well.

Try scoring any group we've discussed in this book, or one you are thinking of joining, on each of the following factors, on a scale of one-to-ten:

1. *Internal Control:* amount of internal political and social power exercised by leader(s) over members; lack of clearly defined organizational rights for members.
2. *External Control:* amount of external political and social

---

*The list that will follow is from Version 2.6, copyright 1979 and 2004. A current version can always be found on my Web site at www.neopagan.net/ABCDEF.html, with translations into multiple languages.
†This led indirectly to the legalization of same-sex marriage there.

influence desired or obtained; emphasis on directing members' external political and social behavior.

3. *Wisdom/Knowledge Claimed by leader(s):* amount of infallibility declared or implied about decisions or doctrinal/scriptural interpretations; number and degree of unverified and/or unverifiable credentials claimed.

4. *Wisdom/Knowledge Credited to leader(s) by members:* amount of trust in decisions or doctrinal/scriptural interpretations made by leader(s); amount of hostility by members towards internal or external critics and/or towards verification efforts.

5. *Dogma: Rigidity of reality concepts taught:* amount of doctrinal inflexibility or "fundamentalism;" hostility towards relativism and situationalism.

6. *Recruiting:* Emphasis put on attracting new members; amount of proselytizing; requirement for all members to bring in new ones.

7. *Front Groups:* number of subsidiary groups using different names from that of main group, especially when connections are hidden.

8. *Wealth:* amount of money and/or property desired or obtained by group; emphasis on members' donations; economic lifestyle of leader(s) compared to ordinary members.

9. *Sexual Manipulation of members by leader(s) of nontantric groups:* amount of control exercised over sexuality of members in terms of sexual orientation, behavior, and/or choice of partners.

10. *Sexual Favoritism:* advancement or preferential treatment dependent upon sexual activity with the leader(s) of nontantric groups.

11. *Censorship:* amount of control over members' access to outside opinions on group, its doctrines or leader(s).

12. *Isolation:* amount of effort to keep members from communicating with nonmembers, including family, friends, and lovers.

13. *Dropout Control:* intensity of efforts directed at preventing or returning dropouts.
14. *Violence:* amount of approval when used by or for the group, its doctrines or leader(s).
15. *Paranoia:* amount of fear concerning real or imagined enemies; exaggeration of perceived power of opponents; prevalence of conspiracy theories.
16. *Grimness:* amount of disapproval concerning jokes about the group, its doctrines or its leader(s).
17. *Surrender of Will:* amount of emphasis on members not having to be responsible for personal decisions; degree of individual disempowerment created by the group, its doctrines, or its leader(s).
18. *Hypocrisy:* amount of approval for actions, which the group officially considers immoral or unethical, when done by or for the group, its doctrines or leader(s); willingness to violate the group's declared principles for political, psychological, social, economic, military, or other gain.

Remember, if someone is selling you something, observe their *actions* as much as their *words.* There are plenty of different Meso- and Neopagan Druid (and Wiccan) groups around to choose from today, no one needs to give their money to—let alone entrust their physical and spiritual safety to—blatant con artists.

PART FIVE

◎

Current Druidic Beliefs and Practices

II

What Do Modern Druids Believe?

The collective noun for a group of druids, ancient or modern, is a "disputation." If you gather nine druids together today, you are likely to get at least 27 opinions on nearly every topic. The question of Mesopagan or Neopagan Druidic beliefs is no exception. Some are monotheists (usually the Mesopagans), some polytheists (usually the Neopagans), and some are both. Some are vegetarians, others are omnivores. Yet, as this chapter will demonstrate, modern druids often have more in common than not.

Common Mesopagan Druid Beliefs

According to the United Ancient Order of Druids, as outlined in their pamphlet, *The Story of Druidism: History, Legend and Lore,** the Druidic philosophy inculcates the recognition of:

1. Belief in the Supreme Power of the Universe [a "Supreme Being"]
2. Immortality of the soul
3. Dignity of the individual man and woman
4. Respect for the rights of others
5. Development of the mental faculties
6. Development of the finer sensibilities of the heart

---

*Copyright sometime in the 1970s by UAOD.

7. Mutual protection
8. Development of the social virtues
9. Americanism [or other national patriotism]
10. Brotherhood.

[The pamphlet continues:] The Druids of today confine themselves to the moral, fraternal, patriotic, and benevolent philosophy exemplified by the druids of old. Their teachings and principles are derived from ancient druidism, founded on reason and sound morality. The greatest of all druidic teachers was Merlin, and his Seven Precepts are considered as a moral way of life, the finest oral virtues ever laid down for the guidance of man. These *Seven Precepts of Merlin* have been observed down through the ages by all druids:

First: Labor diligently to acquire knowledge, for it is power.

Second: When in authority, decide reasonably, for thine authority may cease.

Third: Bear with fortitude the ills of life, remembering that no mortal sorrow is perpetual.

Fourth: Love virtue—for it bringeth peace.

Fifth: Abhor vice—for it bringeth evil upon all.

Sixth: Obey those in authority in all just things, that virtue may be exalted.

Seventh: Cultivate the social virtues, so shalt thou be beloved by all men.

The motto of the Druids the world over is "United to Assist." The aim of the Druids is Unity, Peace, and Concord.

This obviously sounds a great deal more like monotheism and Freemasonry than anything the Paleopagan Druids would have recognized.

According to another group calling itself the Druid Order ADUB (*An Druidh Uileach Braithrearchas,* affiliated with the Mother Grove *An Tigh Geatha* mentioned in Chapter 5), these monotheistic druids believe, based on "ancient druidic triads" (three-part statements mostly provided by Iolo, based loosely on legitimate Irish and Welsh three-part wisdom sayings):

1. God is of necessity three things: the greatest part of life, the greatest part of science, and the greatest part of force; and of each thing there can be but one greatest part.
2. Three things are continually increasing: fire or light, intelligence or truth, and spirit or life; and these things will end by predominating over all others. *Abred* (the plane of material life and cyclic incarnation) will be destroyed.
3. The three gifts of music: sleep, laughter, tears.
4. Courses of instruction are given in the Groves of the Outer Order to prepare students for the Druidic teachings which are given in the Groves of the Inner Order.
5. Understanding is cultivated by ritual and wisdom by triads increasingly appreciated, mastery of the body and brain [are cultivated by] by exercises and meditations.
6. The three intentions of Druid instruction: the training of the mind, the cultivation of the heart, and the making of true manliness.*

Now some of these (1, 2, 6) come closer to reflecting the Indo-European triplicities, in the emphasis on light and the obvious correlations to the Dumézilian three functions, like so:

	First Function: Wisdom/ Knowledge	Second Function: Force/ Courage	Third Function: Strength/ Hard Work
God is:	Science	Force	Life
Three increase:	Intelligence/Truth	Fire/Light	Spirit/Life
Druid instruction:	Mind	Heart	Manliness

*From an essay called *The Ancient Druid Order,* also copyright sometime in the 1970s by the British Circle of the Universal Bond, *An Druidh Uileach Braithrearchas.*

We could probably have thrown the "effects of music" triad in as well, but there are too many arguments about which belongs where. These three effects are, however, said in historical sources to be the three that a master harper is supposed to be able to produce and are based on Irish mythology and legend.

As a ritualist, I strongly agree with the reference that, "Understanding is cultivated by ritual and wisdom by triads," that is to say, true understanding of spiritual matters (and many others) requires *experience* to turn theory into practice, and wisdom comes from organizing knowledge into meaningful *patterns*.

The ADUB is one of several Mesopagan Druid orders that promotes what it calls:

The Druid Prayer
Grant, O God, Thy protection
And in protection—strength:
And in strength—understanding:
And in understanding—knowledge:
And in knowledge—the knowledge of justice:
And in the knowledge of justice—the love of it:
And in the love of it—the love of all existences:
And in the love of all existences—the love of God and of
all goodness.

As an interesting sidelight, let's take a look at the Unitarian Universalist Association's "Principles and Purposes":*

We, the member congregations of the Unitarian Universalist Association, covenant to affirm and promote:

- The inherent worth and dignity of every person;
- Justice, equity, and compassion in human relations;
- Acceptance of one another and encouragement to spiritual growth in our congregations;
- A free and responsible search for truth and meaning;
- The right of conscience, and the use of the democratic process within our congregations and in society at large;

*Taken from their Web site at www.uua.org/aboutuua/principles.html.

- The goal of world community with peace, liberty, and justice for all;
- Respect for the interdependent web of all existence of which we are a part.

Is it only a coincidence that Mesopagan Druidism, so heavily influenced by an early Unitarian, and modern Unitarian Universalism are so similar? I think not.

What Members of OBOD Believe

Unlike the previously discussed Mesopagan Druid groups, the Order of Bards Ovates & Druids doesn't have short and pithy belief statements. Here, however, are some highlights from *What Do Druids Believe?* by Philip Carr-Gomm:*

Since Druidry is a spiritual path—a religion to some, a way of life to others—Druids share a belief in the fundamentally spiritual nature of life. Some will favor a particular way of understanding the source of this spiritual nature, and may feel themselves to be animists, pantheists, polytheists, monotheists, or duotheists. Others will avoid choosing any one conception of Deity, believing that by its very nature, this is unknowable by the mind.

The greatest characteristic of most modern-day Druids lies in their tolerance of diversity: A Druid gathering can bring together people who have widely varying views about deity, or none, and they will happily participate in ceremonies together, celebrate the seasons, and enjoy each others' company. . . .

Whatever beliefs they hold about Deity, all Druids sense Nature as divine or sacred. Every part of nature is sensed as part of the great web of life, with no one creature or aspect of it having supremacy over any other.

*A slightly longer version of the following can be found on the OBOD Web site: www.druidry.org. I believe it is being turned into a book by the same title.

A cornerstone of Druid belief is in the existence of the Otherworld—a realm or realms which exist beyond the reach of the physical senses, but which are nevertheless real.

While a Christian Druid may believe that the soul is only born once on Earth, most Druids adopt the belief of their ancient forebears that the soul undergoes a process of successive reincarnations—either always in human form, or in a variety of forms that might include trees and even rocks, as well as animals.

Druids seek above all the cultivation of wisdom, creativity, and love. A number of lives on earth, rather than just one, gives us the opportunity to fully develop these qualities within us.

The goal of wisdom is shown to us in old teaching stories. . . . These tales, rather than simply teaching the virtues of innocence and helpfulness, contain instructions for achieving wisdom, encoded within their symbolism and the sequence of events they describe, and for this reason are used in the teaching of Druidry.

The goal of creativity is also central to Druidism because the Bards have long been seen as participants in Druidry. Celtic cultures display a love of art, music, and beauty that often evokes an awareness of the Otherworld, and their old Bardic tales depict a world of sensual beauty in which craftspeople and artists are highly honored. Today, many people are drawn to Druidry because they sense it is a spirituality that can help them develop their creativity.

Druidry can be seen as fostering the third goal of love in many different ways to encourage us to broaden our understanding and experience of it, so that we can love widely and deeply.

Druidry's reverence for Nature encourages us to love the land, the Earth, the stars and the wild. It also encourages a love of peace: Druids were traditionally peacemakers, and still are. The love of Justice is developed in modern Druidry by being mentioned in "The Druid's Prayer," and many believe that the ancient Druids were judges and law-makers, who were more interested in restorative than punitive justice.

In addition to all these types of love that Druidism fosters, it also recognizes the forming power of the past, and in doing this encourages a love of history and a reverence for the ancestors. The love of trees is fundamental in Druidism, too, and as well as studying treelore, Druids today plant trees and sacred groves, and support reforestation programs. Druids love stones, too, and build stone circles, collect stones, and work with crystals. They love the truth, and seek this in their quest for wisdom and understanding. They love animals, seeing them as sacred, and they study animal lore. They love the body and sexuality, believing both to be sacred. Druidism also encourages a love of each other by fostering the magic of relationship and community, and, above all, a love of life, by encouraging celebration and a full commitment to life—it is not a spirituality which tries to help us escape from a full engagement with the world.

The primary philosophical posture of Druidism is one of love and respect towards all of life—towards fellow human beings and animals, and all of Nature. A word often used by Druids to describe this approach is reverence, which expands the concept of respect to include an awareness of the sacred. This attitude of reverence and respect extends to all creatures, and so many Druids will either be vegetarian or will eat meat, but support compassionate farming and be opposed to factory farming methods. Again, the belief that we should love all creatures is likely to be tempered with a robust realism that will not exclude the possibility that we might want to kill certain creatures, such as mosquitoes.

Woven into much of Druid thinking and all of its practice is the idea or belief that we are all connected in a universe that is essentially benign—that we do not exist as isolated beings who must fight to survive in a cruel world. Instead we are seen as part of a great web or fabric of life that includes every living creature and all of Creation. This is essentially a pantheistic view of life, which sees all of Nature as sacred and as interconnected.

Related to the idea that we are all connected in one great web of life is the belief held by most Druids that whatever we do in the world creates an effect which will ultimately also affect us. The two beliefs—that all is connected and that we will harvest the consequences of our actions—come naturally to Druids because they represent ideas that evolve out of an observation of the natural world.

As we shall see in the next few sections, these beliefs (which I have shortened considerably) can be seen as linking those of the Mesopagan and Neopagan Druids. They also make it abundantly clear that modern druidry is about far more than merely dressing up in costumes and performing pageants!

Common Reformed Druid Beliefs

According to one Reformed Druid document, "The Book of the Law,"* the basic beliefs of Reformed Druidism run thusly:

> The object of the search for religious truth, which is a universal and a never-ending search, may be found through the Earth-Mother; which is Nature; but this is one way, yea, one way among many. And great is the importance, which is of spiritual importance, of Nature, which is the Earth-Mother; for it is one of the objects of Creation, and with it do people live, yea, even as they do struggle through life are they come face-to-face with it.†

---

*Not to be confused with Aleister Crowley's *Book of the Law*, which is a great deal longer and 93 times as arcane.

†*The Druid Chronicles (Evolved)*, which can be found in several formats, the latest of which is *A Reformed Druid Anthology*, available online at www.geocities.com/mikerdna.

This has since been abbreviated, in "The Outline of the Foundation of Fundamentals," to the following statements:

1. Nature is good! and the second is like unto the first:
2. Nature is good!*

The material realm in Reformed Druid belief is personified as the Earth-Mother (or Mother Nature), one of the oldest archetypes known to humanity. Many Pagans now apply this name to the biosphere as a whole, in order to emphasize our dependence upon Her (though She is usually called Gaia then). However, the early RDNA included the stars, the sun, and the moon as part of the Earth-Mother, so the correlation to Gaia is far from absolute. The nonmaterial essence of the universe(s) is called Béal, which was believed to be an ancient Celtic name of an abstract divinity, based on *Bel* or "shining one." The concept is rather similar to some versions of the Native American idea of the Great Spirit (their attempt to put a monotheistic spin on their polytheistic beliefs for the benefit of pushy missionaries). Thus a polarity (not a dualism) of matter and energy, female and male, darkness and light, is established in RDNA cosmology; but it is vital to realize that neither half of the polarity is believed to be superior to the other.†

The "object of humanity's search" is called "awareness," and is defined as "unity with Béal," a task that can only be accomplished by also attaining unity with the Earth-Mother. Thus Reformed Druids are urged to develop all the different aspects of their beings—physical, mental, emotional, psychic, artistic, and spiritual—in order to attain the required state of dynamic balance that will lead them towards awareness.

Beyond these fundamentals, the philosophy and (poly)theology of Reformed Druidism are kept deliberately vague. It is up

---

*Ditto.

†Interestingly, something somewhat similar to this Earth/Sky polarity shows up in current ADF liturgy in the form of the "Two Powers meditation" (see Chapter 17).

to each Reformed Druid to work out her or his own path towards awareness.

Common Neopagan Beliefs

Explaining the differences between common beliefs held by Neopagan Druids and those held by other Neopagans can be difficult, and it's mostly my fault. I founded ADF with the intent that we would be squarely within the ranks of the overall Neopagan movement. So the following is excerpted from material that has been written and rewritten by me many times over the last thirty-plus years. This information is essential for Neopagan Druids to know, but also for others, so if you are already familiar with this background information, feel free to jump to the next section, where I'll discuss specific Neopagan Druid issues.

Most Neopagans today believe most of the following ideas, most of the time:

- Divinity is both immanent (internal) and transcendent (external), with immanence being far more important for people to pay attention to after centuries of emphasis on transcendence. Deities can manifest at any point in space or time which They might choose, whether externally (through apparent visitations) or internally (through the processes known as inspiration, conversation, channeling, and possession). This belief often develops among Neopagans into pantheism ("the physical world is divine"), panentheism ("the Gods are everywhere"), animism ("everything is alive"), or monism ("everything that exists is one being"), all of which are concepts accepted by some Neopagans.
- Children are born holy, since they have no barriers of consciousness between them and their indwelling deities. So the concept of "original sin"—the idea that all children are born innately evil and have to be cleansed by a magical

ceremony before they can become good—is alien to us. Because of this reverence for children, Neopagans do not approve of any form of child abuse.

- Divinity is as likely to manifest in a female form as it is in a male form, and the word "Goddess" makes just as much sense as "God." Women and men are spiritually equal, and "masculine" and "feminine" attitudes, values, and roles are of equal importance, regardless of the physical gender of those exercising them.

- There are a multiplicity of gods and goddesses, as well as "lesser" beings, many of whom are worthy of respect, love, and worship. We have a wide variety of non-exclusive concepts as to the nature of these entities. Neopaganism, as a whole, is polytheistic and focuses its attention on the deities associated with our planet.

- Within that overall polytheism, much of Neopaganism is "duotheistic" (with female deities seen as aspects of a single Goddess, and male deities as aspects of a single God).

- Along with polytheism comes a logical tendency towards pluralism, leading thoughtful Neopagans to reject dualistic or "binary" logic systems that paint the universe in terms of black vs. white, in favor of multivalued or "fuzzy" logic systems that accept the astonishing complexity and ambiguity of life, the universe, and everything.*

- There is no divine or semidivine figure of ultimate Evil. Those who insist that our beloved deities are "really demons in disguise," are simply exhibiting their ignorance, their dualism, and their bigotry, as their predecessors have been doing for centuries.

- It is necessary to respect and love Nature as divine in Her own right, and to accept ourselves as part of Nature and not Her "rulers." Many of us accept what has come to be known as "the Gaia thesis." As first articulated by Neopagan polytheologian Oberon (then Tim) Zell-Ravenheart (and later in secular terms by scientist James Lovelock), it

---

*The answer to which is 42.

states that the biosphere of our planet is a living Being who is due all the love and support that we, Her children, can give Her.

- There are many positive aspects of Western science and technology—most of us love our computers!—but we are wary about claims that science and technology can be ethically neutral. We consider it important that scientists and engineers (like everyone else) pay as much attention to their methods as they do to their goals. Most Neopagans are hostile towards unnecessary testing of commercial products on animals, for example.

- Knowledge and wisdom are good for all people to cultivate. Scholars and philosophers can teach us a great deal that is worthwhile knowing, even though we need to be aware of their biases and limitations.

- Ethics and morality should be based upon joy, love, self-esteem, mutual respect, the avoidance of actual harm to ourselves and others—human or nonhuman—and the increase of public benefit. Most Neopagans believe in some variant or another of the principles of "karma," and many Neopagans will affirm that the results of their actions will always return to them, sooner or later. This belief that "what goes around, comes around," whether thought of as karmic retribution or as an ecological principle, has a major influence on the ethical choices made by most Neopagans.

- Human beings were meant to lead lives filled with joy, love, pleasure, beauty, and humor. Neopagans may be carnivores, vegetarians, or omnivores, depending upon their individual religious beliefs, but we all approve of good cooking! Some Neopagans abstain from alcoholic beverages, but most neither abstain themselves nor disapprove of others drinking. Neopagans are enthusiastic about many different forms of music and dance, both ancient and modern, especially tribal and ecstatic forms.

- Sexual ecstasy can be both a divine blessing and a potential source of spiritual growth and enlightenment; we vary widely though in how, with whom, and under what circumstances we seek such ecstasy. By and large, the Neopagan community is sympathetic towards many sexual minorities and alternative relationship styles, which have been persecuted by monotheistic religions for sexist or erotophobic reasons. A Neopagan may be in a monogamous relationship, in one or more polyamorous ones, or have no romantic relationships at all. As long as all parties involved are happy and healthy, Neopagans will generally approve (or at least not actively disapprove).

- With proper training, art, discipline, and intent, human minds and hearts are fully capable of performing most of the magic and miracles they are ever likely to need. Magical and/or miraculous acts are done through the use of what most of us perceive as natural (some say "divinely granted") psychic talents, or occasional divine intervention. Most Neopagans seem to accept the laws of magic* as accurate descriptions of the way magical phenomena usually behave, though they might not say that they "believe" in these laws any more than a physicist "believes" in the laws of thermodynamics.

- There is an art and/or a science to creating, preparing, and performing magical and religious rituals. Our ceremonies are continually evolving as we search for the most intellectually satisfying, artistically beautiful, spiritually powerful, and magically effective rites possible. The use of human or animal sacrifice, though a common accusation, is not part of Neopagan worship, though some meat-eaters may say a blessing over their animals before preparing them for cooking. Animal sacrifice is often a part of some Mesopagan religions such as Santeria, Macumba, Voudoun, etc. (but not among any of the Mesopagan Druid groups of which I am aware).

- It is important to celebrate the solar, lunar, and other cycles of our lives. We consciously observe the solstices,

*As discussed in my first book, *Real Magic.*

equinoxes, and the halfway points in between, as well as the phases of the moon. Such "rites of intensification" are human universals, as are the various ceremonies known as "rites of passage"—celebrations of birth, puberty, personal dedication to a given deity or group, marriage, ordination, death, and so forth. Together these various sorts of observations help us to find ourselves in space and time.

- There is some sort of afterlife, probably involving rest and recovery in an Otherworld before reincarnating. There is a common belief that we grow spiritually through each lifetime and will continue reincarnating until we have learned all we need to. This aspect of Neopagan polytheology has not been developed very far, perhaps because of Neopaganism's emphasis on the joys and duties of one's present life.

- People have the ability to solve their current problems, both personal and public, and to create a better world, even though we might not all think of ourselves as "utopians." This vision, tempered with common sense, leads us to a strong commitment to personal and global growth, evolution, and balance.

- People can progress far towards achieving personal growth, evolution, and balance through the carefully planned alteration of our "normal" (culturally defined and limited) states of consciousness. Neopagans use both ancient and modern methods of concentration, meditation, reprogramming, and ecstasy, including both shamanic and other trance-inducing techniques, practiced by Paleopagan and Mesopagan peoples around the world.

- A major collection of tools for altering our own and others' consciousnesses are the arts, and most Neopagans believe that music, poetry, drama, painting, carving, and other arts are an essential part of both worship and spiritual growth. The Neopagan community is one in which artists of all varieties are honored and respected.

- Human interdependence implies community service. Some of us are active in political, social, ecological, and charitable organizations, while others prefer to work for the public good primarily through spiritual means (and many do both).

- If we are to achieve any of our goals, we must practice what we preach. Neopaganism, like any other religion, should be a way of life, not merely a weekly or monthly social function. So we must always strive to make our lives consistent with our proclaimed beliefs, difficult as that may be under our particular historical, cultural and economic conditions. Yet an insistence on such effort does not imply an expectation of impeccability—Neopagans know that mortals make mistakes, sometimes grievous ones.

- Healthy religions should have a minimum amount of rigidity and a maximum amount of flexibility. Neopaganism is an assortment of organic religions, which are growing, changing, and producing offshoots, and (though we do have our "orthodox" types) most of us accept these changes as natural (if sometimes painful) processes. Neopagans almost all believe that monolithic religious organizations and would-be messiahs are a hindrance to spiritual growth. As a general rule, Neopagan groups score very low on my Cult Danger Evaluation Frame (see Chapter 10).

- It's difficult for ordinary humans to commit offenses "against the Gods and Goddesses," short of major crimes such as ecocide or genocide. Our deities are perfectly capable of defending Their own honor without any need for us mortals to punish people (inside or outside of our community) for "blasphemy" or "heresy." We have no divine mandates to force our beliefs down other people's throats. Therefore, Neopagans believe in freedom of worship and belief for all religious groups and individuals who are willing to grant us our freedoms in return.

- It is good to cooperate and engage in ecumenical activities with those members of other faiths who share all or most of these beliefs. It is clear that we have much in common with members of the liberal religious community, such as

Unitarian Universalists, Reform Jews, Liberal Catholics, and others. However, most Neopagans also believe in resisting efforts by members of dysfunctional religions who seek to take advantage of our idealism.

Specifically Druidic Neopagan Beliefs

How do those of us who call ourselves Neopagan Druids take these general Neopagan beliefs and specifically apply them to our druidic paths? I would say that we do it by emphasizing particular elements. For example, while we recognize (and research) the similarities between deities fulfilling similar functions, polytheism rather than duotheism is stressed, so that every deity invoked or honored in ritual is appreciated as the unique God and/or Goddess She/He was originally worshipped as. We see "theodiversity" as an important parallel to biodiversity and are neither confused nor dismayed by the wide variety of deities and other spirits in existence.

Obviously, Neopagan Druids are literally nature worshipers—we see Gaia as a real, living Goddess within whose body we are "cells." For us, ecological awareness and environmental activism aren't just good ideas, they are religious duties incumbent upon us all. The vast majority of Neopagan Druid worship takes place outdoors or in small temples surrounded by nature. When looking for philosophical or spiritual principles, we look first to nature for our examples and metaphors. That commitment to nature ties in with one to scholarship and science—the more we know about the physical world around us, the more accurate our religious beliefs about it are likely to be.

As with the other Druid organizations mentioned in this chapter, we emphasize the importance of beauty and creativity, especially in ceremonial circumstances. As a public Pagan religion, ADF has made a major commitment to providing powerful and effective public religious rituals—for which the arts are a crucial factor—for all the commonly celebrated holidays in the Neopagan calendar (see Chapter 12), as well as for rites of passage needed in our groves.

Beliefs of the Henge of Keltria*

The Henge of Keltria shows another variation of the common Neopagan beliefs as perceived by Druids. In this case, they do have a short numbered list, though, of course, the members have discussed these principles at great length in their publications and online forums. Note the similarities to those previously discussed in this chapter.

1. We believe in divinity as it is manifest in the Pantheon [group of deities]. There are several valid theistic perceptions of this Pantheon.
2. We believe that nature is the embodiment of the Gods and Goddesses.
3. We believe that Natural Law reflects the will of the Gods and Goddesses.
4. We believe that all life is sacred and should neither be harmed nor taken without deliberation or regard.
5. We believe in the immortality of the spirit.
6. We believe that our purpose is to gain wisdom through experience.
7. We believe that learning is an ongoing process and should be fostered at all ages.
8. We believe that morality should be a matter of personal conviction based upon self-respect and respect for others.
9. We believe that evil is not a matter of inheritance but of intent, therefore, actions are not in themselves evil. Rather, it is through intent behind actions that evil can manifest.

*Taken from their Web site: www.keltria.org.

10. We believe in the relative nature of all things, that nothing is absolute, and that all things, even the Gods and Goddesses, have their dark sides.
11. We believe that individuals have the right to pursue knowledge and wisdom through his or her chosen path.
12. We believe in a living religion able to adapt to a changing environment. We recognize that our beliefs may undergo change as our tradition grows.

Any or all of these belief systems can serve as a template for creating your own Druidic set of beliefs. One could even sum them up in a Dumézilian fashion thusly:

- Be open to new wisdom
- Be brave enough to fight for your beliefs
- Be practical and grounded in your lifestyle
- Be willing to do the dull, dirty work necessary
- Be a dancer along the edge of the Otherworld

Do all that and you will be your own Archdruid!

12

Druidic High Days and Festivals

The Modern Druid "Wheel of the Year"

There are eight holidays in the Druidic year shared by most
Mesopagan and Neopagan Druids. The following chart will
give you their names as used by most modern Druids:

When	Common Pagan Name	Irish Names	Welsh Names
Early November	Samhain	*Lá Samhna*	*Calen Gaeof* (First Day of Winter)
Winter Solstice	Yule	*Meán Geimhreadh* (Midwinter)	*Alban Arthan* (Light of Arthur)
Early February	Feast of Bridget, Oimelc, Candlemas	*Lá Fhéile Bríde, Oimelc*	*Calen Gaeaf* (Middle of Winter)
Spring Equinox	Eostre, Ostara	*Meán Earrach* (Mid-spring)	*Alban Eilir* (Light of the Earth)
Early May	Beltane	*Lá Bealtaine*	*Calen Mai* (First Day of May)

179

When	Common Pagan Name	Irish Names	Welsh Names
Summer Solstice	Litha, Midsummer	*Meán Samhradh* (Midsummer)	*Alban Hefin* (Light of the Shore)
Early August	Lunasa, Lammas	*Lá Lúnasa, Lughnasa, Lughnasadh*	*Calen Awst* (First Day of August)
Fall Equinox	Mabon	*Meán Fomhair* (Midfall)	*Alban Elfed* (Light of the Water), *Mabon*

While the solstices and equinoxes are easy to obtain from any good astrological ephemermis or almanac, the methods for the calculation of the other holidays will vary from group to group and individual to individual. These same eight holidays are celebrated in most branches of Wicca, where they make up the spokes of the "Wheel of the Year."

Why do Wiccans and modern Druids celebrate the same eight holidays? Because Gerald Gardner, the father of Wicca, and Ross Nichols, the father of OBOD, were friends, having met at a naturist (nudist) resort in England. Gardner was a member of the ADO before Ross schismed from it to begin OBOD. As Damh the Bard puts it:*

Between them, they set about creating the now familiar "Wheel of the Year," the cycle of eight seasonal festivals that divided the year up into approximately six-week parts. Each festival celebrated the changes in the agricultural and celestial worlds, which symbolically represented the dance between the Pagan God and Goddess of the Land. At that time Druids only celebrated the two Equinoxes of Spring

*"The Order of Bards Ovates and Druids," essay at www.witchvox.com/va/dt_va. html?a=ukgb2&c=trads&id =8464.

and Autumn, and the Summer Solstice.* Gardner intro-
duced the wheel into his then-fledgling Wicca almost immediately. Druidry, on the other hand, had to wait until
Ross formed the OBOD.

Ross and Gardner discussed the question of whether the
Celtic "fire festivals" or the Germanic and Mediterranean solstices and equinoxes were the most important to preserve. Ultimately, according to my sources, the decision rested on the
convenient fact that keeping all eight would provide an opportunity for a ritual and a party every six weeks! Fortunately, the
decision also was a way to reconcile conflicting calendars in
Britain, where people of both Celtic and Anglo-Saxon cultures
have lived side by side (however unhappily) for centuries. A festival cycle including all eight celebrations would provide something for everyone.

According to Michael Scharding:

> The RDNA actually came up with the four fire festivals
> and solstices on their own from reputable books on Celtic
> religion; and didn't do the equinoxes until the mid-'70s,
> because of a lack of supporting material, but gave in when
> they, too, realized a party every six weeks was the way to
> go. It's kind of a parallel evolution of the calendar actually.
>
> You might wish to note that while Druids have a dozen
> ways to calculate their festivals, many in fact observe the
> celebration on weekends to accommodate the meeting of
> far-flung members.

To this day, however, Celtophile Druids have difficulty coming up with plausible ritual symbolism or associated deities for
the two equinoxes.

In the RDNA, ADF, and other Neopagan Druid groups, the

---

*This was possibly because of the symbolism of the Awen, to be discussed in Chap-
ter 13.

"nonsolar" holdays were called the "Major High Days" and the obviously solar ones the "Minor High Days." In large part this choice was made because the former were Celtic in origin and the founders of ADF were mostly Celtophiles. These holidays have been referred to as "fire festivals" for at least the last hundred years or so, because (1) to the ancient Celts, as with all the Indo-European Paleopagans, fire was a physical symbol of divinity, holiness, truth, and beauty; and (2) fires play important roles in the traditional customs associated with these festivals; and (3) several early Celtic scholars called them that. Whether in Ireland or India, among the Germans or the Hittites, sacred fires were apparently kindled on every important religious occasion.

In OBOD, the Welsh names are used for the solstices and equinoxes, while variations on the Irish or common Pagan names are used for the Major High Days. Since I'm most comfortable with the Irish names, that's what I'll use for the rest of this discussion.

The most common Neopagan practice for the calculation of Samhain, Oimelc, Beltaine, and Lughnasadh is to use the civil calendar days (or their preceding eves) of November 1, February 1, May 1, and August 1, respectively. Another way is to use one or more of the days of the secular weekend closest to each of these dates (which may arguably be closer to how the Paleopagans did it—i.e., by maximum convenience).

Still others choose to use the sixth day after the new moon closest to each of these dates (the so-called "Druid New Moon," see below). Astrologically oriented Neopagans use the days upon which the sun enters 15 degrees of each of the "fixed signs" of the Zodiac, to wit: "Eagle Point" (15 degrees of Scorpio in early November); "Angel Point" (15 degrees of Aquarius in early February); "Ox Point" (15 degrees of Taurus in early May); and "Lion Point" (15 degrees of Leo in early August). Still others use those days upon which the Sun hits 16 degrees and 18 minutes declination north or south of the Celestial Equator—this was the method taught me by my RDNA initiator Robert Larson, who claimed it was based on the sighting lines at Stonehenge. Like the astrological method, this also makes the Major High Days come halfway between the Solstices and Equinoxes, and usually gives calculation results within a few hours of the astrological ones.* Those druids who pay attention to subtle energy currents in the earth claim that using these latter methods for dating their holiday celebrations enables them to connect more accurately with changes in those currents, ones that the Paleopagan Druids might have paid attention to.

Using either the astrological or the Stonehenge method, Samhain in the early decades of the twenty-first century will usually occur on November 7, Oimelc on February 3 or 4, Beltaine on May 5, and Lughnasadh on August 7 or 8. Most modern Druids will celebrate these events beginning at sunset of the night before, according to the ancient Celtic custom of beginning days with their "dark half." Obviously, when the whole world is convinced that Halloween (Samhain) is the night of October 31 and May Eve (Beltaine) is that of April 30, it can be swimming upstream against the psychic energies of the English (and Spanish) speaking world to celebrate them on November 6 or May 4, so many modern druids simply celebrate them two or three times!

Samhain is pronounced "Sô-un" or "sow-" [as in female pig] "-en"—not "Sam Hain" because in Irish the "mh" sound becomes a soft "w." Samhain is the original festival that became "All Saints' Day," or "All Hallow's Evening," which was contracted into "Hallow-e'en," now usually called Halloween. Samhain is often said to have been the most important of the fire festivals, because (according to most Celtic scholars) it may have marked the Celtic New Year. Whether it was the Celtic New Year or not, Samhain was the beginning of the winter or "dark half" of the year (the seasons of Geimhreadh and Earrach—Winter and Spring) as Beltaine was the beginning of the summer or "light half" of the year (the seasons of Samhradh and Fomhair). The day before Samhain is the last day of summer (or the old year) and the day after Samhain is the first day

---

*For yet another method, visit the Web site of Ireland's Druid school, at www. druidschool.com.

of winter (or of the new year). Being "between" seasons or years, Samhain was (and is) considered a very magical time, when the dead walk among the living and the veils between past, present, and future may be lifted in prophecy and divination.

Samhain basically means "summer's end" (trust the Celts to begin something with an ending) and many important mythological events are said to have occurred on that day, most of them involving the temporary victory of the forces of darkness over those of light, signaling the beginning of the cold and dark half of the year. Samhain begins the winter quarter of the year.

The Winter Solstice usually occurs around December 21 or so on the current civil calendar. While the Celts don't seem to have paid much attention to it, the Anglo-Saxons and other Germanic cultures certainly did. Also known as Yule and Midwinter, this is a day sacred to sun, thunder, and fire deities. Large fires were built outdoors and "Yule logs" lit indoors, in order to symbolically "rekindle" the dying sun and help it return brightly to the northern skies. Burnt logs and ashes from the Midwinter fires were kept in their houses as talismans against lightning and house fires. This is considered by some modern druids, along with Midsummer, to be the best day of the year to cut mistletoe.

Oimelc ("ee-melc") or Lá Fhéile Bríde is strongly associated with the Irish multifunctional fire goddess Brighid, Bride, or Bridget. This goddess was best known as a triple-aspected deity (originally a sun and fire goddess) of poetry/divination, healing, and smithcraft, whose followers kept an eternal flame burning in Her honor. She was known to the British Celts as Brigantia and may have been, like Lugh/Llew/Lug, a pan-Celtic deity.

Oimelc may originally have been the festival of the lactation of the ewes. An alternate name for it, Imbolg, means "in the belly," so both of these referred to the importance of the cattle, goats, and sheep giving birth at this time of year. In Paleopagan days (and, indeed, until the recent past) these very important animals provided both food and clothing. The occasion of the birth of lambs (not to mention kids and calves) was a cause for rejoicing and a sign of life in the "dead" world of a northern winter.

The name "Candlemas" (candle-mass) is a Roman Catholic term for a holiday occurring February 2. To them it is the "Feast of the Purification of the Blessed Virgin Mary" (a reference to a traditional Jewish ceremony done to "purify" women six weeks after giving birth). At this festival, the priests bless candles, which are then used on February 3 in a fire magic ritual to bless people's throats, supposedly in honor of a "Saint Blaise." Naturally, this has no connection with "Saint" Bridget and her cult of fire, nor with the fact that this day was one of the four major fire festivals of Paleopagan cultures throughout Western and Northern Europe. Of course, they also neglect to mention a certain Slavic god named Vlaise, who was the patron of cattle, wealth, and war, and who was worshipped with fire—perhaps another omnifunctional deity like those discussed in Appendix F.

February 2 is also known as Groundhog's Day, a holiday so-called because American groundhogs were the local counterpart to the Irish hare that was sacred to Bride. Celtic belief is that good weather on Oimelc means that winter will continue, and that bad weather means winter is on the way out—hence the importance of the presence or absence of a sacred animal's shadow. Oimelc begins the spring quarter of the year.

The Spring Equinox usually takes place around March 21. As Ostara, it is named after the German Fertility Goddess Eostre (source of the name for the Christian festival called "Easter"). It is a celebration of the returning of life to the Earth. Rabbits, eggs, and children are sacred at this feast, and Pagans in need of fertility talismans now color hollow eggs and pass them through the ceremonial fires (quickly) to take home and hang over their beds and in their barns. A fascinating source of almost forgotten Paleopagan symbols can be found by examining carefully the fantastically decorated eggs produced by folk artists from

Europe (especially Eastern Europe and Russia), Mexico, and South America. Among some Paleopagan cultures in Southern Europe, the Spring Equinox was the date of the New Year.

Beltaine is, of course, the day we know in English as May Day. It is also called by a variety of other names, such as Roodmas, Summer Day, Walpurgistag, St. Pierre's Day, Red Square Day, etc. It is the beginning of the "summer half" of the Celtic year (the seasons of Samradh & Foghamhar—Summer and Fall) and is a festival of unalloyed joy.

A very large number of important Celtic mythological events are connected with this day, which balances out Samhain on the opposite side of the Wheel of the Year. It was on a Beltaine that Partholan and his followers, the first inhabitants and partial creators of Ireland, landed on that isle. Three hundred years later, on the same day, they returned to the Otherworld. It was on a Beltaine that the Tuatha De Danann and their people invaded Ireland. It was on a May Eve that Pryderi, the missing son of Rhiannon and Pwyll (rulers of the Welsh Otherworld), was lost by them and later (on another May Eve) found by Teirnyon Twryf Vliant (and eventually restored to them). Most of these events, again, as all over Northern and Western Europe, have to do with stories of the forces of light/safety defeating the forces of darkness/danger. Why did you think the Marxists chose May Day as their international holy day? Beltaine begins the summer quarter of the year.

The Summer Solstice usually occurs around June 21 or so. Also known as St. John's Day and Midsummer, it shares mythical elements with both Beltaine and Lughnasadh. It is a feast celebrating the glory of summer and the peak of the sun deity's power. But in some systems of belief, it is the day of the biggest battle of the year between the Dark Sun God and the Light Sun God (the dangerous vs. the safe one), who are usually brothers or otherwise intimately related. Midsummer is a peak from which the sun can only fall, for it is the day on which the hours of light slowly begin to shorten.

Lughnasadh is the first harvest festival of the Irish year, signaling the beginning of the harvest season and the ripening of the apples (as well as other fruits and vegetables). Applejack, hard cider, mead, and other alcoholic beverages are consumed at this time (it's almost a duty!) by many enthusiastic Neopagans. It is strongly associated with the pan-Celtic god Lugh/Llew/Lug, though in official Irish myth it was created when Lugh held funeral games to honor his deceased mother, Tailtu.

This holiday is a day of mixed joy and woe (Irish wakes are an old tradition), for it is by now obvious that the days are getting shorter. Stories of the battles between Lugh and Balor (the light Sun/Fire God and the dark one) are retold. Horse racing, county fairs, and matchmaking are some of the traditional amusements associated with this festival. Lughnasadh begins the fall or autumn quarter of the year.

The last big holiday of the year, the Fall Equinox (sometimes called Mabon or Michaelmas) usually occurs around September 21 or so. This is a thanksgiving and harvest feast, and signals the beginning of the hunting season (for deer and other large game) in many parts of Europe and North America. Thus, it is dedicated to the hunting and fishing deities and the deities of plenty, in thankfulness for benefits received and hoped for. Outdoor picnics in the woods are a popular tradition in those areas where the weather is still good at this time of year.*

About Those Druid New Moons

According to Pliny's famous mistletoe harvesting scene, the "sixth day after the new moon" was the best time of month to do this and many scholars have assumed that Celtic months began at this odd-seeming time of the moon's cycle. I've even speculated that this was a way to split the month into light and dark halves, beginning with the light half in contrast to how the day and the year began. A probable solution to the puzzle has finally been published.

According to Garrett S. Olmsted, in his *A Definitive Recon-*

---

*Hunting magic may be minimized by those living in areas where game is a little deer.

*structed Text of the Cologny Calendar,** at the time Pliny was writing, the Gauls had been using a 30-year solar-lunar calendar for 1,000 years,† one that had originally begun each month on the first day of the new moon. With such a 30-year cycle, the calendar would move ahead of the moon one day every 199 years, so 1,000 years later, the months would be starting on the sixth day of the new moon. The second century CE Gaulish calendar dug up in Cologny, France, was based on a 25-year cycle, apparently in an attempt to lose the extra days.

This means that modern druids are now "free" to start their ceremonial months at the new moon, should they choose to do so, without fearing that they are being "inauthentic." But if it's Celtic inauthenticity you want, there's one writer sure to provide it to you . . .

Robert Graves's "Tree Calendar"

Those of you who have read my works on the history of witchcraft and Wicca will remember my comments about this (usually trustworthy) author's one clunker of a book, *The White Goddess*. As I put it in *Bonewits's Essential Guide to Witchcraft and Wicca*,

> The purpose of *The White Goddess* was to prove that the Universal Goddess Worship theories the early anthropologists and archeologists had come up with were correct. To accomplish this took considerable acrobatics. He jumped back and forth from the Mediterranean to the British Isles and across great gaps of time. He constantly asked his readers to accept a "slight" bit of illogic and error, then built these up into gigantic megaliths of theory. While ad-

---

*He came to his conclusions in part due to a clever use of modern technology. He used Adobe PhotoShop™ to copy parts of scanned images of the fragments of bronze upon which the calendar was inscribed, then pasted them into various locations virtually, to discover what could or could not have been on the missing bits of the original.

†Making it actually pre-Celtic!

mitting he spoke no Celtic language, he appointed himself
an authority on Welsh language and customs. He used obsolete and inaccurate translations of Celtic poetry, when
there were good ones around in 1948, perhaps because
the accurate translations wouldn't have supported his
ideas as well.

In this work, Graves claimed that the Welsh poem, *Câd
Goddeu, the Battle of the Trees,* provided clues to an ancient
druidic calendar, in which the thirteen lunar months of the
year were supposedly named after sacred trees. Unfortunately
for this very pretty system, it's complete nonsense, and bears
no resemblance to the one ancient Celtic calendar (discussed
above) that we know of for sure. Here's what Graves's idea
looks like:

Ogham Letter	Sacred "Tree"	Supposed Dates
Beth	Birch	Dec. 24 to Jan. 20
Luis	Rowan	Jan. 21 to Feb. 17
Nion	Ash	Feb. 18 to March 17
Fearn	Alder	March 18 to April 14
Saille	Willow	April 15 to May 12
Uath	Hawthorne	May 13 to June 9
Duir	Oak	June 10 to July 7
Tinne	Holly	July 8 to Aug. 4
Coll	Hazel	Aug. 5 to Sept. 1
Muin	Vine	Sept. 2 to Sept. 29
Gort	Ivy	Sept. 30 to Oct. 27
nGetal	Reed	Oct. 28 to Nov. 24
Ruis	Elder	Nov. 25 to Dec. 22

Despite the fact that Graves's own grandfather was an Ogham expert and that a well-known expert on Ogham and Irish Studies in general (Robert MacAlister) told Graves his Ogham theories were untrustworthy, he went ahead and published them anyway. In fact, he went so far as to assert that the thirteen months of the "Celtic Tree Calendar" were related to thirteen signs of a "Celtic Zodiac"—thus launching the current Celtic Astrology nonsense.

I am far from alone in having a "bad attitude" about Graves's writing on these topics. In his excellent book *The Druids' Alphabet,* Robert Lee (Skip) Ellison puts it this way:*

> Graves was a very good poet, but he really was *not* an expert in Celtic material. His main field of study was poetry and Greek history. In those fields, he was very good and deserves respect.
>
> One place where this lack of Celtic scholarship really shows is in the "Celtic Tree Calendar," actually the association of thirteen of the trees from Ogham with months of the year that he devised in the *White Goddess.*
>
> This was really made up strictly by him and has no historical basis. This "calendar" has been very heavily reprinted and many people believe that it is a calendar that was used by the Druids—completely not true! It only dates back to the 1940s.
>
> At the start of his "re-telling" of the *Câd Goddeu, the Battle of the Trees,* he specifically tells the reader that he didn't understand Welsh and was not a Welsh scholar. [Graves said:]
>
>> "Here I must apologize for my temerity in writing on a subject which is not really my own. I am not a Welshman, except an honorary one through eating a leek on St. David's Day while serving with the

---

*Ellison's book includes an Appendix where Graves's translation is compared to three other translations by competent scholars.

Royal Welsh Fusiliers and, though I have lived in Wales for some years, off and on, have no command even of modern Welsh; and I am not a mediaeval historian."

He then proceeded to deconstruct the translation of the poem, not the original mind you, because he could not understand its meaning. He redid it so that it made sense to him.

It didn't matter to him that many people had been able to understand what Taliesin, the original author of the poem, had meant through the years; because he couldn't understand it, the poem had to be wrong, so he had to rewrite it.

It is unfortunate that it is this rewriting that gets reprinted all the time and many people today do not understand that it isn't the original, but a 1940s retelling.

What this comes down to is that the Paleopagan Celts did *not* name their months after trees, no matter how popular this notion has become among modern Neopagans and New Agers. Use it if you like, but don't tell people it's authentic.

If you are looking for a set of names to call months for druidic purposes, you might like the system Robert Larson came up with for the Orthodox Druids of North America (his Gaelic version of the RDNA):

English	Irish	Meaning
November	Mí na Samhna	Month of Samhain
December	Meán Geimhridh	Middle of Winter
January	Deireadh Geimhridh	End of Winter
February	Mí na hOimelc	Month of Oimelc
March	Meán Earraigh	Middle of Spring
April	Deireadh Earraigh	End of Spring

English	Irish	Meaning
May	Mí na Bealtaine	Month of Beltaine
June	Meán Samhraidh	Middle of Summer
July	Deireadh Samhraidh	End of Summer
August	Mí na Lúnasa	Month of Lughnasadh
September	Meán Fómhair	Middle of Fall
October	Deireadh Fúhmhair	End of Fall

The names for the months were based on the ones in Modern Irish for the fall months. Of course, exactly when to *begin* any of these months is up to you.

Other Druidic Holy Days

Because Neopagan Druidism is focused so much on public service, local groves may also celebrate holidays from the secular and mainstream calendars, such as All Snakes Day on March 17 or the Festival of Liberty on July 4 in the United States. Here are some additional optional holidays taken from the SDNA, the HDNA, and various Indo-European sources, together with suggested celebratory activities:*

November 10–11: *Festival of Thanksgiving* to the Gods of harvest, hunting, fishing, and plenty. Have an absolutely gigantic feast. This festival is often postponed until the fourth Thursday of the month in the United States.
November 22: *Feast of Oberon and the Divine Musicians.* Have the biggest bardic revel you can manage. Do something nice for the bards in your grove.

---

*It will soon become obvious that some of these holidays were invented by a bunch of Americans in our teens and twenties!

November 30: *Feast of the Gods of the Crossroads.* Dedicated to the deities who guard the paths between the living and the dead, and between this world and all others. Time to consider your attitudes about death, to study shamanism, and to practice teleportation and aportation.

December 8–9: *Festival of the Conception of the Earth-Mother.* Meditate upon the immaculate conception of life from the primeval seas, billions of years ago. Make a statue of the Mother out of clay or rock.

December 13: *Feast of Belisama* (Goddess of Light, Wisdom, and at least one river in Britain). A young woman with a crown of candles in her hair could wake the members of your household, carrying a tray full of coffee and various munchies.

December 25–27: *Festival of the Birth of the Sun.* Gifts should be exchanged and many parties held.

December 28: *Feast of the Divine Children.* In honor of all the gods of youth, special events should be held for all the girls and boys in your grove.

December 29–31: *Winter Festival of Wine and Pleasure.* It is obligatory to become at least mildly intoxicated and flirt vigorously.

January 6: *Feast of Sirona* (a Goddess of Rivers). Rivers in your vicinity should be blessed by your local archdruid/ess and hymns of praise sung to various river deities. Go fishing.

January 24–26: *Festival of Braciaca* (God of Brewing, Intoxication and Altered States of Consciousness). It is obligatory to become at least mildly intoxicated.

February 14–21: *Festival of Love* (dedicated to Danu, Cernunnos, Aphrodite, Eros, and other deities of fertility and passion). It is obligatory to make love.

March 1: *Feast of Merddyn* (patron of wizards). Do something magical. Read an Arthurian legend.

March 3: *Feast of Rhiannon* (Welsh Goddess of horses, protector of mothers, and queen of the Otherworld). Spend the day reading or telling her stories.

March 11: *Feast of Angus Og* (warrior and god of passion). Practice using your ritual weapons. Learn to sword fight. Read a book on erotic techniques. Practice all three.

March 17: *All Snakes Day.* Celebrate Irish Paganism and the revival of Druidism.

March 21–25: *Spring Festival of Wine and Pleasure.* Hold a wild party and invite all your friends. The 25th is also the *Feast of Young Mothers,* so do a good deed for the ones you know.

April 1: *Feast of the Spring Fool.* Do something silly just because it feels good. Or take the day off and go fishing. Or sit on a hill and herd clouds.

April 5: *Feast of Alexander Nevsky* (warrior). Nevsky was a Slavic Viking who led a Pagan army into battle on April 5, 1242 CE against the Christian Teutonic Knights, luring them out onto the thin ice of Lake Chud (near Pskov). His victory over them marks one of the very few clear-cut victories of a Pagan people against the forces of Christian imperialism (even if the Russian Orthodox Church did later turn him into a "saint"). This is a day on which to practice pride in being Pagan, and on which to contemplate our hopes for total religious freedom.

April 23: *Feast of Oghma* (the God who binds). He is a mighty warrior and the inventor of Ogham writing. Spend the day learning and practicing this alphabet.

May 1: *Feast of the Illuminati.* Anniversary of the public founding of the Bavarian Illuminati, the world's most famous secret conspiracy.* Investigate a conspiracy, or start one.

May 18: *Feast of Cernunnos* (the horned God of lust, hunting, wealth, and the Cythonic Realm). Go hunting. If you can't go hunting, go lusting.

May 24: *Feast of the Dark Goddess.* Celebration of the Goddesses Babh, Morrigu, Macha, and other demon killers. This is based on the Romany feast for their patron Goddess, the Black Kali from India. Meditate upon the beauty of an angry woman.

*See the *Illuminatus Trilogy,* by Robert Anton Wilson for details.

May 25: *Feast of the Two Ladies.* Celebration of sisterhood in the face of the patriarchy. Meditate upon your concepts of womanhood and why you have them.

June 13: *Feast of Epona* (Irish goddess of horses). Go horseback riding and spend the day appreciating our equine friends. Buy a kid a horse book.

June 18–22: *Festival of the Bards.* Hold a big bardic revel, with as much singing and dancing as possible.

July 2: *Feast of Expectant Mothers:* Meditate upon the mysteries of conception and pregnancy. Bring some pickles and ice-cream to a friend.

July 22–24: *Summer Festival of Wine and Pleasure.* Time to hold an outdoor feast and wild party.

August 15: *Feast of Our Lady Queen of the Heavens.* Celebration of the Star/Moon/Mother Goddess. Take a High Priestess out to dinner and give her the best night you can.

August 23–25: *Festival of the Heroes.* Dedicated to all those brave Pagan warriors who fell before the invading Christian armies or who have fallen in recent years. Meditate upon the values of the honorable warrior.

September 8: *Feast of the Birth of the Mother.* Celebrating the birthday of the physical incarnation of the Goddess. Give a birthday celebration for every mother in your grove.

September 26: *Feast of the Druid Taliesin.* Spend the day reading or telling the stories of this most famous of mythical Welsh bards. Celebrate Welsh Paganism. Compose a poem.

September 27–28: *Festival of the Demon Slayers.* Now that the days are really starting to get short, it is good to meditate upon the fact that not all dark deities are evil. This festival is to honor both the light and the dark gods who slay demons, giants, and other enemies of life.

October 1: *Feast of Chwerthin* (the "laughing one"). Tell jokes, make outrageous puns, and pontificate at ridiculous length, while being as flirtatious as possible, in order to honor this most famous of druids.

October 2: *Feast of the Guardian Spirits.* Give love, respect, and honor to your own guardians.

October 7–9: *Autumn Festival of Wine and Pleasure.* Hold a midharvest feast and get as intoxicated as you can safely manage. Then hold a good enough party to keep you warm through the next few months.

October 12: *Feast of the Autumn Fool.* Play practical jokes upon those who actually enjoy them. Talk pompously all day, make fun of ascetic occultists, and make a Great Beast out of yourself.

October 24: *Feast of the Inhabitants of the Air.* Meditate upon and try to communicate with nature spirits. Attempt intimate relations on the astral.

October 31: *Feast of the Faeries.* Have fun, get scary, get scared, and consume chocolate.

November 1: *Feast of All the Gods.* Think about all the deities you know and love. Look up a few new ones.

November 2: *Feast of the Ancestors.* Spend the day reading and thinking about your ancestors. Light a candle or two for them. Invite them to the *Samhain* feasting to take place next week.

In addition to, or instead of, these holidays, you may wish to celebrate specific natural events such as the first leaf-fall in autumn, the first snowfall, the first flowers of the spring, and so forth. Or you could celebrate social or political events in your grove's history, such as its founding date or the inauguration of officers.

13

Druidic Customs and Costumes

Symbols of Druid Identity*

One of the many reasons why people join organizations and movements is to gain a sense of belonging, of having a family of others who share their worldview. To this end, most groups use certain images as signs of membership. These shared symbols of identity help to create the psychological, social, and psychic connections necessary for effective group action. Provided that these images are used as positive signs of inclusion, rather than as negative signs of exclusion, they can only be of benefit to us.

So what are some of the symbols of being a Mesopagan or Neopagan Druid? The most obvious ones are the "Druid Sigil," the "Awen," organizational logos, the use of special clothing and various signs of "rank."

The Druid Sigil

The Druid Sigil is most often rendered as a circle with two vertical lines passing through it. Frequently this is drawn, painted, embroidered, etc. as a wreath of leaves with two staves (or spears for the warrior types) passing through. Twenty years

---

*Most of this comes from an essay of the same title published in *The Druids' Progress*, circa 1985.

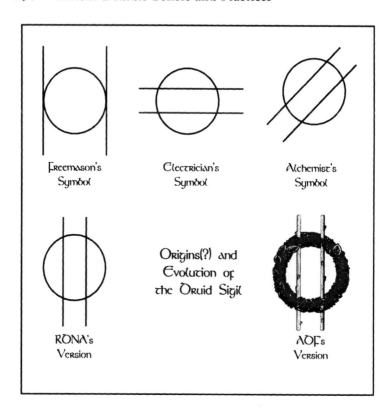

Freemason's
Symbol

Electrician's
Symbol

Alchemist's
Symbol

RDNA's
Version

Origins(?) and
Evolution of
the Druid Sigil

AODs
Version

back, a ceremonial tabard* was made with a tree in full leaf on the front and the sigil on the back with its wreath and stave-wood matching. I always thought it would be nice to have more vestments that followed this pattern, changing the leaf colors or tree species for each season.

Where did the Druid Sigil come from? Nobody knows for sure. It first became associated with Druidism in modern times by the founder of the Reformed Druids of North America, David Fisher, in 1963. He claimed that it was a symbol of Druidism in general and the Earth Mother in particular. In 2005, he said that he may have gotten it from a Masonic sym-

*A tabard is a garment made of two rectangles sewn together at two corners and worn over other clothing.

bol of a circle with two vertical lines outside it.* However, with the two lines running horizontally, the Druid Sigil is known to electricians as the sign for a female plug/socket, and with the lines diagonal, it's an old alchemical sign for oil, both concepts that could lead to some fruitful meditations.

Regardless of its historical origins, I think that it is a quintessentially female symbol and is thus psychologically powerful. For political and metaphysical reasons, I think it's important for members of a religion that many folks erroneously assume is male dominated to have a constant reminder of the eternal power of the female force(s) of nature. As a magical sign, I've used the Druid Sigil for over thirty years as both a blessing symbol and as a banishing sign. From a magical point of view, it is fully as powerful as a pentagram, Seal of Solomon, or cross, and meditation upon it will provide many insights.

While the Reformed Druids of North America and their immediate offshoots have kept the Druid Sigil as their primary organizational symbol, and many members of Ár nDraíocht Féin: A Druid Fellowship (ADF) use it as well, other Neopagan and Mesopagan Druid groups have altered it or ignored it completely.

The Awen

The Mesopagan Druids have, as their most common symbol, the "Awen" or "three bars of light." The word *awen* means "inspiration" in Middle Welsh. In Mesopagan Druidism it represents the primal sound and light caused by "the Supreme Being" pronouncing "His" name to create the universe. Mesopagan Druids have a great deal of metaphysical theory based on this and related triplicities—most of it coming from Iolo Morganwyg.

According to the *Barddas*:

When God pronounced His name, with the word sprang the light and the life; for previously there was no life ex-

---

*Letter from Michael Scharding.

cept God Himself. And the mode in which it was spoken
was of God's direction. His name was pronounced, and
with the utterance was the springing of light and vitality,
and man, and every other living thing; that is to say, each
and all sprang together. And Menw the Aged, son of Men-
wyd, beheld the springing of the /|\, in three columns; and
in the rays of light the vocalization—for one were the
hearing and seeing, one unitedly the form and sound; and
one unitedly with the form and sound was life, and one
unitedly with these three was power, which power was
God the Father.

These three marks are alternately described in the *Barddas* as
rays of divine light and as staves growing from the mouth of a
dead giant, who supposedly had invented writing by carving
marks on wooded staves (as is done in ogham). There is a great
deal of nonsense about /|\ being the first three letters, with their
values being listed as OIV, OIU, and/or OIW. This is argued
through a confusing mess of metaphysics, oghams (Irish letters), runes (Germanic letters), and a complete ignorance of linguistics and paleography. To be fair about it, those two
disciplines hadn't really been invented yet . . .

The Order of Bards Ovates & Druids commonly places the
Awen inside a set of three concentric circles, representing Iolo's
three "circles of existence:" the Circle of Abred, "in which are all

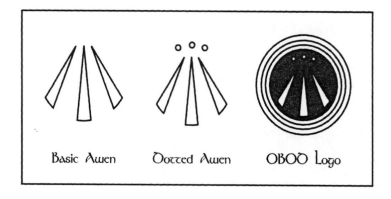

Basic Awen   Dotted Awen   OBOD Logo

corporal and dead existences" in the center, surrounded by the Circle of Gwynvd, "in which are all animated and immortal beings," and the outermost Circle of Ceugant, "where there is only God." Iolo drew the third circle as rays coming out of the second, but OBOD's version is easier to use in making talismans.

OBOD also, like other groups, adds three dots above the three rays. These are thought by some to represent the directions of the sunrises of the Summer Solstice, the two Equinoxes, and the Winter Solstice: east-north-east, due east, and east-south-east respectively. Others use a single dot to represent a Supreme Being.*

The word "awen" is used by some modern Druids as a Celtic equivalent to the Sanskrit word "aum," intoning it when doing trancework, raising energy in ritual, and so on, thusly: "aah-ooo-enn . . . "

Organizational Logos

The original (1983) ADF logo was inspired by the badge for the Scottish clan of MacEwen, which depicts new branches sprouting from a chopped oak tree stump. It was drawn by the well-known Neopagan, science fiction and fantasy artist Nybor, based on my vague description. It had one thin shoot with five leaves rising from the stump. The symbolism of ADF's logo is obviously that of survival and revival—indeed, the MacEwen clan motto is, *Reviresco,* which is Latin for "We (re)grow green." The axe marks in Nybor's original rendition made it clear that the tree of Druidism, like that of the MacEwen clan, was reviving after having been deliberately chopped down. Nybor added the interlacing below the stump to show that, although ADF is a Pan-Indo-European tradition, "we have Celtic roots." In 1993, I edited the logo to update it, with a slightly thicker trunk rising from the stump and more leaves.

The ADF logo usually appears only in black and white, al-

---

*I like to think of the three rays and three dots as symbolizing the Three Gates and Three Kindreds, with the three circles showing the Three Worlds and Three Realms. Hence, the awen on the cover of this book.

though several colored versions of it have been done. Usually the heavy lines of the roots, stump, and branch are black or dark brown, with the outside stump lines fading into dark green on the horizontal line, which in turn fades into dark blue as it rises into the circle. The oak leaves are green, the inside above-ground sky is blue, and the inside below-ground area is light brown.

Keltria has kept the Druid Sigil as a wreath and added the Awen in the center. Various local groves of ADF have done variations of the sigil with additional symbols added (Mugwort Grove, ADF, for example, uses the sigil with a large sprig of mugwort leaf in the center).

Other druidic groups have their own logos, of course, most of which involve oak trees, leaves, acorns, triple spirals, triskelions, trilithons, etc.

Varieties of Vestments and Tools

The specific clothes and ceremonial tools used by druids are related to the topic of identity but are also about appropriate and effective ritual use. These can be broken down into matters of headgear, robes, sacrificial/offering tools, and musical instruments.

Druidic Headgear

At one time, wearing white berets was an identifying symbol for ADF members. The story behind the white berets is this: When we first started having local grove meetings in the New York City area, we were meeting in coffeehouses in Greenwich Village. Since many of the folks at the early gatherings knew about ADF only through the mails, and had never met me or each other, we needed some sort of identification signal to help us find our fellow Druids. Since I was wearing a white beret at the time (along with a lot of other white clothing), I suggested that the others do the same. There was no particular reason why one's "Druid hat" should be a beret, I just thought that it looked appropriately ancient and was a way of honoring my

Breton and Gaulish ancestors. Red, brown, black, and other color berets were and are still worn in the Village, but white ones were and are fairly rare. This enabled us to find each other easily.

Later, when I sent out a mailing to Midwest ADF members about plans for an upcoming Pagan festival, I suggested that those who were going to attend could also wear white berets. Some did so, and more did at subsequent festivals. With anywhere from 100 to 500 people at the average Pagan festival back then, this easily visible symbol came in handy. Then we found out that the Ku Klux Klan was using white berets as an identifying symbol for its members! The mother grove immediately decided to abandon the use of them, for fear of confusion. In some ways this was a pity, for the hats were an easy symbol that could be spotted from a distance, and the ADF T-shirts never caught on the same way. Today, I still wear my white beret to Druid events and it makes me, at least, easy to find at large festivals.

Popular among members of the Mesopagan Druid orders is a loose detached hood called a "nemyss," which resembles nothing so much as Egyptian headgear, apparently because of Masonic associations of the Druids and the Egyptians with Atlantis, and, therefore, with each other. John Michael Greer, Archdruid of AODA (the Ancient Order of Druids in America), explains:

> One of the things the Hermetic refugees [from the Golden Dawn and Stella Matutina] brought with them was the nemyss. A black and white striped version was standard issue in the Golden Dawn, of course, and by the 1920s you start seeing photos of Druids at Stonehenge in white nemysses. I can tell you from personal experience that it's an exceptionally comfortable piece of headgear for outdoor rituals; push the hanging part back behind your shoulders on a hot day and it channels any breeze right to the back of your neck, where it does the most good; when it's cold, pull the corners forward, in front of your shoul-

ders, and you have a nice pocket of still air right around the back of your neck, which keeps you from getting chilled.

Also popular with Mesopagan Druids are various crowns, breastplates, rings, and other items, many of which are taken from the (very obsolete) scholarship of the early antiquarians, including misidentified items that are really pre-Celtic.

Certainly those druids who wear robes (see next section) will often have hoods of various sorts, vaguely monkish looking,

John Michael Greer, Archdruid of AODA,
in a nemyss from www.rogueregalia.com

Photo courtesy Rogue Regalia

and useful for the same purposes that Christian monks traditionally use them—keeping the sun out of one's eyes and blocking out the world while meditating. Also, the Roman and other Indo-European clergy would often cover their heads when making sacrifices, so the Paleopagan Druids *might* have done the same. It is, however, important for Druid groups that wear white robes to *not* have matching pointed hoods that hide their faces—especially south of the Mason-Dixon Line in the United States! As public Pagan clergy, Neopagan Druid ritual leaders should not hide their faces in any event, but rather show the courage of their convictions.

Perhaps someone else will come up with a different sort of hat for druids to wear—preferably something with a brim that will keep the sun out of our eyes during long rituals!

Robes

Long white robes have been popular for Mesopagan and Neopagan Druids for a long time. When they go to Stonehenge to celebrate the Summer Solstice, some of the Mesopagan Druids, especially the members of OBOD, wear solid white, blue, or green robes to signify who among them are the druids, bards, or ovates, respectively. We do know that the color white was associated with the Paleopagan clergy. This is one reason why I tend to wear white clothing (with various colors of decoration) as my public and private "clergy garb," a habit some other Neopagan Druids have picked up. If we were going to use the Indo-European colors for subcastes of the druids, then the ovates should probably be wearing red robes and the bards blue-green ones, but it's a little late to change the Mesopagan customs now.

Early in the history of ADF, one of our members (Elspeth of Haven) presented us with a sewing pattern for what we called the "bog people robe." This was based on the clothing worn by the ancient Celts found buried (and probably sacrificed) in the peat bogs of Scandinavia and Ireland. It obviously is an efficient way to get the maximum use out of a minimum amount of

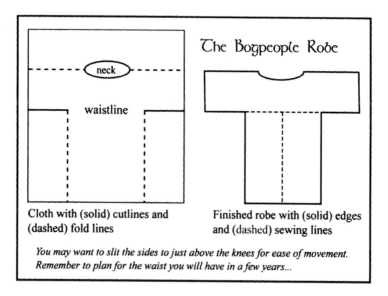

The Bogpeople Robe

Cloth with (solid) cutlines and
(dashed) fold lines

Finished robe with (solid) edges
and (dashed) sewing lines

You may want to slit the sides to just above the knees for ease of movement.
Remember to plan for the waist you will have in a few years...

cloth, a very important factor to people who had to weave their
own fabric.

Another authentic style would be a "great kilt," which is
really nothing but a heavy wool or linen toga—that is, a big rec-
tangle of cloth wrapped around and around the wearer, belted,
then pinned at the shoulder to keep it in place. The "small kilt,"
is the modern pleated skirt with which readers may be familiar.

Signs of Druidical Rank

The founders of the RDNA, in imitation of the garb worn
by Episcopal priests, "stole" the idea of using ribbons draped
around the neck to indicate who was a Druid of the Third
(clergy) Order. Originally these were given to new clergy in sets
of two—a red ribbon for the summer half of the year and a
white one for the winter half. Later, as "higher orders" were invented, many of them used differently colored ribbons to indicate membership. The big advantage to defining ribbons as the
minimal clergy gear was that they could be carried in a pocket
and quickly draped around one's neck over normal school

clothing, should either security or lack of sewing skills be a problem. They looked nice over elaborate robes as well.

What about signs of rank among the Neopagan Druids? While I'm not too sure it's a good idea to encourage them, they seem to be a universal human need. The idea I originally came up with for ADF was to use narrow bands of interlace or similar designs (Celtic, Norse, Slavic, Greek, etc.) climbing up the sleeves and hems of our robes: black/brown/green for First Circle members; red/blue for Second; white (with green and blue outlining) for Third; with perhaps silver and gold colored threads for Fourth and Fifth Circle members (none of whom exist as of 2006). The magnificent white robe that Karen Dougherty embroidered for me (see the frontispiece, facing the title page) uses this color-coding combined with symbols for the Three Worlds of Land, Sea, and Sky, plus lunar and solar symbols. This system wasn't used very much, but many of our members come up with their own, often stunning, ceremonial costumes based on their own research and artistic skills.

Druidic Ceremonial Tools

Every religion has certain objects that are used in rituals to focus the attention of the participants and, thus, to shape the flow of the invisible energies used for magical, psychic, and spiritual purposes. Most Neopagans are familiar with the standard Wiccan ceremonial tools: wands, knives, cups, and pentacles. Some, but not all, of these can be used in druidic rituals as well. Most Meso- and Neopagan Druids seem to prefer to have historical references for the tools they use, rather than just adopting those of other faiths.

There are several Irish and Welsh references to druids using wands of various woods, and sometimes staves. These were usually used as pointing objects to show the direction or target the druid wished her or his power to go. The "silver branch" was apparently a symbol of bardic authority, being a forked twig made of (or decorated with) silver and strung with silver bells.

This could be shaken to gain attention during a ritual or bardic performance.

Ceremonies that involve consecrating liquids obviously need vessels, which can range from small cups or drinking horns to large cauldrons or bowls. The latter can hold consecrated water to be sprinkled upon the congregants or else be used to represent the sacred well that links us to the cythonic realm.

Plates or "pentacles" aren't used much in Druidic ceremonies (that I know of) and neither are ceremonial daggers or athames. The latter could be used in rites involving war and peace, but are likely to be replaced by swords, as more effective in medium to large group rites. Indeed, the Mesopagan Druids have used the sheathing or unsheathing of swords, indicating whether their nation is at peace or at war, as an important step in their rituals for 300 years.

Sickles have been associated with druids ever since Pliny. At first I considered them to be a hopelessly lame cliché, until it dawned on me that they are a perfect symbol for sacrifice—a key concept of druidic philosophy. You cannot have a harvest without a whole series of sacrifices, even when we are looking only at the mundane, secular aspects of agriculture: Someone has to sacrifice long days of hard work to clear land, plow fields, plant seeds, hoe weeds, water and fertilize the plants, and finally cut the grain, grapes, or vegetables from their stalks. A sickle or scythe is a key agricultural implement in most of the world's cultures, one that is critical to bringing in a harvest. As such, a sickle becomes an obvious metaphor for spiritual sacrifices as well.

The Paleopagan Druids included doctors and herbalists in their class, so those folks at least might well have carried small sickles for cutting herbs, including mistletoe, though they probably weren't made of gold! While the Paleopagan Druids might have been recognized by carrying a wand or silver branch, Neopagan ones are most likely to be recognized as such if they wear a sickle in their belt (but not on airlines).

For ceremonial uses, the larger the number of people attending a rite, the larger the ritual tools should be (within reason). This is both so they can be seen from a distance and because their dramatic effects are stronger, so the energies raised in your ceremonies will be greater and more focused.*

A bag of ogham sticks or disks, runes, cards, or other divinatory tools (see Chapter 19) is also something that a druid should have available in rituals, meditations, or counseling sessions. Musical instruments are also a common druidic tool. These can include drums, guitars, harps, bagpipes, etc. It really doesn't matter much that the Paleopagan Druids didn't have them, or had ones that looked quite different from current instruments. If they had had them, they would have used them!

---

*See my *Rites of Worship: A Neopagan Approach* for a discussion of this.

14

Druidic Responsibilities

Responsibilities? Oh, No!

Druids have always been associated with *duties*—to their tribes, to the deities and other spirits, and to the universe as a whole. Like the brahmans in India and other Indo-European clergy, the Paleopagan Druids were charged with the responsibility of making sure that safety and order ruled over danger and chaos, that the annual sacrifice rituals were done properly, so that the universe would be recreated correctly each year, and that the knowledge of the past would be preserved into the future.

As we have seen, different members of the druid caste handled different responsibilities. Some would provide moral and practical advice to their tribes' rulers and warriors; others would perform the magical and religious ceremonies needed; others would use their psychic skills to perform divination, so that the future would be less vague and necessary precautions could be taken; yet others would memorize and teach to new generations all the accumulated wisdom their predecessors had gathered in various arts and sciences. In a time when death and chaos was never far away, the ability of druids to perform their duties often determined whether a tribe prospered or was destroyed, either by nature, internal dissension, or other tribes.

We still live in dangerous times, though the sources of many current dangers are different from those of the distant past.

Short of a total political and/or environmental collapse, it's unlikely that the knowledge accumulated over the past few centuries will be completely lost, for we have them enshrined in millions of books in libraries throughout the developed world (albeit the ability of the average American to read big words has suffered dramatically over the last forty years). But the common people and our political rulers still need to hear the wisdom of the Earth-Mother and the calm advice of subtle counselors. Certainly, there is plenty of magic waiting to be done by those with the moral courage to take action. Let's look at some modern druidic duties.

Cultural Responsibilities

The druids have always been the preservers of the best of their traditional cultures. The Mesopagan Druids of Brittany and Wales, for example, are directly responsible for the revival of the Cornish language and tradition from the very edge of extinction. The various cultural preservation and independence movements, such as the Celtic, Flemish, Baltic, and other related movements in Europe, need religious and cultural leadership based in their own cultures. Druidism can help create an environment in which such leadership can develop, not just for Celtic or other endangered Indo-European cultures, but for many other cultures that are equally at risk of being diluted and homogenized in our modern world.

Druids should be learning the old languages, their music, and their arts, so that they can be preserved for future generations. As for Ireland, the Holy Island will never be free and peaceful until the "white" of Druidism there becomes a major cultural influence again, to stand between the "green" of Catholicism and the "orange" of Protestantism, just as the Irish flag foretells.*

*Of course, it might just get us shot at by both sides there . . .

Magical, Religious, and Philosophical
Responsibilities

Druidism offers a worldview completely different from that of the monotheistic dualisms, with their eternal crusades and jihads, that now endanger our planet. One of the many things that any religion or philosophy does is to shape the ways in which people see the world around them. We need religions and philosophies that offer people a multitude of options, rather than the traditional Western either/or, black/white, win/lose choices.

Druidism, druidry, and *draíocht* are dangerous, at the bedrock level, because they can teach people how to use their Gods-given psychic and other talents to change the way things are. Make no mistake, magic works, at least as often as poetry, music, or political rallies do. Magic is a form of power that we, the people of the Earth, have available to use, not just for psychological "empowerment" (making ourselves feel better), but to actually control the individuals and institutions responsible for our planet's current mess.

Throughout all known human history, people who had hidden knowledge (whether of healing, weather prediction, mathematics, or magic) have used their exclusive possession of that knowledge as a source of power, for purposes that were good, bad, or weird. The warrior caste has always done its best (or worst) to take that knowledge away from the intelligentsia and to put it to political, economic, and military use. Today, almost all the hard and soft sciences have become tools for those who wish to control their fellow human beings. The polluters, the exploiters, the oppressors, and the conquerors are the ones who control nearly all the technology of overt power and a great deal of the technology for covert tyranny.

One of the very few ways we have of defending ourselves and our fellow passengers (human and other) on Earth is through the careful and judicious use of magic. National governments and private enterprises have spent millions of dollars (and rubles and pounds and yen) trying to develop psychic powers into dependable tools for warfare and oppression. Meanwhile, most of us who should have been learning precise techniques and careful timing, in order to use magic and the power of the Gods to defend ourselves and our Mother Earth, have been busy being misty-eyed romantics, not wanting to "sully our karma" by trying to do magic that might really work (that is to say, for which we would have to take personal responsibility).

As a result, those of us in the New Age, environmentalist, druidic, and Neopagan communities have assisted the very forces of oppression which we claim to oppose. We are partly responsible for the poverty, hunger, pollution, disease, and early deaths that dominate so much of our planet. Occultists have assisted by being unwilling to put their talents to the test by using them for "mundane" or "lowly-evolved" purposes. Ecologists, Celtic nationalists, and would-be revolutionaries have assisted by being unwilling to use nonmaterialistic technologies to cause changes in the material world (after all, if Freud and Marx didn't think magic is real, it can't possibly work). Modern Druids may eventually be able to help change those attitudes.

Despite the efforts of liberal mainstream clergymen to make us forget the physical and cultural genocide committed by their predecessors against tribal peoples everywhere, there is simply no way to ignore the fact that conservative monotheists in power always seek to silence competing voices. We cannot look to the mainstream religions for our physical and spiritual liberation, for they are the ones who took our freedom away in the first place. Scientism, leftist atheism, and New Age transcendentalism have no answers either, for they are also products of the monotheistic tunnel-reality, and seek to impose their dogmas and holy scriptures just as strenuously as ever the churches have. Those who want to live in a world of peace, freedom, and cultural pluralism, must look beyond the currently available "respectable" alternatives they have been presented with by the mass media, and consider new alternatives.

If we are unwilling to use magic, then we might as well resign ourselves and our descendants to either a life of slavery in a homogenized, pasteurized world, a world of chaos in which major cities have been destroyed by terrorists, or a slow and lingering death by radiation and/or environmental collapse.

Environmental Responsibilities

Druidism has environmental responsibilities because only nature-honoring religions and/or philosophies can give people sufficient concern for the environment to make them willing to make the many sacrifices that must be made in terms of lifestyle and consumption patterns.* We need strong public religions that tell the polluters, "No, it's not divinely sanctioned for you to rape the Earth, no matter what it says in your scriptures." If there is any religious or philosophical group on the face of the earth that should be supporting the environmental movement, it's the Druids!

And support it they have, especially in England. Arthur Uther Pendragon and the Loyal Arthurian Warband have been actively working for environmental and other noble causes for over a decade. They have taken advantage of the archetypal power of (the original) Arthur as the Sacred King, surrounded by noble knights willing to fight for what's right, and wielding Excalibur, the Sword of Truth. Pendragon and his LAW—there's little coincidence in *that* acronym—have worked with British druids in one outrageous act of political defiance after another against land developers, polluters, and those who would violate civil rights (especially at Stonehenge).

And let's not forget OBOD's Campaign for Individual Ecological Responsibility, which has worked since 1988 to encourage druids and others to take personal action to help the Earth-Mother. As they put it,

> Druid Spirituality isn't just about improving your own life—it's about making a difference to the world, too—it's about becoming environmentally responsible . . .

*See John Michael Greer's disturbing and all too convincing article "Druidry and the Future" on the AODA Web site at www.aoda.org/articles/Druidry.htm.

Recycling and buying environmentally friendly products is a start—but only a start. We need to protect our environment by consuming less and driving less. Our society is based upon massive overconsumption, and it is this overconsumption that is driving the "machinery" (cars and factories) that is ravaging the earth. By following Druidry, by focusing our lives on opening ourselves to the power and beauty of nature and spirit, rather than on consuming more products, we not only reduce some of the damage being done to the earth, but we also free up enormous amounts of time, energy, and money . . .

The Order's *Campaign for Individual Ecological Responsibility* focuses at the level of consciousness change—from which flow practical applications. The Campaign aims to change the idea that we are powerless, and to encourage the taking of individual responsibility. Once we act with personal responsibility, we can turn to the world of industry and commerce—and work to promote the idea of Corporate Ecological Responsibility, and to governments and nations to promote the idea of Global Ecological Responsibility.

Members of OBOD have planted sacred groves in countries all over the world through their wonderful Sacred Grove Planting Programme:

[It offers] support, advice, and financial aid to members of the Order and members of the public who wanted to create new sacred spaces across the world. As a result, thousands of trees, and hundreds of groves, have been planted around the world. These groves form a network of woodland sanctuaries that radiate peace, and offer refuge to both wildlife and humankind.

OBOD also encourages its members to research which of the world's many endangered species of trees can grow in their areas and to obtain and plant seeds of them. This is the sort of environmental "tree worship" that every druid organization and individual should consider getting involved in.

Beyond that, it seems to me that if we druids worship nature, we ought to be doing things in our mundane lives that are congruent with such worship, from recycling our own home waste materials, to shopping with green businesses, to voting for Green (literally or metaphorically) candidates, to joining and supporting environmental organizations. It's not like there's a shortage of the latter—there are hundreds of groups fighting for specific species, particular biomes, the oceans, and the Earth as a whole. If you want to call yourself a druid, of any flavor, you ought to belong to at least one such group (though three would be more druidic) and support it with your money if you can't with your time.

As OBOD puts it:

> In the Order's training, we learn how to work in an Inner Grove—we create a place of beauty and safety in the world of Soul and the Imagination that becomes our own personal sanctuary. The Grove, then, is the hallowed heart of the Druid, the place we create in the Otherworld—a place of learning and wisdom and peace. But the Grove also needs to exist in the Apparent world, for without it there can be no Inner Grove. Only the physical Grove can teach us the aromas, the sounds, textures, visions, flavours and ambience that we might find in our own Inner Groves.

Of what use is a druid in a world without trees? Or wolves, whales, or wombats?

Political Responsibilities

Many druids insist that there is nothing political in what they do, thereby following the Masonic traditions from whence they sprang, which decry discussions of politics and religion in the lodge. But I believe that Mesopagan and Neopagan Druidism, like Paleopagan Druidism—and Freemasonry!—before them, have important political aspects which should be considered, especially by those concerned with the survival and revival of either the Earth Mother or the Celtic peoples. If the Masons had been completely unwilling to discuss politics, there would never have been the American or French Revolutions, and freedom of religion, among other civil liberties, would never have become a modern ideal.

Separating one's spiritual and political lives is rooted in monotheistic dualism, by claiming that "worldly" matters should have nothing to do with spiritual ones. But as druids, we should be wise enough to see beyond this trap—matter and spirit are not separate but entwined. Ironically enough, it's the worst dualists in Western cultures who skip this particular doctrine when it comes to politics and who do everything they can to use secular political systems to force their spiritual opinions upon others. Religious and philosophical liberals need to learn that acting from your core religious beliefs is not the same thing as shoving your beliefs down others' throats, or advocating the removal of the wall between church and state.

One of the primary tasks of the Indo-European clergy caste (and, I suspect, of wise ones of any faith or none), has always been to ride herd on the warriors, to keep them from becoming either tyrannical or chaotically destructive. This may be one reason why Norse and Celtic warriors welcomed the Christian missionaries, because they perceived (correctly) that the Christian priests and monks would be far more likely to let them do what they wanted than the Paleopagan clergy had been. After all, if the world is ending any day now, as most early Christians (and some current ones) believed, why bother controlling your local warriors? Centuries later, the primary threat to life on this planet now comes from out-of-control warriors: soldiers and mercenaries, corporate polluters, and terrorists. So it's time we druids started taking that duty seriously again.

I believe that Druids *should* be involved in mundane politics, at least to the extent of studying, discussing, and taking action about political issues in your own town, region, or nation. Ask yourself whether your political leaders/rulers are really acting in ways that you as a Druid consider both just and honorable. Decide whether voting for your personal profit, your freedom, or your environment, might be your most important priority. Jump into political discussions online and don't let dualist extremists dominate the opinion-forming process—push the world's complexities into the arena of discussion. Write letters to your local newspapers, magazines, and secular online forums. Take to heart the Mesopagan Druid motto, "Truth against the world," and share your truth, however you view it. Remember another old saying, "In order for evil men to triumph it is sufficient that the forces of good do nothing."

As I said in the Introduction, personally I'm a liberal. I believe that thinking about the long-term consequences of human actions is one of the things that distinguishes political progressives, environmentalists, and nature worshippers from those in thrall to what I see as the real forces of evil: stupidity, short-sightedness, and greed. So to me "Druidic wisdom" implies particular political positions. I'm not the only modern Druid with such attitudes. Philip Carr-Gomm wrote in an essay on "Druidry and Politics" in 2001:

> In thinking about what a Druid's relationship to politics might be, I looked back at the attitudes of previous [Druid] chiefs, and discovered a remarkably consistent thread of beliefs, that led them all to promote liberal and socialist ideals that advocate freedom and justice for the underprivileged. In the nineteenth century Gerald Massey campaigned against slavery in the United States, and is now a hero of Afro-American scholars. In the early twentieth century, Robert MacGregor-Reid championed the rights of working men, and apparently stood for election in the American Senate and the British Parliament, as well as leading the Druid Order. I know the most about my predecessor, Ross Nichols, who continued this tradition by championing monetary reform, pacifism, and socialism.

You may well agree or disagree with these British Druids or myself, but for the Gods' sake, please apply what you say are your Druidic principles to everything in your life—including who you vote for and what political organizations you support. Druids know that everything is connected to everything else and, in the words of the ancient druidic saying, "the personal *is* political!"

PART SIX

◉

Current Druidic Religious Rituals

15

OBOD Rituals

The Pattern of OBOD Group Ritual

Philip Carr-Gomm, chosen chief of the Order of Bards Ovates &
Druids tells me, "In the Order's training, members are taught
thirty-six rituals, including tree-planting ceremonies, initiations,
rites of passage, and seasonal rituals." Their public group rites
follow a standard pattern:

- Grounding meditation
- Opening statement
- Call to the spirit(s) of the place, the grove, the God(s), etc.
- Peace to the quarters
- The "Universal" Druid's Prayer
- Awen chant
- Casting the circle
- Consecrating the circle
- Opening the quarters
- The working
- Unity prayer
- Awen chant
- Thanking the quarters
- Unwinding the circle
- Ending statement

This is clearly a combination of the Masonic-style rites of the
AOD, the BCUB, and so forth, groups with some influences

from Wicca. The following is a good example of one of OBOD's seasonal rites done according to this pattern.

An OBOD Group Ritual for Imbolc*

A meditation on what, in our selves and in our lives, needs healing and/or renewal is an ideal preparation for this ceremony.

> Roles: *Druid 1, Druid 2, Herald, North, South, East, West, Southeast, Northeast, Southwest, Northwest, Lady Brighid.*
>
> Prepare: *a bowl of water, two candles or lanterns to create the gateway in the Northeast, a pot of snowdrops or similar very early flower to place in the center. Each participant carries a candle lantern with a small candle lit: the same as, or representing, the one that was extinguished and relit at Alban Arthan. Lady Brighid carries a bowl of water and a somewhat larger candle lantern if available. Druid 1 will need to know the names of the participants in the Northeast, Southeast, Southwest, and Northwest.*

The Opening

Each person enters from the West and circles sunwise (clockwise, via the North) to salute the East before taking their place in the circle.

HERALD: By the power of star and stone,
By the power of the land within and without,
By all that is fair and free,
We welcome you to this rite of Imbolc,
In the grove/seed group/family/etc. of . . .

WEST   We have come from East and West, North and South to be here together today. *(All join hands)*

DRUID 2:   Let us take three breaths. . . .
Together with the Earth beneath us . . .

*Provided to me by Phillip Carr-Gomm.

Together with the Sky above us . . .

Together with the Sea around us . . .

NORTH: With the blessings of Earth, Sea, and Sky may our ceremony begin! *(All release hands)*

DRUID 1: *(Saluting East and facing outward)* O Spirit/Great Spirit/God(s)/Goddess(es) *(Choose a term you feel comfortable with)* we greet you and honor you, and ask for your blessings! *(face inward)* O Spirit of this place, O Spirit of this circle, we ask your blessings, your guidance, and your inspiration for this our ceremony.

DRUID 2: Let us begin by giving peace to the quarters, for without peace can no work be.

(Moving to salute each direction in turn, crossing the center of the circle, then returning to place in the West)

May there be peace in the North.

May there be peace in the South.

May there be peace in the West.

May there be peace in the East.

ALL: May there be peace throughout the whole world.

DRUID 1: Let us join in this prayer that unites all Druids:

ALL: Grant, O Spirit/Great Spirit/God(s)/Goddess(es),
thy protection,
and in protection, strength,
and in strength, understanding,
and in understanding, knowledge,
and in knowledge, the knowledge of justice,
and in the knowledge of justice, the love of it,
and in the love of it, the love of all existences,
and in the love of all existences,
the love of Spirit/Great Spirit/God(s)/
Goddess(es) and all goodness.

ALL: *(intone)* Awen, awen, awen.

DRUID 1:   Let all disturbing thoughts be laid aside. *(Casts circle sunwise, while Druid 2 says:*

DRUID 2:   The circle of our horizon—of our lives and lands, of time and of the year, of seasons and of goodness, of birth and of growing, of dying and of rebirth . . .

The circle can either be cast with a wand, staff, sword or forefinger, or in the following way—particularly if children are present—

SOUTH: Let us mark out this circle with symbols of the season.

Children/adults sprinkle confetti or seeds, flowers, petals, or leaves in circle sunwise around participants while Druid 2 speaks as above. Then, continue as follows, using the appropriate choices from the alternate terms:

DRUID 2:   As this circle is cast, the enchantment of the apparent world subsides. We stand together in the eye of the sun/by the light of the stars, here and now, between past and future. The earth below us, the heavens above us, and the circle/stones/trees/sea around us. This is sacred time. This is sacred space.

DRUID 1:   Now let us consecrate this circle with Water and with Fire.

WEST OR WATER BEARER: May our circle be purified and blessed with the element of Water. *(moves sunwise with water)*

SOUTH OR FIRE BEARER: May our circle be purified and blessed with the element of Fire. *(moves sunwise with candle/incense)*

DRUID 1:   We gather as equals, in our physical form here upon the Earth. Each presence is a blessing, and with every breath we take, we breathe light and life into this circle.

DRUID 2: Let the four directions be honoured, and let the gateways of the quarters be opened, that power and radiance might enter our circle for the good of all beings.

EAST: *(turning and facing outward):* With the blessing of the hawk of dawn soaring in the clear pure air, we call upon the powers of the East.

SOUTH: *(turning and facing outward):* With the blessing of the great stag in the heat of the chase, and the inner fire of the sun, we call upon the powers of the South.

WEST: *(turning and facing outward)* With the blessing of the salmon of wisdom who dwells within the sacred waters of the pool, we call upon the powers of the West.

NORTH: *(turning and facing outward)* With the blessing of the great bear of the starry heavens and the deep and fruitful earth, we call upon the powers of the North.

(All four then turn to face into the circle.)

ALL: May the harmony of our circle be complete.

The Rite

HERALD: Within this circle and in the apparent world, I declare the opening of this ceremony of Imbolc. Its symbol is the snowdrop, sacred symbol of the Goddess, that blooms bright in the snow.

DRUID 1: *(name of participant in NE)* is in the place of the young child, a place of winds and water, at the place of Imbolc, the season of Brighid. With water are we refreshed and cleansed, and in the wind does the spirit speak.

NORTHEAST: Lady, the snowdrops have pushed their way through the cold, wet earth, and we dream of your return.

ALL: Come back to us Lady, and bring the spring.

DRUID 1: (*name of participant in SE*) is in the place of the rising light, a place of energy and fertility, Beltaine, and the Hawk of May. Let our inspiration not fail us.

SOUTHEAST: The birds are ready to return from their winter homes, and the trees are waiting to bring forth new leaves.

ALL: Come back to us Lady, and bring the spring.

DRUID 1: (*name of participant in SW*) is in the place of high summer, the feast of Lugh. S/he guards and feeds the fire. His/Hers is the heart of the ceremony. May it be warm.

SOUTHWEST: The plants which were harvested and returned to you in the earth, are close to renewal.

ALL: Come back to us Lady, and bring the spring.

DRUID 1: (*name of participant in NW*) is s/he who chants and leads the rhythms of movement in the place of the caves of the soul, during the dark time of Samhain. May his/her voice, and our actions, be strong. May we ride well the storm of sound.

NORTHWEST: On this night we remember the Goddess of Winter, the Cailleach ("kai-e-och"), whose time is passing. Now we await the return of the Maiden.

ALL: Come back to us Lady, and bring the spring.

DRUID 2: See how all around us are air and fire. The leaves of the trees speak to us with the breath of air; and in the heart of the wood is the seed of fire. The leaves whisper of one who has come in youth and hope. The Lady is close.

NORTHEAST: *(steps forward with snowdrops and says)* Welcome Brighid, gentle maiden, bathed in the white milk of nurturing. The fire of spirit shines through your eyes. Bless us with the breath of life. *(then walks to stand beside South.)*

SOUTH: *(steps forward with candle and says)* Welcome Brighid, Queen of the South, whose inner fire touches the sun. May the radiant warmth of your love be felt in our hearts. Bless us with your inspiration.

Both NE and S walk to stand either side of NW who steps forward and says:

NORTHWEST: Welcome Brighid, seer and guide, lead us safely through the sacred maze to the centre of the spiral. Let the light of the young one bless us with healing.

All three spiral around to the centre led by NW. NE places snowdrops by central fire. S lights the two large candles or lanterns.

NORTHWEST: Brighid, guard your fire, this is your night.

The three retrace the spiral to the Northeast, where S places the two lanterns/candles to form the Northeastern gateway. They then return to their places.

DRUID 1: In the name of the guardians of this Order, and of all those here to greet you, I bid you welcome O Lady Brighid. Come and bless us with your presence once again.

Lady Brighid, bearing water and lantern approaches the Northeastern gateway. She may have been waiting outside or, if she has been present in the circle, she moves from her position sunwise around the outside. She steps through the gateway into the center of the circle where she puts down her lantern and raises the bowl of water, saying:

LADY BRIGHID: I bring this water of healing and renewal, that all who would walk in my footsteps might bring joy and inspiration to these lands.

She circles sunwise, starting with Druid 1, to pour a little water into the outstretched palms of each participant. They can then sip the water or bathe their brows, or do both as she says to each:

LADY BRIGHID: May this water bless you. *(returns to center, raises lantern)* Behold the light I have nurtured. Through the dark and the cold of winter we have each carried forward from Alban Arthan a tiny flame. Soon the light of the Sun will be strong enough to truly warm the Earth once more. Guard well the seed of your light! *(Goes to stand in NE gateway)*

Brighid is the goddess of the well and the flame, of fire and water. But she is also the goddess of poetry and of healing. The central section of the ceremony may be used for meditation, for healing, and/or for a reading of poetry. Participants can be invited beforehand to bring poems on the feminine and on the Goddess. After readings/meditation/healing, enact:

The Closing

DRUID 2:   It is the hour of recall. As the fire/light dies down let it be relit in our hearts. May our memories hold what the eye and ear have gained.

All hold hands.

ALL: *(three times, pausing between each)*
           We swear, by peace and love to stand,
           Heart to heart and hand in hand.
           Mark, O spirit, and hear us now,
           Confirming this, our sacred vow.

ALL: *(chant "cascading")* Awen, awen, awen *(etc.)*

DRUID 1:   May the spirits of the four directions be thanked for
           their blessings.

NORTH: In the name of the great bear of the starry heavens
           and of the element of Earth, we thank the powers of
           the North.

WEST: In the name of the salmon of wisdom and the ele-
           ment of Water we thank the powers of the West.

SOUTH: In the name of the great stag and of the element of
           Fire, we thank the powers of the South.

EAST: In the name of the hawk of dawn and of the ele-
           ment Air, we thank the powers of the East.

All turn to face the centre again.

ALL: May the harmony of the land be complete.

Circle is uncast countersunwise.

DRUID 1:   May the blessings of the Goddess/God/Spirit/
           Great Spirit be always with us. I declare this cere-
           mony of Imbolc is closed in the apparent world.
           May its inspiration continue within our beings.

16

Reformed Druid Rituals

The Pattern of RDNA Group Ritual

The Reformed Druids use a very simple pattern, one which nonetheless fits within what I call "a common worship pattern" for Indo-European cultures:*

- Invocation
- Procession
- Praise
- Sacrifice
- Reply
- Catechism of the waters
- Consecration
- Communion
- Meditation
- Benediction

There were two major variations on this pattern, one for summer and one for winter. Most of the other original RDNA, NRDNA, and SDNA public rituals are elaborations of one of these two, supplemented by songs, poems, chants, seasonal readings, or festive activities.

---

*See my *Rites of Worship* for details.

An Order of Common Worship for Summer, NRDNA*

This service is for use from Beltaine to Samhain. It starts with all participants standing some distance away from the area where the ritual is to take place. If both safe and legal, a fire should be started in or near the altar. The Druid/ess who is presiding (usually, though not always, the grove's archdruid/ess) should already have cut the sacrifice (a small branch) and have it tucked into his or her robe (or it may be held in one hand). The presiding Druid/ess may choose to speak the opening invocation to Béal alone, or may ask the Preceptor and/or the people (depending on local grove custom) to join in speaking the invocation.

The Invocation

DRUID:	O Lord, forgive these three errors that are due to our human limitations: Thou art everywhere,
PREC:	but we worship thee here;
DRUID:	Thou art without form,
PREC:	but we worship thee in these forms;
DRUID:	Thou has no need of prayers and sacrifices,
PREC:	yet we offer thee these prayers and sacrifices;
DRUID:	O Lord, forgive us these three errors that are due to our human limitations.
PREC:	O Mother, cleanse our minds and hearts and prepare us for meditations.†

---

*As published in *A Reformed Druid Anthology, Second Edition*. This is from the mid-1970s and predates most of the changes I made to the NRDNA liturgy and those made by others in later years.

†This is based on a Hindu prayer translated by Houston Smith in *The World's Religions*.

The Procession

Here occurs the procession, often with the grove singing an appropriate Druidic hymn. Upon arrival near the altar, the Preceptor and the Server or any two others designated by the grove use their staves to mark the Druid Sigil upon the ground in front of the altar (usually on the South side), leaving the bottom of the circle incomplete. The Druid/ess steps into this Sigil, which is then closed by the two staves.

The Praise

Here an incantation, poem or hymn of praise is recited or sung by the Druid/ess, the bard(s) or the entire grove.

The Sacrifice

The Druid/ess holds up the sacrifice to the sky, while saying:

DRUID: Our praise has mounted up to thee on the wings of eagles, our voices have been carried up to thee on the shoulders of the winds. Hear now, we pray thee, our Mother, as we offer up this sacrifice of life. Accept it, we pray thee, and cleanse our hearts, granting us thy peace and life.

Here the Druid/ess places the plant offering into the fire, upon the altar, or on the ground if there is no altar. As each of the directions are questioned, the members may turn to face that direction.

DRUID: Hast thou accepted our sacrifice, O our Mother? I call upon the spirit of the North to give answer . . . of the South . . . of the East . . . and of the West.

The Reply

If the sacrifice is accepted, and it almost always is accepted, then continue. If a bad omen occurs, such as lightning striking the Druid/ess, a tree falling over, etc., the service ends at this point.

DRUID: Praise be, our sacrifice, dedicated to the fertility and renewal of life, and to the cleansing of our minds and hearts, has been accepted!

The Catechism of the Waters-of-Life

The preceptor holds the waters-of-life* while the Druid/ess ask the Catechism of the Waters-of-Life. The preceptor or all present may speak the responses, according to local custom.

DRUID: Of what does the Earth-Mother give that we may know the continual flow and renewal of life?

PREC: The waters-of-life.

DRUID: From whence do these Waters flow?

PREC: From the bosom of the Earth-Mother, the ever† changing All-Mother.

DRUID: And how do we honor this gift that causes life in us?

PREC: By partaking of the waters-of-life.

DRUID: Has the Earth-Mother given forth of her bounty?

PREC: She has!

DRUID: Then give me the Waters!

The Consecration

The Druid/ess takes the chalice from the Server, who fills it if it is not already full. The Druid/ess then consecrates its contents with the following:

DRUID: O Dalon Ap Landu, hallow these waters by thy sevenfold powers and by the three ways of day and one of night. Cleanse our hearts and join us together as we take and drink of thy secret essences!

*Water with whiskey!
†Originally "never" changing.

The Communion

The Druid/ess drinks from the chalice and blesses the Preceptor with the words, "the Waters-of-Life," and the marking of the Druid Sigil in the air. The Preceptor returns the blessing and receives the chalice from the Druid/ess. The Preceptor drinks, blesses the Server, is blessed in return, and gives the Server the chalice. The Server drinks, then goes around the circle of the grove (usually clockwise) blessing each person, handing them the chalice, letting them drink, being blessed in return and taking the chalice to the next person. The Server does not drink more than once (not if he/she wants to still be standing by the end of the rite).

In some groves, the Druid/ess may merely turn to the left and exchange blessings with the person to that side, letting the chalice be handed around the circle by the members of the Grove.

In either method, the last person in the circle should not finish the contents of the chalice. This is returned to the Druid/ess with a last exchange of blessings. Then the Druid/ess takes the last sip pouring the remainder on the altar or fire, saying:

DRUID: To thee we return this portion of thy bounty, O our Mother, even as we must return to thee.

The Meditation

Here follows an appropriate reading, from any nature-oriented scripture that the Druid/ess may choose, read by the Druid/ess or by someone appointed for that purpose. After this comes a few brief words of meditation* from the Druid/ess and a period of silence and private meditation (usually two or three minutes in length) by all. Eventually, the Druid/ess signals the end of the service with:

The Benediction

DRUID: Go forth into the world, secure in the knowledge that our sacrifice has found acceptance in the Earth-

---

* *Not* a sermon!

Mother's sight, that she has answered our prayer, and that we go forth with her blessing.

The Priest blesses the grove with three sigils in the air, left to right, saying:

DRUID: Peace! Peace! Peace!

An Order of Common Worship for Winter, NRDNA

This service is for use from Samhain to Beltaine. It is mostly similar to the Summer version, so I will present only the parts that were traditionally done differently during what the Reformed Druids called the Season of Sleep. In these rites, it was assumed that the Earth-Mother was sleeping and that the four winds would not answer to the Druids' calls. Hence, the text diverges at the Reply.

The Reply

DRUID: The four winds are silent; the Earth-Mother sleeps.

The Catechism of the Waters-of-Sleep

The Preceptor holds the waters-of-sleep* while the Druid/ess asks the Catechism of the Waters-of-Sleep. The preceptor or all present may speak the responses, according to local custom.

DRUID: Of what does the Earth-Mother give that we may know the continual flow and renewal of life?

PREC: The waters-of-life.

DRUID: From whence do these waters flow?

PREC: From the bosom of the Earth-Mother, the ever changing All-Mother.

DRUID: And how do we honor this gift that causes life in us?

*Plain water.

PREC:　　By partaking of the waters-of-life.

DRUID:　　Has the Earth-Mother given forth of her bounty?

PREC:　　She has not! The waters are here, but the spirit has gone out of them.

DRUID:　　Of what, then, do we partake?

PREC:　　The waters-of-sleep!

DRUID:　　Then give me the waters-of-sleep!

The Consecration

The Druid/ess takes the chalice from the Server, who fills it if it is not already full. The Druid/ess then consecrates its contents with the following:

DRUID:　　O Dalon Ap Landu, descend once again into these waters, and hallow them. Give us to know thy power and the promise of life that is to return.

The Communion

The Druid/ess drinks from the chalice and blesses the Preceptor with the words, "the Waters-of-Sleep," and the marking of the Druid Sigil in the air. The rest of this part follows the summer pattern, ending with the return:

DRUID:　　To thee we return this portion, O our Mother even as we must return to thee.

The Meditation

Follows an appropriate reading, as in the Summer.

The Benediction

DRUID:　　Go forth into the world, secure in the knowledge that our prayers will be answered, that the bounty of life will return to the face of the Earth, and then will the Earth-Mother shower her blessings upon you.

The Priest blesses the Grove with three sigils in the air, left to right, saying:

DRUID: Peace! Peace! Peace!

I should point out here that, according to Michael Scharding, many current RDNA members are actually listening to the Reply and continuing, changing, or stopping the ritual accordingly.

17

ADF Rituals

The Pattern of ADF Group Ritual

This is a simplified version of my original ADF liturgical design (see Appendix G) matching the way the rites are commonly done today, in which most of the forty-three steps are present but conflated:

- Procession
- Opening prayers
- Grove attunement
- Fire, Well, and Tree
- Purpose and precedent
- Purification
- Opening the Gates
- Kindred offerings
- Key offerings
- Sacrifice and omen
- The blessings
- Work
- Closing

The rite that follows is a "sample," because ADF encourages its members to continually research and evolve their ceremonies, but it is pretty close to being a "standard" one. Words and actions attributed to "the Druid(s)" may be done by one person or several.

A Sample ADF Rite of Worship*

One group of celebrants hallow the Grove; the Fire is lit, the Well is filled, the Tree is blessed.

Procession

With singing, all others arrive and circle the hallows deosil (clockwise). The Druids complete the sigil, by closing the ring and then having two of them walk parallel lines across it. They return to the center and then give the opening prayers.

Opening Prayers

EARTH-MOTHER

All kneel and kiss the earth. The Chief speaks as a Druid makes an offering of grain, bread, or flour.

CHIEF: O beloved Mother of all
        From whose starry womb the green Earth springs
        You who are the bearer of all life
        We pray you bless and uphold this rite.

ALL: Mother of all accept our offering!

AWEN

The Bard invokes, saying:

BARD: Power of inspiration that attends us
        Voice of the fire of wisdom,
        Voice of the well of inspiration

*As taken from the *ADF Grove Organizers' Handbook, Fourth Edition,* 2005. Written by Ian Corrigan, used by permission.

Come into our hearts' shrine
O! Into our hearts' shrine
Let us ken of every good or ill,
Guide our rite in the way of truth
I call you to place the clear heart in us
O power of inspiration in this holy place
O power of inspiration at this holy time
So be it!

Grove Attunement

A Druid leads a meditation intended to attune the company to the Earth and Sky powers and to join the company in spirit. This might conclude with an intoning or a proper chant or hymn.

Fire, Well, and Tree

Druids or members of the grove make offerings to the Sacred Center. Silver is offered to the well, saying:

DRUID: O sacred waters that flow and swirl beneath all being accept our offering! Let us know the elder depths within ourselves the source of all, the Well of elder wisdom.
Sacred Well, flow within us!

ALL: Sacred Well, flow within us!

An offering of oil is made to the Fire, saying:

DRUID: O sacred Fire that consumes and transforms
True and holy light of the Shining Ones
Accept our offering! O sacrificed and sacrificer
Let holy flame warm our spirits and our lives.
Sacred Fire, burn within us!

ALL: Sacred Fire, burn within us!

The Bilé is censed and sprinkled, saying:

DRUID: O sacred pillar, boundary of all worlds,
Stand at the center of the Sky,

Stand at the center of the Sea,
Stand at the center of the Land on which we dwell.
Let us be deepened in your depths
Raised to your heights
Strengthened in your strength
Sacred Tree, grow within us!

ALL: Sacred Tree, grow within us!

Purpose and Precendent

As proper to the work. (This is the announcement of why the people have gathered, the historical precedent for their actions, and who the special divine patron(s) of the ritual are and why.)

Purification

ACKNOWLEDGMENT OF THE OUTSIDERS

An offering is made to the South of the grove, saying:

DRUID: Ancient dark ones, we make this offering to you.
You who dwell in the outer dark
You who stood against the Gods
You twisted and misshapen
You cold of heart and dim of mind
Take this offering and trouble not our working.
Likewise we acknowledge in ourselves
Weakness and perversity
Hatred and spite
Cowardice and ignorance
We contemplate these ills and enemies
And for this sacred time
We set them aside!

Fire and Water

Druids draw water from the Well and light a censer from the Fire. They quickly cense and asperge the company, while the company intones or chants.

Opening the Gates

A Druid makes an offering to Manannan, saying:

DRUID: O Manannan, Lord of the Gates, Lord of Wisdom, open the ways for us. We walk in your holy ways, we walk the Sacred Road. Share your magic with us, ward us as we walk in safety. Manannan mac Lir, accept our sacrifice!

ALL: Manannan mac Lir, accept our sacrifice!

An offering of oil is given to the Fire. The Druid then conjures the Gates, making an opening triskel (three-legged sun wheel) on the Fire and Well, saying:

DRUID: Now, lord of ways, join your magic with mine and let the Fire open as a Gate, let the Well open as a Gate, let the Tree be the crossroads of all worlds. Open as a road to our voices and to the spirits. Let the gates be open!

ALL: Let the Gates be open!

Kindred Offerings

The druids make proper offerings to each of the kindreds, standing at the Fire.

ANCESTORS

DRUID: The children of the Earth call out to the Mighty Dead. Hear us, our ancestors, our kindred.
           To all those whose bones lie in this Land, whose hearts are tied to it, whose memory holds it; ancient tribes of this place, we offer you welcome.
           To all of our grandmothers and grandfathers, our own beloved dead, blood kin and heart kin; ancient tribes of our blood; we offer you welcome.
           To all those elder wise ones who guide their peo-

ple, poets and seers, judges and magicians; wise women and men of ancient days, we offer you welcome.

So, O mighty ones, we call to you as our kin, in the love of the all-Mother, to join in our magic. Come to our fire, spirits; meet us at the boundary. Guide and ward us as we walk the elder ways.

In some groves, members may call out the names of their belovéd dead. Then an offering of food and/or drink is made onto the ground or into a shaft previously dug.

DRUID: Ancestors, accept our sacrifice!

ALL: Ancestors, accept our sacrifice!

NATURE SPIRITS

DRUID: The children of Earth call out to the spirits of this Land. Hear us, companions and teachers.

To all our allies, kindreds of stone and stream, crystal and fertile soil, pools and every water; kins of the Earth, we offer you welcome.

To all our allies, kindreds of the growing green, herb and flower, shrub and mighty trees, root and stem and fruit. Green kins, we offer you welcome.

To all our allies, kindreds of fur and feather and scale, all who walk or fly or swim or crawl, we offer you welcome.

So, O noble ones, we call to you as our allies, in the joy of life upon Earth, to join in our magic. Come to our Fire, spirits; meet us at the boundary. Guide and ward us as we walk the elder ways.

In some groves, members may call out the names of their guardian spirits. Then an offering of herbs, flowers, and/or trinkets is scattered around the nemeton's edge or hung on the tree.

DRUID: Land Spirits, accept our sacrifice!

ALL: Land Spirits, accept our sacrifice!

DEITIES

DRUID: The children of Earth call out to the Shining Ones. Hear us, eldest and brightest.

To all the Shining Ones, first children of the Mother, wisest and mightiest, loving and comforting; Gods and Goddesses, we offer you welcome.

To the Gods and Goddesses of this place, ancient and powerful, known to us or unknown; Gods of this place, we offer you welcome.

To all the deities of those here gathered, you whom we worship, you who bless our lives; O patrons and matrons, we offer you welcome.

So, O Shining Ones, we call to you as our elders, in reverence and love, to join in our magic. Come to our Fire, Shining Ones; meet us at the boundary. Guide and ward us as we walk the elder ways.

In some groves, members may call out the names of other deities they wish to honor. Then an offering of scented oil is poured on the Fire.

DRUID: Deities, accept our sacrifice!

ALL: Deities, accept our sacrifice!

After all the offerings have been made, the druids recenter the company and lead an attunement to all the spirits that have been called, and a proper chant or hymn is sung to the three kindreds.

Key Offerings

DRUID: Welcome to the Gods and Goddesses, the dead and the *sidhe!* To all of you who have gathered at our Fire, we pray you join us in worshipping the patron of this holy rite here in our Sacred Grove.

The Druids now give the descriptive invocations of the patron powers of the rite. This is followed by any proper customs for the occasion, and by praise offerings. Physical offerings are made, and a portion of each is held back for the final sacrifice.

Sacrifice and Omen

The Druids prepare the final offerings and (using appropriate pronouns) say:

DRUID: So we have given of our love and our wealth to the Lord and Lady. Now let our voices arise on the Fire, let our voices sound in the Well, let our words pass the boundary to the Otherworlds. O Lord, O Lady, we give you our love, our respect, our devotion as we pray you . . .
Lady and Lord, accept our sacrifice!

ALL: Lady and Lord, accept our sacrifice!

All are led to send their energy through the gates to the powers, meditating on the deities.

DRUID: Having prayed to the powers, let us open to them, asking what blessings they offer us in return.

The omen is taken as usual. The seer then interprets the omen, leading the company to contemplate the things they would ask of the powers, especially as suggested by the omen. Company recenters in preparation for the blessing.

The Blessing

THE LITANY OF THE WATERS

DRUID: Ancient and Mighty Ones we have honored you. We pray you honor us in turn, for a gift calls for a gift. Hear your children . . .

ALL: Shining Ones, give us the waters!

DRUID: We thirst for the waters of wisdom, of bounty, of rebirth from the Well of wisdom, from the spring of renewal, from the bosom of the Earth-Mother. Hear us . . .

ALL: Shining Ones, give us the waters!

DRUID: We open our hearts to the Great Ones' blessing. We stand in pride, honor, and friendship with all the powers of the worlds. Hear and answer us now . . .

ALL: Shining Ones, give us the waters!

HALLOWING THE WATERS

Ale is poured into the horns and elevated.

DRUID: We draw blessing from the cauldron of blessing. We pour the ale of inspiration. Behold the holy cup of magic, the outpouring of blessing from the Mighty Ones. When we share the draught of the Gods we drink in wisdom, love, and strength to do as we will in the worlds, in service to the Shining Ones.

Hear us O Lord, O Lady; hallow these Waters! We, your children, rejoice in your gift. Bless our spirits and our lives with love, magic, and bounty as we drink these Sacred Waters.

Behold the Waters of Life!

ALL: Behold the Waters of Life!

The horns are passed and all drink as a proper hymn is sung. With large groups, participants may be asperged instead of drinking.

Work

As needed.

Closing

When all is done, the Druids lead a resettling, then begin to close the grove, saying:

DRUID: The Mighty Ones have blessed us. With joy in our hearts let us carry the magic from our Sacred Grove into our lives and work. Each time we offer to the powers they become stronger and more aware of our needs and our worship.

So now as we prepare to depart let us give thanks to those who have aided us.
O [patron powers], we thank you!

ALL: We thank you!

DRUID: O Gods and Goddesses of elder days, we thank you!

ALL: We thank you!

DRUID: O spirits of this land, we thank you!

ALL: We thank you!

DRUID: O ancestors, our kindred, we thank you!

ALL: We thank you!

DRUID: To all those powers that have aided us, we say again . . . we thank you!

ALL: We thank you!

Druids renew the company's centering once more, signaling the return to common awareness and ease of access to the centered state. Then any unused offerings, return flow, incense, water etc., is given to the Earth, saying:

DRUID: Mother of all, to you we return all we leave unused. Uphold us now in the world as you have in our rite. We thank you!

ALL: We thank you!

The Druids goes to the center, bearing the wand.

DRUID: O Gatekeeper, warder of the ways, for your presence and power, your guiding and guarding we say . . . we thank you!

ALL: We thank you!

Druid makes the closing sign over the hallows with the wand, saying:

DRUID: Now by the keeper of Gates and by our magic we end what we began.

>Now let the Fire be flame
>Let the Well be Water;
>Let all be as it was before.
>Let the Gates be closed!

ALL: Let the Gates be closed!

DRUID: Go now, children of the Earth, in peace and bless-
          ings. The rite is ended!

*The bard leads a proper chant as the company processes out of the
grove.*

A Short Devotional Rite*

*This rite is suitable for daily or frequent performance at a per-
sonal altar or shrine. Deity gender references may, of course, be altered to suit the participant(s).*

*The Druid comes, freshly bathed, before the altar and lights the
altar lamp (which may be any sort of candle or small flame), saying:*

>O blessed spirit of light and magic, flesh of the
>deities' flesh, spirit of my spirit, bring to my shrine
>the divine power of your light. O sacred spirit-fire,
>be welcome in your house. *Beannachta!*

*The visualizations of the deities are built up, and a short prayer of
praise may be offered. The Triple Offering is then made with these
words:*

>I shall offer my offerings in the eye of the mothers
>who bore me, in the eye of the fathers who quick-
>ened me, in the eye of the Gods and the light of the
>Fire.
>Make me your kinswo/man, accept from me: Salt,
>that your power preserve and defend me,

Druid elevates salt, places it on the altar

---

*Also written by Ian Corrigan, used by permission.

Water, that your power cleanse and sustain me,

Druid offers water

Incense, that your power lend my life joy and de-light.

Druid offers incense

Bestow upon me in the hour of my need the love of the Gods, the wisdom of the Gods, the power of the Gods, to do in the Three Worlds as the heroes do in *Tir na nog*. Each shade and light, each day and night, each hour in blessing, give me your spirit.

The Druid meditates on the visualization for a time, then extin-guishes the flame, leaving the incense to burn out, and goes about her/his business.

18

Keltrian Druid Rituals

The Pattern of Keltrian Group Ritual

This is another simplified version of my original ADF liturgical design, matching the way Keltrian rites are commonly done today. Again, most of the 43 steps are present but conflated:

- Procession
- Purifications
- Sacred space marking
- Opening prayers
- Tree Meditation
- Parting of the Veil (Opening of the Gates)
- Unity song
- Triad (kindred) invocations
- Purpose and deities of the occasion
- Primary invocations
- Key offerings
- Sacrifice
- The blessings
- Closing

The rite that follows is a holiday celebration done according to this pattern.

A Keltrian Ritual for Beltaine*

In addition to the usual Keltrian ritual tools, there should be a priapic wand and a flower wreath present. The altar is in the East, decorated with budding branches, spring flowers, and so forth. Also present as remembrances should be hazelnuts for Boann and rose petals for Bilé. This rite assumes two presiding Druids.

All process to the ritual site, receive anointing/blessing, and define sacred space in customary manner.

DRUID #1: We come to celebrate Beltaine, the season of the greening.

Sing unity song, have Tree Meditation, Parting of the Veil, and perform Triad invocations in customary manner. Druid #1 and Druid #2 face each other before altar.

DRUID #1: Wherefore have we come to the grove upon this day [night]?

DRUID #2: We celebrate Beltaine, feast of the flowering.

DRUID #1: And why do we celebrate?

DRUID #2: We welcome the flowering of the Earth as it reflects the time in our lives of spiritual flowering.

DRUID #1: And whom do we honor upon this feast?

DRUID #2: We honor Boann, Cattle Goddess of the Boyne. We honor Bilé, God of the greening.

DRUID #1: And why have we chosen these deities to honor on this occasion?

DRUID #2: We honor Boann for the fertilizing spring floods. We honor Bilé for the strength of the increasing sun.

DRUID #1: And what does this time mean to the Druids?

*Provided by Tony Taylor; used by permission.

DRUID #2: Beltaine is a feast of fertility. We rejoice in the fertility of the Earth, and our own physical and spiritual fertility. The seeds of our yearly plans now put forth flowers that bring the promise of fruit.

DRUID #1: Then let us call the God and Goddess to be honored at this feast.

Druid #2 takes altar candle and transfers Boann from the incense cauldron into the candle flame. Druid #1 does same for Bilé with remaining altar candle. Druid #1 and Druid #2 approach center Fire cauldron/Fire-pit with candles.

DRUID #2: O' Boann . . .

DRUID #1: O' Bilé . . .

DRUID #1 & DRUID #2:   With the flame of your spirits, we kindle the sacred Fire.

Druid #1 and Druid #2 kindle the grove fire with candles, then return to altar. Devotions and offerings/gifts are asked for and presented per standard ritual. Druid #1 then takes sickle and branch from altar and holds over offertory.

DRUID #1: O' Boann, O' Bilé, be strengthened by the energies of these gifts we send to you. So be it.

Druid #1 touches sickle to branch. Offering is placed into Sacred Fire (or wrapped for a later fire), celebration song is sung, and seer divines for messages per standard ritual format.

Druid #1 takes flower wreath and holds forth. Druid #2 takes priapic wand and holds forth.

DRUID #1: Beltaine is the season of fertility. Women, I shall pass this symbol of our fertility. Hold it and meditate upon how you desire fertility to come into your life this season.

DRUID #2: Men, I shall pass to you this symbol of our fertility. Hold it and meditate upon how you desire fertility to come into your life this season.

Druid #1 hands wreath to first woman deosil. Druid #2 hands wand to first man deosil. Both are passed around circle. When items return to Druid #1 and Druid #2, Druid #1 holds wreath above wand held by Druid #2. Druid #1 slowly lowers wreath over wand and says:

DRUID #1: Just as physical fertility requires the coming together of two, know that in your own search for physical, mental, or spiritual fertility, you will need the love and support of those close to you

DRUID #2: Let us come together as a tribe, as a spiritual people, and dance the dance of life.

All join in a circle dance about the central fire. D1 takes bowl of hazelnuts from altar.

DRUID #1: Boann, Goddess of sexual awareness, we remember you through the hazelnuts of knowledge.

Passes bowl of nuts. Each celebrant takes a nut and eats. Druid #2 takes bowl of rose petals from altar.

DRUID #2: Bilé, God of the greening pastures, we remember thee through the flowers of the field.

Druid #2 Passes remembrance bowl sunwise. Each celebrant takes a petal and keeps it as a remembrance.
  Druid #2 takes chalices of water and mead from altar. Druid #1 takes sickle and branch from altar, holds above chalices.

DRUID #1 & DRUID #2: Boann, Bilé, we have given to you our adoration and praise. Now we ask that you give to us your blessings. Boann, bring to us your fertility. Bilé, bring to us your desire. So be it!

Touches branch to sickle blade.

ALL: So be it!

DRUID #1: Behold, the Waters of Fertility and Desire.

Libates from each chalice, then passes sunwise for all to drink.

ALL: Sing "Mead Chant."

DRUID #1: We have received the blessings of the Gods. Our closing draws near. Let us now thank those whom we have called.

Druid #2 returns Boann's spirit to incense cauldron, then extinguishes Boann's candle. Druid #1 returns Bilé's spirit to incense cauldron, then extinguishes Bilé's candle. Then Druid #1 and Druid #2 thank Gods, ancestors, and nature spirits for attending. Close Veil, and reverse the Tree Meditation per standard procedure.

DRUID #1: Let us return now to the world refreshed by our communion with the ancestors and nature spirits.

DRUID #2: Let us return to the world renewed by our communion with the Gods.

DRUID #1: It is done. Walk with wisdom.

ALL: Sing "Walk With Wisdom."

PART SEVEN

※

Draíocht Today

19

Druidic Divination

Draíocht and Divination

Judging from the surviving Classical and Celtic literature, the lines between druidic poets, prophets, seers, and magicians were rather blurry. In large part this is because the Paleopagan Celts seem to have agreed with the Paleopagan Greeks that a poet *was* a type of seer, using his/her skills to peer into the past or to forecast the future. The Celts extended this to imply that a poet was also a magician who was able to change the future. The term *draíocht* could be used for all these activities. Let's look at divination first.

"Divination" is a general term for the art and science of finding out hidden information about the past, present, or future through the use of the various, mostly passive (or receptive), psychic talents. This can be done through such systems as astrology, tea-leaf reading, rune-casting, tarot, and so on. They are all essentially props to keep the diviner's conscious mind busy while her or his subconscious is using clairvoyance, precognition, or retrocognition to ferret out the desired information.*

One of the primary means of divination used by the Paleopagan Druids (and some modern ones) was what the Romans would have called "augury," which draws its insights from ob-

---

*See *Real Magic* for details on this.

servations of the natural world. Things such as the flights of birds, the blowing of a Sacred Fire's smoke, the calls or appearance of certain animals, the bumps on the liver of a sacrificed animal, or the blood splashes of a sacrificed human (if we can believe the Romans) could all be used as druidic Rorschach tests to reveal that which was otherwise hidden. We have records of druidic poets shutting themselves up in darkened rooms, or using other methods in order to go into the necessary trance state, summoning *imbas/awen* (the state of inspiration) to assist them in composing their poems.

Learning how to do specifically "druidic" augury requires spending a lot of time out in the natural world talking to trees, watching birds and insects, observing clouds and weather patterns, paying attention when animals show up, etc. Over the course of living through several years of seasonal turnings, you will learn what events are usually followed by what other events in your local bioregion, and with a little imagination and intuition you will be able to apply these seasonal observations as sometimes being symbolic indicators of events in the human realms.*

It's in the Cards?

Obviously the Paleopagan Druids did not have tarot cards, since those were invented in the Renaissance. Many modern druids use tarot cards with Celtic themes or other decks of divination cards, however, such as the stunning *Druid Animal Oracle Deck* by Philip and Stephanie Carr-Gomm and Bill Worthington. This deck of large cards has pictures of all the birds and beasts who were symbolic to the ancient Celtic peoples, plus four elemental dragons. These three also have produced *The Druidcraft Tarot,* which is a Celtic version of the traditional

*For example, if a dead fish falls out of the sky and hits the Archdruid on the head, this may indicate that he or she should retire to become the group's extinguished flounder.

78 card tarot deck with images relating to their "Druidcraft" blending of Mesopagan Druidism and Wicca.

While there are plenty of druidic purists (that is, snobs) who refuse to use anything so modern in their rituals, our experience in ADF has been that the three kindreds are perfectly willing to communicate with us through modern tools such as divination cards. I have noticed a bit better response with cards that are ethnically congruent with the particular pantheon or ethnic set of ancestors being honored. Norse themed cards or runes, for example, would work better in Norse rituals than Celtic or Slavic ones, but because these are historically, linguistically, and genetically related cultures, all of these tribal variations could do the job. Standard tarot cards almost always have European pictures on them, so they will work in a pinch, while casting the *I Ching* or throwing African cowrie shells might not work at all in Indo-European rituals.

But for purely Celtic rites (especially Irish), many modern druids swear by the oghams, so let's look at them closely.

Ogham

Ogham was the name used for the alphabet designed by Irish druids to inscribe words onto tombstones and other memorials. It had just the letters necessary for Old Irish and was made by cutting marks across straight lines, either vertically or horizontally, making it ideal for use on the corner edges of big rocks. Eventually it found its way into various manuscripts and many different systems were invented. Robert Lee "Skip" Ellison's excellent book, *The Druids' Alphabet*, gives examples of over 120 versions. Irish myths and sagas show the characters of the ogham alphabet (called "oghams") being used to cast spells, usually by making talismans or other magical objects. There is little that looks like divination being done with them by the Paleopagans, according to Damian McManus, author of *A Guide to Ogam*. By the way, you will also see the word spelled *ogam*, because the original spelling was with a dotted "g," signifying "aspiration" of it, which is handled in Modern Irish by putting an "h" after such letters. Ellison explains:

> The Oghams are broken down into five groups, called "aicmes." Each aicme is composed of five further divisions, each equal to an individual letter, called "fews."
>
> Another difference of opinion arises over the use of the fifth aicme. Again, these are known by the name of *Forfeda* and are not part of the original set of twenty trees that were used. They represent the Greek diphthongs and were certainly added after the original group of four aicmes was developed.

Neopagan Druids, however, having heard of or even studied Norse runes, another Paleopagan alphabet that *was* used for both magic and divination, decided to try using oghams for divination as well. Runes as divinatory tools are a form of "sortilege," in that they are carved or painted upon small objects. They are then randomized in some fashion, such as by tossing a bunch of them onto a cloth or drawing some blindly from a bag, often to place into a predetermined pattern similar to a tarot spread. Oghams, carved or painted onto small sticks or disks of wood, can be used the same way. The meaning of each ogham letter depends upon a cluster of images associated with each, usually of traditional categories of things that began with the same letter in Old Irish. Then you have to pick from the dozens of meanings each ogham could have, based on what other oghams are near and/or its position in your spread.

Trees and other plants were the original associations for oghams, which are generally called by those botanical names. Other categories included birds, animals, occupations, activities, etc., as described in Ellison's book. And as he said, to extend the system just look for Old or Modern Irish words that begin with the same sound as each ogham. For example, using English words, I could make a set of occupational meanings for the oghams thusly: Baker, Locksmith, Farmer, Sailor, etc., though it

The Ogham Alphabet
(with notes for the aspiring diviner)

F A **i i** **r c** **s m** **t e** labials	⊤	⊣	*Beith*	Birch	B	*beginnings, white, cow, fertility, love, lust, worker*
	⊤⊤	⊨	*Luis*	Rowan	L	*protection, clarity, beauty, frog, grey, piloting*
	⊤⊤⊤	≡	*Fern*	Alder	F, V	*shielding, guidance, red, mare, poetry*
	⊤⊤⊤⊤	≣	*Sail*	Willow	S	*mysteries, waters, deathly pale, fox, female, handicraft*
	⊤⊤⊤⊤⊤	≣	*Nion*	Ash	N	*ancient knowledge, peace, clearness, weaving, adder*
S A **e i** **c c** **o m** **n e** **d** dentals, aspirants	⊥	⊢	*Uath*	Hawthorn	H	*counseling, protection, blanched, piglet, fear, poetry*
	⊥⊥	⊨	*Dair*	Oak	D	*wisdom, strength, order, wizardry, black, ox*
	⊥⊥⊥	⊫	*Tinne*	Holly	T	*justice, balance, fire, dark grey, boar, turning-work*
	⊥⊥⊥⊥	⊫	*Coll*	Hazel	C	*wisdom, intuition, puns, brown, hound, harping*
	⊥⊥⊥⊥⊥	目	*Ceirt*	Crab Apple	Q	*Otherworld, choices, mouse colored, cricket, shelter, fluting*
T A **h i** **i c** **r m** **d e** gutturals	⟋	⟋	*Muin*	Vine	M	*prophecy, inhibition, strength, variegated, otter, soldiering*
	⫻	⟋⟋	*Gort*	Ivy	G	*introspection, inner wisdom, blue, goat, smithing*
	⫻⫻	⟋⟋⟋	*nGéadal*	Broom	NG	*working, tools, green, hare, modeling*
	⫻⫻⫻	⟋⟋⟋⟋	*Straif*	Blackthorn	ST, STR, Z	*trouble, negativity, bright colored, stallion, deer-stalking*
	⫻⫻⫻⫻	⟋⟋⟋⟋⟋	*Ruis*	Elderberry	R	*Otherworld gates, faeries, red, seal, dispensing*
F A **o i** **u c** **r m** **t e** **h** vowels	+	+	*Ailm*	Silver Fir	A	*farseeing, precognition, piebald, donkey, sovereignty*
	++	++	*Onn*	Gorse	O	*collecting, attracting, dun, sheep, harvesting*
	+++	+++	*Úr*	Heather	U	*healing, homelands, soil, resinous, lamb, brassworking*
	++++	++++	*Eadhadh*	Aspen	E	*communication, trembling, red, eel, fowling*
	+++++	+++++	*Iodhadh*	Yew	I	*death, rebirth, age, very white, salmon, fishing, ancestors*
F A **i i** **f c** **t m** **h e** diphthongs	✳	✳	*Éabhadh*	White Poplar	EA, CH, E, K	*buoyancy, floating above problems, astral projection*
	◇	◈	*Ór*	Spindle	OI, CH	*community, working in the home, spinning, axis*
	✖	✖	*Uilleann*	Gooseberry	UI, IO, PH	*the Kindreds, esp. nature spirits, sweetness*
	⌖	⌖	*Ifin*	Honeysuckle	IA, IO, P, PE	*drawing things together, binding, synergy*
	▦	▦	*Eamhancholl*	Witchhazel	AE, X, XI	*magic, hidden knowledge*
punctuation	⟩—	Y	*Eite*	Arrow	Beginning of line	Divinatory meanings above are mostly taken from
	• :	••	*Spás*	Space	Either 1 or 2 between words	Ellison's *Druids' Alphabet*, with additions by the author.

would be good to pick meanings that go with the other meanings you are using for each ogham. Just remember, this probably isn't the way the Paleopagan Druids did divination, yet by the magical Law of Pragmatism, "if it works, it's true!"

For an example, I will do a reading on the future of this book, drawing the oghams from their bag and placing them into the positions I also use for tarot readings, as shown opposite.

In this particular spread, the positions have the following meanings:

1. The past *or* the beginning of a process
2. The present *or* the middle of a process
3. The future *or* the end of a process
4. Helping factors in the environment
5. Good luck or bad luck determiners
6. Hurting factors in the environment
7. The gem, the concentrated center that affects the preceding six positions
8. Irony, your blindspot, or how Murphy's Law will affect the situation
9. The will of the Gods, what should be done from a spiritual point of view.

How the first three positions function depends on the diviner's intent when drawing the oghams (or runes or cards). In this case, the question was all forward-looking, so the positions focus on the beginning, middle, and end of the situation or process. The gem position modifies the six others around it, while the irony and Gods positions are independent. Positions on the opposite sides of the layout affect each other: 1 and 4, 2 and 5, 3 and 6, and sometimes 8 and 9.

So the ogham sticks that I pulled were:

1. *Beith* or Birch—fertility, growth, lushness, new beginnings
2. *Dair* or Oak—strength, stability, durability, wisdom, wizardry

A Sample Ogham Layout

Beith~Birch
1 ⊤
Dast/Beginning

Eadhadh~Aspen
6 卌
Hurting

Dair~Oak
2 ⊥
Present/Middle

Ailm~Silver Fir
8 +
Irony

Ceirt~Crab Apple
7 ⊪
Gem

Nion~Ash
9 ⅢⅢ
Gods

Straif~Blackthorn
5 ⫿⫿
Luck

Coll~Hazel
3 ⊪
Future/End

Gort~Ivy
4 ⧺
Helping

3. *Coll* or Hazel—wisdom, magic, intuition
4. *Gort* or Ivy—inner wisdom, self-actualization, grace
5. *Straif* or Blackthorn—trouble, negativity, deer stalking
6. *Eadhadh* or Aspen—communication, friends, quaking
7. *Ceirt* or Crab Apple—the Otherworld, choices
8. *Ailm* or Silver Fir—far seeing, knowing the future
9. *Nion* or Ash—Ancient knowledge, weaving, peace, and war

All in all, it would seem to indicate that the book will sell well (1) be a steady text for years (2) and be a source for people to find their own magic (3). It is helped by the author (and the readers?) applying inner wisdom (4)—so maybe I don't need all those footnotes? Its good or bad luck in the marketplace and history will depend on how well it stands up to hostile criticism (5). It may be hurt by negative reviews or other communications (6) or if the publisher doesn't succeed in marketing it properly (which is true of all books). The key to its fate is the influence of the Otherworld (7) on the author and the readers—I've done a lot of ancestor invocation during the writing of it! The irony of this book's "career" will be found in the far future, in its long-range effects (8). The Gods and Goddesses wish it to carry ancient knowledge to the world, weaving links between different varieties of druidism, druidry, and *draíocht,* bringing peace rather than war between druids of all persuasions (9). Whatever grace (4) is in the writing will influence the new beginning (1), and the new beginning will be graceful. Strife and trouble (5) will crash futilely against the sturdiness (2) of the book, which will be a defense against attackers. Communication problems (6) may hurt the effort to bring wisdom and magic, but that wisdom and magic may be used to ease the communication difficulties. Long-range planning (8) influences the ability of the ancient knowledge to manifest (9) and druids of the past will become part of a peaceful weave with those yet to come.

Other druidic diviners, who may have slightly different meanings memorized for the oghams, and who aren't so close to the subject of the reading as I am, may well come up with different interpretations for this spread, and I would be glad to see them. In any event, whether my rose-colored glasses are giving me a correct picture or not, at least you now know *one* way to use oghams for divination!

Sets of ogham sticks or disks are now available for sale, both in metaphysical stores and online, including some through druid Web sites. Skip includes instructions on how to make them in his book and nothing results in a set of divination tools more attuned to you than making them yourself!

20

Druidic Magic

What Makes *Draíocht* Different?

On one level of reality, not much! When Paleopagan or Neopagan Druids did/do magic (and when Mesopagan Druids admit it), they still were/are/will be working with the same laws of magic as any other system of magic in the world. The laws of personification, invocation, evocation, and names mean that Druids address the deities, ancestors, and nature spirits by name when they can. We think of them as "people" whose energies can be experienced directly through living persons, places, and things. The laws of knowledge and self-knowledge apply and have long been associated with Druids. The laws of association, sychronicity, cause and effect, and perversity all mean that Druids do magical and/or religious rituals with the help of visualizations and physical objects that resemble the people or objects they wish to affect—and that they have to watch out for unanticipated consequences.*

What makes *draíocht* different is the *style* in which it is done. Druidic spells, incantations, invocations, blessings, and banishings are done *beautifully*, with the best and most emotionally powerful poetry, music and/or other arts the druids involved can create or borrow. This takes a bit more work than just reading a spell out of a book, but the results are worth it! Before we

---

*See *Real Magic*.

look at some ancient spells, or think about creating our own, however, let's look at a little discussed but often noticed kind of *draíocht.*

Unplanned Magic

I'm talking about the kind of magic that happens when no one mortal was intending it to happen, at least not consciously. I began to notice this kind of magic happening when I was leading a grove of the Schismatic Druids of North America in Minneapolis, back in the mid-1970s. According to my notes, there were a few occasions when the regular 2:00 P.M. Sunday services were canceled because it was raining at 1:00 P.M., only to have the skies clear up at 1:45, stay clear until about 2:45, then start raining again at 3:00 P.M. That was when we figured out that the Earth-Mother and the Gods really wanted those rituals done! We started going out to the park every Sunday, rain or shine, and were only rained on once. For one winter ceremony, a full-scale Minnesota blizzard thoughtfully paused for an hour to enable us to gather. "And this was taken to be a sign."

We also received signs that we shouldn't bother trying to tape-record our praise offerings. My first wife was the bard of our grove and she used to go into a trance when it was time to offer praise. She would recite some wonderful poem or sing a glorious song, then not remember a word after the ceremony was over. Being technodruids, we figured that the solution was to bring a tape recorder and turn it on just before that part of the ritual came. But we kept "forgetting" to push the switch, or the cord became unplugged, or the tape snarled, or the battery died. After several attempts we finally decided to accept the situation as one that we were not going to be able to change—although I'm not sure if we ever tried consecrating the recorder as a ritual tool . . .

I have in subsequent years learned that magic and electrical devices don't always mix well* unless you plan ahead. I suspect

*As the famous Chicago wizard Harry Dresden has pointed out in *The Dresden Files.*

that *draíocht*, with its emphasis on beauty and inspiration, may have even more such difficulties than other kinds of magic. If you want to record a powerful druidic spell or liturgy, you might want to try using shotgun mikes and telescopic lenses.

The serious lesson here is that druids work with the primal forces of nature, and once they notice your activities, they start working with you and not always in the ways you expect. The deities, the ancestors, and the nature spirits—not to forget the Outdwellers—have their own agendas, which must always be taken into consideration when planning your workings. This is another important use for divination in your *draíocht*. It can be really helpful to find out what the spirits have in mind *before* you call to them and ask for their attention and/or help.

How does one call to them? Beautifully, of course!

Celtic Spells

When the Milesians were trying to conquer Ireland from the Tuatha dé Danaan, having honorably discussed the issue with them, the Milesians got back on their ships and went back out to sea, from whence they would formally begin their invasion. The druids of the Tuatha dé Danaan cast a magical wind that swept the nine ships of the Sons of Mil out into the ocean. The Milesian druid Amergin calmed the seas with this incantation.*

"I invoke the land of Ireland.
Much-coursed be the fertile sea,
Fertile be the fruit-strewn mountain,
Fruit-strewn be the showery wood,
Showery be the river of water-falls,
Of water-falls be the lake of deep pools,
Deep pooled be the hill-top well,
A well of the tribes be the assembly,
An assembly of the kings be Tara,

*From the Irish Texts Society edition, translation by R. A. S. MacAllister, 1941.

Tara be the hill of the tribes,
The tribes of the sons of Mil,
Of Mil be the ships, the barks,
Let the lofty bark be Ireland,
Lofty Ireland, darkly sung,
An incantation of great cunning;
The great cunning of the wives of Bres,
The wives of Bres of Buaigne;
The great lady, Ireland,
Eremon hath conquered her,
Ír, Eber have invoked for her.
I invoke the land of Ireland."

I strongly recommend reading as much Irish, Welsh, Scots, etc., poetry as you can find, to give you a feel for the rhythms of the languages. Obviously it would be better if we could read them in their original languages, but good translators will help with this process. I also recommend that all would-be druids begin a study of one of the Celtic languages as soon as possible. As I have said for many years, when you invoke a spirit in their own tongue, or at least a modern descendant of it, you are far more likely to receive a powerful and positive response. This collides with American monolingualism, but I don't recall anyone saying that becoming a druid was going to be easy!

Something that should be in every druid's library is the *Carmina Gadelica,* a collection of Scots Gaelic spells, hymns, prayers, and incantations from the 1800s, available in many editions*. Almost all of the items in it have Christian names and references, but after reading a lot of them it becomes easy to see that they were originally Pagan, and then to repaganize them. I

---

*By Alexander Carmichael, a nineteenth century folklorist who collected Scottish Gaelic folklore. Many of the prayers and spells from the first volume of this can be found at www.smo.uhi.ac.uk/gaidhlig/corpus/Carmina/. Of course, it's all in Scots Gaelic, so you may want to buy one of the English translations. "Re-Paganized" versions of these and other materials from the later volumes can be found at www.wildideas.net/cathbad/pagan/carmina.html, www.iit.edu/~phillips/personal/contents/carmind.html, and www.geocities.com/pagantheology/carmina/carmina.html.

have done this with traditional Irish materials such as the well-known St. Patrick's Breastplate, which is a meditation for psychic protection. I turned it into:

The Shield of the Dagda

I bind unto myself today, the strong name of the Dagda,
By invocation of the same, the Three in One, the One in Three.

I call this day to me forever, the Dagda's many arts:
His mounting of the River Women, his siring of the God of Love
His fury on the field of battle, His druidry so strong
His majesty as High King, His sympathy for the despised.

I bind unto myself today, the Good God's mighty seed
His eye to watch, His might to stay, His ear to harken to my need
His wit to teach, His hand to guide, His shield to ward
His fire to enflame my speech, His mighty club to be my guard.

Dagda be with me, Dagda within me
Dagda behind me, Dagda before me
Dagda to my left, Dagda to my right
Dagda beneath me, Dagda above me
Dagda in quiet, Dagda in danger
Dagda in the hearts of all that love me
Dagda in the mouth of friend and stranger.

I bind unto myself the name, the strong name of the Dagda,
By invocation of the same, the Three in One, and One in Three,
The mightiest of all the Gods, Father of the Queen of Arts,
The Supreme Knower, Lord of Fire, and King of Druids.
So be it!*

*Complete instructions for using this spell is found in my recent book, *The Pagan Man*.

In this particular case, I chose my patron deity the Dagda, the omnifunctional (see Appendix F) all-father of the Gods of Érin, and worked into the poem as many descriptions of his characteristics as possible. All of his different functions are included: ruler/Outdweller, druid, warrior, stud, and so on. This is the sort of scholarly and artistic approach to *draíocht* that will produce spells, incantations, hymns, and rituals in a truly druidic style.

A Healing Spell

This spell involves invoking the assistance of Bridget, the multifunctional Sun and Fire Goddess who is a smith, bard, and healer. Begin by obtaining a photograph or object link of the person you wish to heal, unless they can be in the same room with you (which would be ideal). Light a fire of nine different woods, or at the very least a candle, in front of a depiction of Bridget. If it is a fire magically connected to the one in Ireland (as discussed in Chapter 9), so much the better!

While looking at the image or idol, or visualizing Her in your mind's eye as a beautiful, strong Irish woman of gentle and loving nature, chant or sing:

A HYMN TO BRIDGET*

A Bhríd, ár gcroí, an-gheal Bheanríon;
lo de thoil é beannachta sinn.
Is sinn bhur leanaí, is tu ár mamaí;
bí ag isteacht dúinn mar sin.
Is tu an coire, anois inár doire,†

---

*© 1983, 2006 CE, words by Isaac Bonewits, music Irish trad. ("Roving Galway Boy/Spancil Hill," mutated), Key of C. This was one of the first bilingual songs I wrote, and shows my childlike Irish vocabulary. *Mamaí*, for example, is closer to "mommy" than to "mother." However, for a Goddess of Mothers, the phrasing seems appropriate.

†Alternate Irish wording for ritual use: *fane* = circle, *seomra* = room—neither of which rhymes with *coire* (which is an Irish pun on the words for "sheep" and "cauldron," both of which are appropriate for Bride), but then classical Old Irish songs didn't rhyme either!

a Bhean-Feasa tinfim orainn.
A thine ghrá, a thine bheatha;
lo de thoil é ag teacht Bhrid dúinn!

O Bridget, our heart, o brightest Queen;
cast your blessings unto us.
We are your children, you are our mother;
so hearken unto us.
You are the cauldron, now in our grove;
Wise Woman inspire us.
O fire of love, o fire of life;
please Bridget, come to us!

A Bhrid, ár gcroí, an-gheal Bheanríon;
lo de thoil é beannachta sinn.
Is sinn bhur leanaí, is tu ár mamaí;
bí ag isteacht dúinn mar sin.
Is tu an coire, anois inár doire;
a Bhean-Feasa tinfim orainn.
A thine ghrá, a thine bheatha;
lo de thoil é ag teacht Bhrid dúinn!

Chant or sing the hymn three times through (nine verses in all), while visualizing power flowing from Bridget into you. Place your hands upon the person or their magical link and let the power flow into them while you visualize them as completely healed and healthy. Repeat as needed the following:

Bridget of the holy fire
Bridget of the singing heart
Bridget of the healing hands
Let your power flow through me
And into s/he whom I now hold
As mother's milk into a babe.
Blest once by you and then again
Blest twice by you and then again
Blest thrice by you and s/he is whole!

When you are finished, thank Bridget, then let the fire burn out naturally while you keep vigil.

Prosperity and Love

This is another area of life where the Dagda can be of use to the aspiring druid. He is the owner of the "un-dry cauldron," a source of never-ending nourishment (at least for the brave). As a special patron God of druids and an earthy deity of fertility, and the prosperity that comes from it, he is inclined to bless his druids with sufficient resources to meet their needs—provided we remember to ask!

For love, rather than lust, the Irish deity to invoke is the Dagda's son, Angus Og. The Dagda sired him while loving the River Goddess Boann—in the river! Angus represents the Indo-European symbol of "fire in the water," known as *soma* to the Vedic peoples, and exemplifies the paradoxical characteristics of intoxicating substances and emotions (why do you think they called it "fire water"?) that can carry us away from our daily selves.

Cut a green sucker shoot from the base of a birch tree, after asking permission, of course. You should end with a wand of flexible wood about 36 inches or one meter long, about a quarter of an inch thick. With a sharp knife cut the appropriate oghams into the wood at least three and preferably nine times (see chart). To attract wealth use the name of the Dagda, to attract love use the name of Angus Og. For the former carve the oghams for *maoin agus saibhreas* ("gifts and riches"). For the latter, carve the oghams for *gra do chroí* ("love of your heart") without thinking of any one person in particular.

Make a sacred fire from nine woods. Wrap the carved wand around into a circle large enough to go around your head with three inches to spare. Tie it closed with short lengths of vine or twine. Pass the hoop through the smoke of the fire nine times, asking the Dagda or Angus Og to bless and empower it. Write an appropriate chant to the god of your choice to recite while

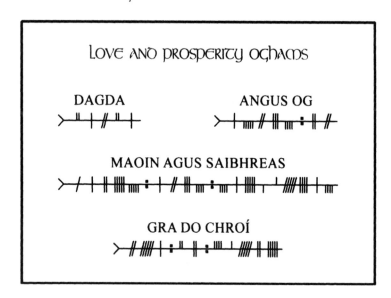

charging the hoop. Then place the hoop over your head and wear it for nine days. Yes, it will get scratchy—did you think attracting love and wealth was easy?

To Guide a Warrior Home

The purpose of this working is not a spell-casting as such, but rather to help someone who is dying to find their way safely to the Otherworld where they may join the ancestors. This particular song/chant can be used for anyone's dying, but is most appropriate for a warrior.

It should be integrated into whatever other deathwatch prayers and ceremonies are being done for the dying person, near the end. If necessary, it may be whispered over their head or sung silently in your mind.

A HYMN TO THE MORRIGAN*

O Morrigan, we call your name
Across the dusty years.

*© 1986, 2006, words by Isaac Bonewits, music Irish trad. ("Lagan Lad/Quiet Joys of Brotherhood"), Key of A.

You speak to us, of blood and lust.
You show us all our fears.
You are a Goddess, old and wise.
Of holy power you have no dearth.
Beneath your wings, black, red, and white,
We learn of death and birth.

You walk about, this ancient land,
Your hungers raw and clear.
You make the crops, grow rich and strong,
As well your geese and deer.
A flirting maid, a lusty hag,
A mother of great girth:
Without the touch, of your black wings,
We cannot heal the Earth.

You float upon, a blood red wave,
Of swords and spears and knives.
Your voice inspires, fear and dread,
That you'll cut short our lives.
You try the warriors', courage sore,
Our inner souls unearth.
Without the touch, of your red wings,
We cannot know our worth.

You fly above, the silver clouds,
To Avalon's shining gate.
You lead the dead, along that path,
To meet our final fate.
The joke's on us, we find within,
A land of laughter and of mirth.
Without the touch, of your white wings,
We cannot have rebirth.

O Morrigan, we call your name
Across the dusty years . . .

The Morrigan ("Great Queen") is an omnifunctional Goddess. In this case, we are concentrating on invoking Her in Her

role as psychopomp. This song may be sung or chanted several times (three, nine, or twenty-seven are always appropriate for Celtic magic). When the person has to leave (or you do), thank the Morrigan for her blessings.

The key in all of these acts of *draíocht* is to use your own creativity to contact the Gods or other powers and to show them honor by your art. *Please* feel free to use your own invocations or chants rather than mine. I don't claim to be a great poet and my grasp of Modern Irish is primitive, to say the least. These materials are included here to give you the general idea of how to do magic in a druidical fashion—not to become holy scripture!

PART EIGHT

❀

Conclusions

21

The Future of Druidism, Druidry, and Draíocht

Current Population Figures

The Order of Bards Ovates & Druids has approximately 8,000 members worldwide, as of the end of 2005, with over 90 groves. The RDNA and its offshoots have had over 4,000 members over the last forty years, with dozens of groves, all of whom may or may not be active at any given date. ADF has about 1,000 members with around 60 groves. Keltria has about 200, with two groves and five study groups. AODA has 70–150 members (numbers are vague due to missing records), with two groves and three study groups. The Druid Order of the Sacred Grove in Las Vegas has around 100 members, with one main grove and two seed groves. Other Druid groups pop up and/or disappear every year, and thousands of solitary Druids are wandering about in the modern Celtic mists.

So it looks like Meso- and Neopagan Druid groups are multiplying like Bridget's hares! That bodes well for the future, but what sorts of Druids will we be seeing?

My Vision of Neopagan Druidism

What makes the Neopagan Druidism, that is, the *religion* of Druidism for Neopagans, that I envision different from other Neopagan as well as other Druidic traditions—and how is it

similar to those that have gone before? To a great extent, both
the differences and the similarities are rooted in my vision of the
past, the present, and the future. That vision leads me to express
much of it in terms of a commitment to achieving *excellence.*

The Earth-Mother and the other Goddesses and Gods do
not need us to tell lies on their behalf, nor can we truly understand the ways of our Paleopagan predecessors by indulging in
romantic fantasies, no matter how "politically correct" or emotionally satisfying they might be. So we should promote no tall
tales of Stonehenge being built by Druid magic, nor of the ancient Druids originally having been shamanic crystal-masters
from Atlantis. We need not whitewash the occasional barbarism
of our predecessors, nor exaggerate it. We should use real arche-
ology, history, and comparative mythology—by which I mean
current (within the last thirty years or so) academic research and
theory that reflects the highest aspirations of honest scholarship. We should be willing to change our opinions when new
information becomes available, or more sensible interpretations
are offered, even if to do so damages our favorite theories. Until recently, this approach has been rare in the history of both
Druidic revivals and the Neopagan community. Nevertheless, it
is vital if we are to avoid the sorts of doctrinal traps that other
religions so often fall prey to, which force them to suppress
whatever new learning contradicts their dogmas.

The Earth-Mother and the Gods and Goddesses deserve the
very best that we can give them, so we should encourage each
other to develop our creative skills to the highest levels that
each can attain. Our bards, storytellers, painters, woodcarvers,
needleworkers, smiths, and dramatists should be among the
best in the Neopagan community, and their artistic skills should
be available to our liturgists, teachers, temple builders, and
grove keepers.

Good leadership is vital for any healthy, growing religion. To
that end Neopagan Druid religious groups should create leadership training programs equal in difficulty and superior in results to anything done by the world's other religions. Unlike
many New Age and otherwise alternate religions, we should be

willing to spend the necessary years becoming clergy, bards, diviners, teachers, or other sorts of religious leaders. We don't have to assume that every member of our communities will have a genuine vocation to reach a leadership role, though it's likely that a high proportion will for the first few decades. Instead we can expect that eventually the vast majority of our people will be Neopagan laity; there is nothing wrong with that status.

Nonetheless, everyone should be expected to communicate with the Goddesses and Gods in her or his own way—spiritual growth should never be a monopoly of those called "leaders." Every lover of the Earth needs to learn how to contact the divine Fire within, how to communicate reliably with plant and animal spirits, and how to unleash the power of magic to save the Earth. This is an area where "church-style" druidism and "magical order-style" druidry can meet and cooperate in mutual encouragement.

Excellence in ritual is rooted in these other forms of excellence. Sound scholarship (especially historical and mythological), beautiful art, genuinely competent clergy and bards, and people who are ready, willing, and able to channel divine energies are all crucial to creating the powerful religious and magical ceremonies that we and the Earth so desperately need.

I believe that Neopaganism is becoming a mainstream religious movement, with hundreds of thousands (and perhaps millions) of members, and that this is a good thing, both for the individuals involved and for the survival of the Earth-Mother. Many people who grew up in the 1960s and 70s are discovering us at about the same time that they are realizing both the desperate state of our planet and the eternal relevance of our youthful ideals. Younger people, even teenagers, are flooding into our communities, eager to learn what we have to teach them, as well as to do their own research and perhaps teach some of us! Membership in the Neopagan community is growing at a geometric rate, both through word of mouth and the many do-it-yourself books now available, giving us an ever-greater impact on the mainstream culture as a whole.

Many, if not most, of these Neopagans want publicly accessible worship, teaching, counseling, and healing. Before 2020, I expect to see Neopagan temples and/or sacred groves throughout North America, Europe, and Australia, some of them staffed by full-time paid professional clergy. They'll provide the full range of needed services to the Neopagan community, with no more "corruption" than the Unitarian Universalists, the Buddhists, or the Taoists usually experience. I foresee globally televised Samhain rites at Stonehenge, and Beltaine ceremonies attended by thousands in every major city. Neopagan clergy will take part as equals in international religious conferences with clergy from other faiths (which is already happening in some places). Our children will be able to wear Pagan religious emblems to school as easily as others now wear Jewish, Christian, or Islamic ones.

I see talented and well-trained Neopagan clergy leading hundreds of thousands of people in effective magical and mundane actions to save endangered species, stop polluters, and preserve wilderness. I see our healers saving thousands of lives and our bards inspiring millions through music, video, and drama in other media not yet invented. I see Neopaganism as a mass movement, changing social, political, and environmental attitudes around the world and stopping the death mongers in their tracks.

This vision is very different from that of most previous Neopagan traditions, as well as most previous Druidic movements, almost all of which have focused on small esoteric groups as their ideal. Those small groups will always be an essential part of both the Druidic and the Neopagan religious communities, operating both within and apart from larger organizations, just as their equivalents have throughout human history. As I see it, the future of both Neopaganism and Druidism will require a wide variety of different group sizes, structures, and ritual styles. To lose any of the currently existing approaches risks impoverishing our spiritual "gene pool." So Neopagan Druids have no need to replace other Neopagan or Druidic traditions, even though we think that we have some unique and wonderful things to share with the world.

If Neopagan Druids are going to have large congregations with inclusive ceremonies and other services, how do we integrate those people who have needs for smaller, perhaps exclusive, groups? Imagine a Druid grove twenty years from now, with three to four hundred people as regular attendees. Such a grove might include several closed lunar circles (which might consider themselves "covens"), healing circles, bardic groups, an ecology action committee, a scholarly group, a lodge of ceremonial magicians, artistic and craft guilds, a liturgical committee, a groundskeeping committee, etc., all with overlapping membership and all joining together for major events. They would have to work out their own etiquette, internal membership requirements, and so on, but the emphasis would be on fellowship and cooperation, rather than on exclusivity and competition.

I believe that Neopagan Druidism has an important role to play in the future of the Neopagan community as a whole, and in the survival of the Earth. Already, Wiccan and other Neopagan traditions are imitating Neopagan Druid training programs, our liturgical techniques, and our emphases on the arts. If we can attract enough people who are willing to dedicate their time, energy, and money to achieving these goals, this vision can be manifested. We can save the Earth-Mother, create a global culture of prosperity and freedom, and usher in a genuine "New Age."

Achieving such grand goals is going to require the Neopagan community in general, and Neopagan Druids in particular, to begin wrestling with many difficult social, political, economic, and spiritual issues—most of which we've been avoiding for the last thirty years. Becoming a "public Pagan church" style of Neopagan Druid means supporting and working towards such a vision and beginning the wrestling process. Together we can do it. But we're going to need as many coconspirators as possible. If this vision excites you, share it with your friends and family. Then become part of Druidism's future by joining a Neopagan Druid group or by starting your own. The rest is up to you!

The Future of Druidry

I know far more about druidism than I do about druidry, because the former has always been my area of focus. But I know enough about druidry, whether seen as part of a three hundred-year-old initiatory lineage of mystics; as a form of solitary druidism; or as a new movement for ecological philosophy and symbolism, to safely predict that it will continue to grow rapidly over the next few decades. I expect to see more and more political and ecological activism taking place in cooperation with members of other faith communities.

Groups such as OBOD, ADOA, SOD, GOD, SOA, etc. will probably become more Neo- and less Mesopagan in the next few decades, due in part to the growing dualism within the mainstream monotheistic faiths. Conservative Jews, Christians, and Atheists will become more and more conservative, and want nothing to do with such "heathen" ideas as druidry. Liberals, on the other paw, will become increasingly liberal. Many will drop out of their former faith communities, while those attracted to druidry will just go ahead and become Neopagans!

That dualistic polarization in the mainstream faiths, however, will be a central part of the global culture wars of the twenty-first century that, along with the deindustrialization of the modern world, drastic climate changes, and environmental collapses in many bioregions, will endanger the very survival, let alone the evolution of our species. I am sure that followers of druidry will be there in the (we hope metaphorical) battlelines fighting for our holy Mother Earth and all Her children alongside Neopagans, whether druidic or not, and liberal religionists of all persuasions.

The Future of *Draíocht*

When we focus on *draíocht*, as the theory and practice of magic and divination in a specifically druidic style, we can see that it, too, will grow by leaps and bounds over the coming years.

There are now thousands of Mesopagan and Neopagan Druids experimenting with and creating new forms of *draíocht* today, soon there will be tens of thousands of them. And most of us talk to each other and share our notes!

I expect to see and hear new magical chants, songs, poems, and spells being created by the hundreds, if not the thousands—just in time, for we will surely need them! I expect to see cyber-*draíocht* happening with thousands participating in the magic.

With druidism, druidry, and *draíocht* working together we can, and will, save the Earth and usher in the next phase of human evolution!

The Book of Meditations, Chapter Seven: *

1. For what reasons is that ye sit here under the oak? Why is it that ye have come out together under the stars?
2. Have ye come that ye might not be alone? If so, it is good.
3. But verily I say unto you: many there are who have come together, yet remain alone.
4. Do ye sit in the open that ye might come to know nature? If so, it is good.
5. But verily I say unto you: many there are who have sat for hours and have risen up knowing less than when they sat down.
6. Rather, in your coming together, seek to know in what way ye may help him who is next to you, and strive to act justly toward him.
7. And in your sitting down in the fields of the Earth-Mother, open your minds as well as your eyes. Let your meditation grow and branch out as the oak, which is over your head.
8. Except that ye have done these things, your sitting is in vain and coming is futility.

*From *The Druid Chronicles (Evolved)*.

9. And why is it that ye do stand up before others and speak unto them?
10. Do ye teach unto them the ways of the ancient Druids? If so, it is good.
11. For they had their wisdom, and that is oft forgot. But verily I say unto you: In their day, even they also were young in their traditions.
12. The wise man is not constrained to learn only that which he is taught. Yea, even as there is a time for talking, is there also a time for no talking.
13. In the silence of your being shall ye find that which is not of your being; and in the Earth-Mother shall ye find that which is not of the Earth-Mother; in Béal shall ye be made aware, and your awareness shall fill you.
14. Ye shall be like the morning sun which has risen and whose brightness is already full, but whose path is yet ever upward;
15. and the light of your awareness shall sweep before it all the shadows of your uncertainty.
16. Then shall ye need wait no more; for this is the great end and all else is but beginning.

APPENDIX A

Bibliography and Recommended Reading

The following books (listed in alphabetical order by author) will get you *started* on understanding what both Neopaganism and Druidism originally were and what they someday could be.

Margot Adler. *Drawing Down the Moon*. Penguin (USA), 2006. This is the newest edition of the classic book about Neopagan movements in America. Every member of the Neopagan, Wiccan, and/or Goddess Worship movements in the United States should own this book—at least if they want to understand our history over the last fifty years.

Nathaniel Altman. *Sacred Trees*, Sierra Club Books, 1994.

Philip Baldi. *An Introduction to the Indo-European Languages*, Southern Illinois University Press, 1983. Good basic intro to this topic.

Isaac Bonewits. *Real Magic*. Samuel Weiser, Inc., 1989. A basic introduction to the theory and practice of magic. Includes an extensive bibliography of other titles that will be helpful.

———. *Authentic Thaumaturgy*. Steve Jackson Games, 1998. A rewrite and expansion of *Real Magic* for players of fantasy games. It contains additional materials on the polytheology of worship and magic.

———. *Rites of Worship: A Neopagan Approach*. Earth Religions Press, 2003. A unique textbook on creating, preparing, and performing public worship rituals.

———. *The Pagan Man*. Citadel, 2005.

289

————. *Bonewits's Essential Guide to Witchcraft and Wicca.* Citadel, 2006.

Julius Caesar, translated by Anne & Peter Wiseman. *The Battle for Gaul.* Chatto & Windus (London), 1980. A modern colloquial translation, filled with dozens of explanatory maps, photographs and drawings. Currently out of print, but you can read the Loeb translation of *The Gallic War* while you're waiting for it to come back.

Alexander Carmichael. *Carmina Gadelica: Hymns and Incantations from the Gaelic.* Floris Books, 2004. This one volume edition will be a good introduction to Scots Gaelic folklore.

Philip Carr-Gomm. *Druid Mysteries.* Rider, 2002. Originally published as *Elements of the Druid Tradition.* A brief introduction to the facts and fancies of Mesopagan Druidism, by the current chosen chief of the Order of Bards Ovates & Druids. Overtly romantic, yet honest about absent historical evidence. Includes excellent guided meditations and good ideas about bridging the gaps between Meso- and Neopagan Druids.

————. *The Rebirth of Druidry.* Thorsons, 2003. Originally published as *The Druid Renaissance.* Includes a chapter by myself on "The Druid Revival in Modern America" and chapters by leaders and members of many Druidic paths. It belongs on every modern Druid's bookshelf!

————. *The Druid Way,* Thoth Books, 2006. The story of a vision quest/pilgrimage through the landscape of southern England.

————. *What Do Druids Believe?* Granta, 2006. An overview and manifesto.

Luigi Luca Cavalli-Sforza, *Genes, Peoples, and Languages,* University of California Press, 2000.

Nora K. Chadwick. *The Celts.* Penguin, 1985. A now classic work, somewhat out of date but well worth reading.

————. *Imbas Forosnai.* Oxford University Press, 1935. Available as an ebook from eDruid Press at www.edruid.com.

Peter Crawford. *The Living Isles: A Natural History of Britain and Ireland.* BBC Pubs, 1991. This beautiful book provides the essential biological background to any pictures we may care to paint of what life in the Islands was like during Paleopagan and Mesopagan times.

Barry Cunliffe. *The Celtic World: An Illustrated History of the Celtic Race, Their Culture, Customs and Legends.* Greenwich House, 1986. Some great photos!

H. R. Ellis Davidson. *Myth and Symbols in Pagan Europe: Early Scandinavian and Celtic Religions.* Syracuse University Press, 1989. This book emphasizes the many similarities between Celtic, Germanic, and Scandinavian Paleopaganism, winding up supporting the Dumézilian approach.

Guy Deutscher, *The Unfolding of Language,* Henry Holt & Co., 2005.

Georges Dumézil. *The Destiny of a King.* University of Chicago Press, 1988.

———. *The Plight of a Sorcerer.* University of California Press, OOP.

———. *The Stakes of the Warrior.* University of California Press, 1983.

———. *Archaic Roman Religion: With an Appendix on the Religion of the Etruscans.* Johns Hopkins University Press, 1996.

———. *Mitra-Varuna: An Essay on Two Indo-European Representations of Sovereignty.* Zone Books, 1996.

———. *Loki.* Flammarion, 1997. All of these are worth reading if you want to know what pre-Christian European Paganism was really like.

Mircea Eliade. *Shamanism: Archaic Techniques of Ecstasy.* Princeton University Press, 1972. This book will demonstrate why it's a misapplication of the term to call druids "shamans."

———. *A History of Religious Ideas, Vol. 1—From the Stone Age to the Eleusinian Mysteries.* University of Chicago Press, 1981.

———. *A History of Religious Ideas, Vol. 2—From Gautama Buddha to the Triumph of Christianity.* University of Chicago Press, 1985. While just about everything he wrote about myth and religion is worth reading, this is some of the best material on the history of religious ideas available, organized both chronologically and thematically.

Peter Berresford Ellis. *The Druids.* Wm. B. Eerdmans Pub. Co., 1995. A more recent work than Piggott's, just as grouchy but multidisciplinary and informed by both Dumézilian theory and the latest scholarly research. Recently updated as *A Brief History of the Druids.*

————. *Chronicles of the Celts.* Carroll & Graf, 1999. Mythology from all six Celtic nations, not just the Irish and Welsh.

————. *Celtic Women: Women in Celtic Society and Literature.* Eerdsman, 1995. A well-balanced book on the topic.

————. *The Celts: A History.* Carroll & Graf, 2003. A revised edition of a solid work.

Robert Lee "Skip" Ellison. *The Druids' Alphabet.* Earth Religions Press, 2003. An excellent introduction to the topic.

————. *The Solitary Druid: A Practitioner's Guide,* Citadel Press, 2005. A good counterpart to this book's emphasis on Druids in groups.

Patrick K. Ford. *The Mabonogi and Other Welsh Medieval Tales.* University of California Press, 1977.

Mara Freeman, *Kindling the Celtic Spirit.* Harper San Francisco, 2001. She also has a CD of *Celtic Spirit Meditations.*

Philip Freeman, *War, Women, and Druids,* University of Texas Press, 2002. A collection of new translations of the major Greek and Roman writings about the Celts and their druids.

Paul Freidrich. *Proto-Indo-European Trees.* University of Chicago, 1970. Primarily a linguistic monograph, this is the only book to cover in detail the various species of trees known to have had names in the PIE language.

Jeffrey Gantz. *Early Irish Myths and Sagas.* Penguin, 1988.

Mirija Gimbutas. *The Balts.* Praeger, 1968. One of the few works on this topic in English.

————. *The Slavs,* Praeger, 1971. A valuable overview of the Paleopagan Slavic peoples.

Miranda Green. *The Gods of the Celts, Revised Edition.* Sutton Publishing, 2004.

————. *Celtic Goddesses: Warriors, Virgins, and Mothers.* George Braziller, 1996.

————(ed.) *The Celtic World.* Routledge, 1995. An anthology of articles by scholars from several disciplines.

John Michael Greer. *The Druidry Handbook.* Weiser, 2006. A new book from the Archdruid of the AODA.

Godfrey Higgins. *Celtic Druids.* Kessinger Pub., 1997. This is a reprint of the classic antiquarian text.

Ellen Evert Hopman. *Tree Medicine Tree Magic.* Phoenix Pub. Co., 1991.

————. *A Druid's Herbal for the Sacred Earth Year.* Destiny Books, 1994. These are by a modern Druid who is also a trained herbalist.

———— and Lawrence Bond. *Being a Pagan: Druids, Wiccans, and Witches Today* (originally published as *People of the Earth*). Destiny Books, 2001. This book of interviews is an excellent introduction to current thinking in the Neopagan community.

Ronald Hutton. *The Pagan Religions of the Ancient British Isles, Their Nature and Legacy.* Blackwell Publishers, 1993. A brilliant review of the history, prehistory, and pseudohistory of British Paleopaganism.

————. *The Rise and Fall of Merry England: the Ritual Year 1400–1700.* Oxford University Press, 1994.

————. *The Stations of the Sun: a History of the Ritual Year in Britain.* Oxford University Press, 1996.

————. *Witches, Druids, and King Arthur.* Hambledon and London, 2003.

Kevin Jones. *The Keys of Knowledge: Ogham, Coelbren and Pagan Celtic Religion.* eDruid Press, available at www.edruid.com. An odd book, combining academic research with the author's unverifiable claims about his "secret Irish traditional knowledge."

T. D. Kendrick. *Druids and Druidism.* Dover, 2003. A current printing of a classic, originally published as *Druids or A Study in Celtic Prehistory.*

Thomas Kinsella. *The Tain.* University of Philadelphia Press, 1985. A key source for understanding Irish mythology.

Erynn Rowan Laurie. *A Circle of Stones: Journeys and Meditations for Modern Celts.* Eschaton Productions Inc., 1995.

Bernard Lewis. *History—Remembered, Recovered, Invented.* Simon & Schuster, 1987. A succinct introduction to the ways in which people filter history through their personal and cultural needs, fears, and wishes, even when they're trying to be unbiased.

Dmitry Likhachov. *The Great Heritage: the Classical Literature of Old Rus.* Progress Publishers (Moscow), 1981. Like the Norse, Irish, and Welsh, the ancient Slavs had great stories that reveal much of their common Indo-European heritage to the discerning eye.

Bruce Lincoln. *Priests, Warriors, and Cattle.* University of California Press, 1981.

C. Scott Littleton. *The New Comparative Mythology, An Anthropological Assessment of the Theories of Georges Dumézil, 3rd Edition.* University of California Press, 1982. This is the best critical introduction to Dumézil's work, with an extensive bibliography of relevant books and articles by Dumézil and others. A new edition of this will be coming out soon.

Proinsias MacCana. *Celtic Mythology.* Hamlyn, 1970.

Ramsay MacMullen. *Christianizing the Roman Empire,* AD *100–400.* Yale University Press, 1984.

Jean Markale. *The Druids: Celtic Priests of Nature.* Inner Traditions, 1999.

———. *Women of the Celts.* Inner Traditions, 1986.

Caitlin Matthews. *The Celtic Spirit: Daily Meditations for the Turning Year.* Harper SanFrancisco, 1999. A book of meditations, one for each day of the year, rooted in the Celtic cultures.

John Matthews. *The Druid Source Book.* Blandford, 1996. An anthology of writings about the ancient druids, mostly from obsolete sources.

Carl McColman, *Complete Idiot's Guide to Celtic Wisdom.* Alpha, 2003.

Damian McManus. *A Guide to Ogam, Maynooth Monographs #4,* An Sagart, St. Patrick's College, Maynooth, Ireland, 1991. Read this with Ellison's book on Ogham.

F. Marian McNeill. *The Silver Bough*. Cannongate, 1989. Genuine Celtic magic!

———. *The Bardic Source Book*. Blandford, 1998. Ditto for ancient bards.

John F. Michell. *The New View over Atlantis*. Thames & Hudson, 2001. This is the later edition of the book that launched the whole ley-line concept.

———. *A Little History of Astro-Archeology*. Thames & Hudson, 2001.

Brendan Cathbad Myers. *Dangerous Religion*. Earth Religions Press, 2004. An entire book about the political and cultural implications of Neopaganism.

———. *The Mysteries of Druidry: Celtic Mysticism, Theory, and Practice*. New Page, 2006. A good book on Celtic mysticism, written by a modern Irish mystic.

Muin Mound Grove, ADF. *A Druidic Wheel of the Year*. ADF, 2003. Spiralbound book and CD of ritual scripts with music. Also available as an ebook from eDruid Press at www.edruid.com.

Joseph F. Nagy. *The Wisdom of the Outlaw: The Boyhood Deeds of Finn in Gaelic Narrative Tradition*. University of California Press, 1985. This will give you some insights into the ambiguity of the warrior caste in ancient Ireland.

Ross Nichols, et al. *The Book of Druidry*. Thorsons, 1992. Core concepts from the founder of OBOD.

Robert O'Driscoll, ed. *The Celtic Consciousness*. George Braziller, 1987.

Wendy Doniger O'Flaherty. *Women, Androgynes, and Other Mythical Beasts*. University of Chicago Press, 1982. O'Flaherty (now known as Doniger) gives an extensive discussion of the sexual politics of the Indo-European myth system.

Daithi O'Hogain. *The Sacred Isle: Pre-Christian Religions in Ireland*. Boydell Press, 1999. An excellent introduction to the topic, with cross-cultural insights from other Indo-European cultures.

Garrett S. Olmsted. *A Definitive Reconstructed Text of the*

Cologny Calendar, JIES Monograph No. 39. Institute for the Study of Man, 2001.

Emma Restall Orr. *Spirits of the Sacred Grove: The World of a Druid Priestess.* Thorsons, 1998. Through the cycle of the seasons with one of the founders of the BDO.

———. *Druidry.* Thorsons, 2001. Thoughts from a co-founder of the BDO.

Diana Paxson. *Taking Up the Runes.* Weiser Books, 2005. An excellent book to study if you wish to use runes in your divination or magic.

———. *Essential Ástarú.* Citadel (in press). The best one-book introduction to Paleo-, Meso-, and Neopagan Norse religions.

Stuart Piggott. *The Druids.* Thames and Hudson, 1985. The archaeological, classical, and historical evidence concerning the Druids, both Paleopagan and Mesopagan, covered in a very grouchy, Secular Humanist ("all priesthoods are Evil") style.

Alwyn & Brinley Rees. *Celtic Heritage: Ancient Tradition in Ireland and Wales.* Thames & Hudson, 1989. A classic Dumézilian analysis of Celtic mythology and religion, based primarily on Irish and secondarily on Welsh materials.

Julian Richards. *Stonehenge: A History in Photographs.* Barnes & Noble, 2004. This is a fascinating book for any druid or fan of Stonehenge!

Anne Ross. *Pagan Celtic Britain.* Academy Chicago Pub, 1996. Even though it is now somewhat dated, this is a classic text on Celtic cultures.

———. *Druids, Gods & Heroes from Celtic Mythology.* Peter Bedrick Books, 1994. This has some great artwork reconstructing what ancient Celtic life would have looked like.

Anne Ross and Don Robins. *The Life and Death of a Druid Prince.* Touchstone Books, 1991. A brilliant bit of archeological detective speculation.

Merritt Ruhlen. *The Origin of Language: Tracing the Evolution of the Mother Tongue,* Wiley, 1996.

Philip Shallcrass. *Druidry.* Piatkus Books, 2000. Same title, different co-founder of BDO.

Michael Scharding, editor and chief instigator. *A Reformed Druid Anthology, 2nd Edition,* in three huge volumes. 2001–2005. *The Druid Chronicles (Evolved)* can be found within Volume 1 of *ARDA,* but is also available as a stand-alone volume. All of this material is fortunately available online in PDF format at www. geocities.com/mikerdna, along with a great deal of supplementary material, including photographs, grove links, etc.

Marie-Louise Sjoestedt. *Gods and Heroes of the Celts.* Turtle Island Foundation, 1982.

Robin Skelton and Margaret Blackwood. *Earth, Air, Fire, Water: Pre-Christian and Pagan Elements in British Songs, Rhymes and Ballads.* Arkana, 1990.

Brian K. Smith. *Reflections on Resemblance, Ritual, and Religion.* Oxford University Press, 1989. A superb introduction to the complex world of Vedic ritual and metaphysics.

Lewis Spence. *The Mysteries of Britain, The Magic Arts in Celtic Britain, The History and Origins of Druidism,* and many other wretched tomes. Save your time and money.

Leon E. Stover and Bruce Kraig. *Stonehenge, the Indo-European Heritage.* Nelson-Hall, 1978. A harsh but fascinating look at the people associated with the various stages of Stonehenge's construction. The bibliography and research notes are good, but dated.

Norbertas Velius. *The World Outlook of the Ancient Balts.* Mintis Publishers (Vilnius), 1989. It's amazing how similar the Paleopagan Balts were to the Celts! This text on Baltic folklore and customs will be very useful in creating nature-based rituals.

Calvert Watkins, editor. *The American Heritage Dictionary of Indo-European Roots, 2nd Edition.* Houghton Mifflin Co., 2000.

I do *not* recommend Robert Graves's *The White Goddess,* nor any of the works of D. J. Conway *(Celtic Magic, Norse Magic,* etc.), Tom Cross, aka "Tadhg MacCrossan" *(The Sacred Cauldron),* Murry Hope *(Practical Celtic Magic),* Douglas Monroe *(21 Lessons of Hogwash),* Edward Williams, aka "Iolo Morganwg" *(Welsh Triads Vol. 3, The Barddas)*—source of much of

Monroe's garbage—nor any works by others based on the writings of any of these mentioned authors.

Over 90 percent of what is available in print about the Paleopagan Druids is nonsense, so read carefully and look for unverified (and/or unverifiable) assumptions, nationalistic biases, scientistic dogmas, monotheistic reinterpretations, Victorian whitewashes, references to Atlantis and/or ancient Egypt and/or UFOs, claims of intact underground family traditions of Druidism, "sacred druid trees" that are actually North American vines and so on. Also beware of works filled with racism, anti-Semitism, sexism (patriarchal or matriarchal), hetero- or homophobia, chapters (or entire books) on "Celtic Shamanism" or "Culdees," etc.

When in doubt, consult your nearest tree . . .

APPENDIX B

Online and Offline Resources

Here are most of the Mesopagan or Neopagan Druidic and/or Celtic Spirituality organizations discussed in this book. Names and Web site addresses, especially for the smaller groups, may change at a moment's notice. I suggest staying up-to-date with the Druid Network, as they seem to be doing a splendid job keeping track of zillions of groups.

Ancient Order of Druids in America
P.O. Box 1181, Ashland, OR 97520, USA
www.aoda.org
info@aoda.org

An Ceile De
Duncauld, Cauldhame Kippen Scotland FK8 3HL
www.ceilede.co.uk

Àr nDraíocht Féin: A Druid Fellowship
P.O. Box 17874, Tucson, AZ 85731–7874, USA
www.adf.org
adf-office@adf.org

Avalon College of Druidry
www.avaloncollege.org
alferian@avaloncollege.org

Avalon Mystery School
www.avalonmysteryschool.net

Axe and Oak
excoboard.com/exco/index.php?boardid=337

British Druid Order
P.O. Box 635, Halifax, England HX2 6WX
www.druidry.co.uk
sparrowhawk@britishdruidorder.co.uk

Cathbad's Wild Ideas
www.wildideas.net/cathbad

Celtic Christian Webring
www.webring.com (requires search)

Council of British Druid Orders
Liz Murray, Liaison Officer, BM Oakgrove, London WC1N
3XX, England

CR Journal
www.livejournal.com/community/cr_r

Daughters of the Flame
www.obsidianmagazine.com/DaughtersoftheFlame
daughters_of_the_flame@yahoo.ca

Druid Clan of Dana
Olivia Robertson Fellowship of Isis Clonegal Castle,
Enniscorthy, Ireland
www.druid-clan-of-dana.de/DCODwelc.htm
info@fellowshipofisis.com

Druid Network
P.O. Box 3533, Whichford, Shipston on Stour Warwickshire,
CV36 5YB England
www.druidnetwork.org
office@druidnetwork.org

Druid Order of the Sacred Grove
www.geocities.com/jaronmcllyr/Homepage.html
druid_order_sacred_grove@yahoo.com

Henge of Keltria
PO Box 4305, Clarksburg, WV 26302 USA
www.keltria.org
Keltria-Office@keltria.org

Imbas
www.imbas.org
imbas@imbas.org

Insular Order of Druids
www.insular.org.uk
contact@insular.org.uk

International Grand Lodge of Druids
www.igld.org
john.butler@fsma.com.au

Ireland's Druid School
www.druidschool.com
info@druidschool.com

Loyal Arthurian Warband
www.warband.org
pendragon@warband.org

Modern Druids Collection
www.geocities.com/druidarchives/
mikerdna@hotmail.com

Nemeton
technovate.org/web/nemeton

Ord na Brighideach
www.ordbrighideach.org
Christie@ordbrighideach.org

***Ord na Darach Gile:* Order of White Oak**
www.whiteoakdruids.org
membership@whiteoakdruids.org

Order of Bards Ovates & Druids
OBOD, PO Box 1333, Lewes, East Sussex BN7 1DX,
England
www.druidry.org
OBOD@druidry.org

Order of the Mithril Star
www.mithrilstar.org
groups.yahoo.com/group/mithrilstar

Reformed Druids of North America
The Archdruid Carleton College, Northfield, MN 55057 USA
www.geocities.com/mikerdna
groups.yahoo.com/group/RDNAtalk/
mikerdna@hotmail.com

Secular Order of Druids
www.warband.org/secular_order_of_druids.htm

Sisterhood of Avalon
PO Box 842, Pagosa Springs, CO 81147, USA
www.sisterhoodofavalon.org
BoardSecretary@sisterhoodofavalon.org

Summerlands
The Summerlands, Inc., 7015 University Drive NW,
Huntsville, AL 35806 USA
summerlands.com
searles@summerlands.com

APPENDIX C

*Paleo-, Meso-, Neo-, and Reconstructionist Paganism**

The history of the term *Pagan* is long and complex, and during most of it the word was used as an insult. Today there are many people who proudly call *ourselves* Pagan, and we use the word differently from the ways that most mainstream Westerners do. To us, "Pagan" is a general term for religions that are polytheistic (have multiple deities) and/or pan(en)theistic (believing that the divine is everywhere and/or is in everything), and usually focused on nature, whether those faiths are old or new.

That, however, tends to be too broad a definition for many uses, so subcategories have been named:

Paleopaganism refers to the original tribal faiths of Europe, Africa, Asia, the Americas, Oceania, and Australia, when they were (or in some cases, still are) practiced as intact belief systems. Of the so-called "Great Religions of the World," Classic Hinduism (prior to the influx of Islam into India), Taoism (before the arrival of Buddhism), and Shinto (ditto) fall under this category. Druidism as it existed prior to the genocide campaigns of the Roman Empire and the Roman Church was all Paleopagan.

Mesopaganism is the word used for those religions founded as attempts to recreate, revive, or continue what their founders *thought of* as the "traditional" Paleopagan ways of their ances-

---

*This discussion is taken from my other works, especially *Bonewits's Essential Guide to Witchcraft and Wicca* and *The Pagan Man*.

303

tors (or predecessors), but which were heavily influenced (accidentally, deliberately, or involuntarily) by the monotheistic and dualistic worldviews of Judaism, Christianity, and/or Islam (or nontheistic Buddhism). Examples of Mesopagan belief systems would include Freemasonry, Rosicrucianism, Spiritualism, the many African diasporic faiths (such as Voudoun, Santeria, or Macumba), Sikhism, and most of Modern Hinduism, all of which have been influenced by Islam and/or Christianity. Hinduism has also been influenced by Buddhism, as have Taoism, Shinto, and the Tibetan Bon religion. Many liberal religious movements, such as Christian Science, New Thought, Unity, etc., can be thought of as Mesopagan, though their founders and some current members might be horrified to do so. Most of Europe's Christians through much of its history were unconscious Mesopagans. Druidism, as it was practiced by the Masonic-influenced fraternal movements in Europe and the Celtic Isles, is a classic example of Mesopagan philosophy, if not always religion. Druidism as it was revived/re-invented by the Reformed Druids of North America (see Chapter 6) in the 1960s definitely began as a Mesopagan movement, but for many of its members became Neopagan in the 1970s and later.

Neopaganism refers to those religions created since 1960 or so (though many of them had literary roots going back to the mid-1800s), that have attempted to blend what their founders perceived as the best aspects of different types of Paleopaganism with modern "Aquarian Age" ideals, while consciously striving to eliminate as much as possible of the traditional Western monotheism and dualism. As this book demonstrates, there are many Neopagan Druids around in the early twenty-first century.

Reconstructionist Pagans are people who may be either Meso- or Neopagans. What makes them distinctive is a strong emphasis on scholarship in their work, a wide streak of conservatism in their practices ("if the ancients didn't do it, we won't either") that sometimes leads to snobbery towards other Pagans, and a dislike of organizational structures and leaders. Some Recon-Pagan groups that are liberal about dropping ancient customs (such as celebrating holy days on specific dates) and adopting modern ones (such as celebrating them on the nearest weekend) may choose to use the term "Revivalist" Paganism.

These terms do not delineate clear-cut categories. Historically, there are often periods, whether of decades or centuries, when Paleopaganism is blending into Mesopaganism, or Mesopaganism into Neopaganism. Furthermore, many of the founders and members of Mesopagan or Neopagan groups prefer to believe (or at least declare) that they are being genuinely Paleopagan in their beliefs and practices. This "myth of continuity" (as anthropologists call it) is in keeping with the habits of most founders and members of new religions throughout human existence.

For the purposes of this book, as with my parallel book on witchcraft, we need to stress that the move from Paleopaganism to Christianity in Europe was particularly slow and torturous (sometimes literally). History books will speak of particular parts of Europe as having been "converted" to Christianity in particular years or decades, when all too often the conversions were only skin-deep, and only among the upper classes.

Appendix D

Some Notes on the Irish in This Book

The primary non-English language used in this book from time to time is Modern Irish. Any book on ancient and modern Druids could have easily focused on Welsh instead, since Ireland and Wales were the two cultures whose druidic castes survived the longest as intact social and religious systems, or else Gaulish, since the oldest (presumed) druidic materials, such as the "Cologny Calendar" (see Chapter 12), that we have are written in that extinct tongue. But Irish is the language I have tried to learn and whose culture I have studied the most among the several Celtic strains in my ancestry (Irish, Welsh, Scots, Breton, and Gaulish), not because it is demonstrably superior in any particular sense, but because Érin, Danu, the Dagda, and Bridget have always called to me more strongly than their equally worthy counterparts in Wales, Scotland, Brittany, or France.

When I use Irish in this book, it will almost always be associated with a translation into English (or other vernacular langauges in which this work appears), so the average reader need only know a few important details about the Irish language(s). Firstly, that Old and Middle Irish, and Modern Irish for a century, had no official spelling rules, merely customs that scribes and authors nodded to now and then. So you will often see the same word show up in different texts with different spellings.

Secondly, the "strong" accents that appear on vowels, as in "á, é, í, ó, ú" and "Á, É, Í, Ó, and Ú," called *fadas* by Irish speakers, merely indicate a long vowel with the usual European sounds: "ah, ay, ee, oh, oo."

Thirdly, when you see an "h" after a consonant, that indicates that the consonant is "aspirated" or pronounced with a breathiness that sometimes makes it completely vanish. This use of "h" was a typesetter's solution in the early twentieth century to the problem of setting type with standard (i.e., English) typefonts, none of which had the dotted consonants that Irish typefonts had for aspirated consonants.

Fourthly, you will see many occasions where "impossible" consonant combinations will occur, such as "mb" or "nd" at the beginnings of words. These indicate "eclipsis," where particular grammatical situations call for the initial sound of a word to change dramatically. Usually you can simply ignore the second consonant, which has been "eclipsed" by the first. For example, the word for druidism (or magic) in Modern Irish is *draíocht,* which is pronounced, "dree-ocht." When the possessive adjective "ár" (our) is put in front of it, as in the name of the Druid organization I founded in 1983, *Ár nDraíocht Féin,* the "d" sound vanishes so that the phrase is pronounced, "arn ree-ocht fane," which means "our own Druidism."

Lastly, there are many different dialects of Modern Irish and there were probably many more in the past, so don't worry too much about how you pronounce the Irish to yourself while reading this book. Someone, somewhere, in Irish history probably said the words the same way you are! If you decide to learn Modern Irish, your teacher (and/or your tapes/CDs/DVDs) will have their own preferences for pronunciation—just pick one dialect and stick with it. Personally, I tend to use the Official national Irish taught by the Irish government via radio and the *Buntús Cainte* ("Beginning Speech") teaching books and tapes/CDs.

APPENDIX E

Some Etymological Notes on Indo-European Clergy Terms

As my long-time readers know, I am fond of researching the historical origins and evolution of words used in the fields of magic and religion. In the pages that follow, asterixes at the beginning of words indicate constructed forms, not footnotes.

The English word "priest" or "priestess" comes from a PIE root *per-*, meaning "forward, through, early, before, first," via *-pres-gwu-*, meaning "going before." A priest/ess does go before altars or idols to perform rituals, but this could also have originally meant that the clergy were the "first" or most important social function, which may be why Dumézil called it that. Other PIE roots spelled the same way, *per-*, lead to families of words based on the concepts of "to lead, pass over, try, risk, strike, mediate, sell." Some of the resulting words include "importune," "port," "espresso," "interpret," "oppress," and "pornography"—all of which could lead to fruitful meditations . . .

Godi and *godia*, the Germanic terms for priest and priestess, come from the word "God," not too surprisingly. That word's origins are a little blurry, as there are arguments deriving it from both PIE roots *gheu-*, "to pour (a libation)" and *gheu(e)-*, "to call or invoke." Since these are both things that priests and priestesses do, perhaps it doesn't matter. However, I find it amusing to contemplate the similar sounding PIE roots *gheu-*, "to yawn or gape," and *ghau-*, a variant of a PIE root meaning "gap, chasm" and the source of the Greek word *khaos*, or "chaos." Since the oldest deities in Indo-European myth are associated with chaos (see the "Wars in Heaven" in Chapter 2), the very word "God" itself hearkens back to that time.

The commonest Latin term for priests and priestesses seems to have been *sacerdos,* from the PIE root **sak,* "to sanctify." An extension of this, **sak-ro-,* is the source of "sacred," not too surprisingly. A further extension, **sak-ro-dhot,* "performer of sacred rites," is where *sacerdos* comes from. This, however, was a generic term. If a priest or priestess was a devotee of a particular deity, other terms were used.

Flamen and *flaminica,* other names given in ancient Rome to a priest or priestess (or the wife of a priest), both come from PIE **bhlad-(s)men,* "worship thinker" or a "priest of a particular deity," extended from **bhlad-,* "to worship."

Brahman is the primary term used in Sanskrit for a priest. It comes from the PIE root **bhragh-men-,* meaning "form or ritual form." Sanskrit turned this root into *brahma,* "prayer or ritual formulation" and *brahman,* "priest" or "the one of the prayer," "religious devotion in general," "spiritual knowledge," "a knower of Vedic texts or spells," and *Brahmin,* "a member of the priestly caste," as well as that entire caste.

While there doesn't seem to be a word for "priestess" in Sanskrit now easily available, one of the variant pronunciations of *brahma* refers to a "woman married according to the brahman rite"† (the "highest" of the eight forms of marriage, one where a dowry was not needed) with a symbolic connection to Durga or Sarasvati—the Vedic equivalents to the Irish Morrigan and Bridget—and *brahmanai* can mean a brahman's wife, a female member of the brahmin caste, or the personified female energy *(Shakti)* of the deity Brahma.‡ There are also now *brahmacharinis* ("female students" of priestcraft) who are young women being trained to function as Vedic priestesses (against much opposition from the priests), but they are required to take nun-like vows of perpetual virginity and chastity, which I doubt the brahmans are required to do.

---

† *Capelle's Sanskrit-English Dictionary.*
‡ *Cologne Digital Sanskrit Lexicon.*

When a brahman priest is compared with other kinds of priests (by Hindus and their Vedic predecessors), he is usually considered to be the best educated kind, who would be able to correct mistakes in rituals and supervise the other priests.

Other major Vedic priests are the *hotr, adhvaryu,* and *udgatr.* The *hotr* is the offerer of oblations or burnt-offerings, a sacrificer who at a sacrifice ritual invokes the Gods or recites the *Rg-Veda* (the oldest book of hymns to the Vedic Gods). This term is often applied to Agni, the Vedic fire deity, as is *bramana.*

The *adhvaryu* was one whose job was to "measure the ground, to build the altar, to prepare the sacrificial vessels, to fetch wood and water, to light the fire, to bring the animal and immolate it; whilst engaged in these duties, they had to repeat the hymns of the *Yajur-Veda,* hence that Veda itself is also called *Adhvaryu.*" Interesting, the wife of this sort of priest was called by the same term.

The *udgatr* is a Vedic priest who chants the hymns of the *Sama-Veda,* which, like the *Yajur-Veda,* repeats many hymns from the older *Rg-Veda.*

A less well-known (to Westerners anyway) Sanskrit word for a priest is *rtvijk,* which means "one who sacrifices regularly, at the proper times," and contains the four above mentioned priests as subsets.† However, it is important to remember that all doctors, lawyers, teachers, and other professionals were originally members of the Brahmin caste.

The ancient Greeks had many words for priest and priestess. Probably the most common were *hiereus* and *hiereia,* respectively. These like many others, were based on the root *hieros,* meaning both "superhuman, mighty, divine, wonderful" and that which is "holy or hallowed," or its close relative *hiera,* "offerings, sacrifices, victims." Both are rooted in the PIE *eis-, source of words related to passion, anger, power, holiness, madness, and epilepsy. The *hier-* roots are themselves the sources of dozens of religion-related terms, including *hierophant* ("shower of the sacred") and *hieroglyph* ("sacred sign").

† Ibid.

So at last we finally come to the Paleopagan Druids! *Draoi* in Irish comes from the same root as the English *druid*—the PIE root **deru-* or **dreu-*, "to be firm, solid, steadfast," hence the specialized senses of "wood," "tree," and things made from wood. Several old and current words in English, including "tree," "truce," "true," "trow" "troth," "trust," and "tryst," etc., as well as "dour," "endure," "obdurate" (stubborn), all come from these PIE roots (the latter ones from a variant of it, **dru-ro-*).

The **dru-* variant gives us the Greek *dryad* (tree spirit) via Greek *drus*, oak. The English word is traced not directly to Celtic roots but via the Latin *druides*, assumed to come from the Celtic compound **dru-wid*, "strong seer." *Draoi* seems more directly associated with the Irish *dair*, the primary meaning of which is "oak," but which has secondary meanings via puns to words meaning "by" in religious exclamations (as in "By the Gods!") and "bull." A slightly different pronunciation (and thereby well within druidic punning range), now spelled *dáir*, means "heat" in a cow (being ready to breed), the act of cattle mating, and "urge, fit, frenzy." All of this ties nicely (if crudely) with the Dagda, the Irish God of fire, druidism, and fertility, and his omnifunctional counterparts in the other Indo-European cultures (see Appendix F).

Also worth a closer look is the number of related words† that all tie into the concepts of fire, light, and shining, especially the derivatives of the PIE root **bhel-*, the four major groups of which are:

1. *"To shine, flash, burn; shining white and various bright colors."* This is probably the source of the Gaulish god Belenos, the Arthurian knight Belenus, the Irish festival of Beltaine, the Germanic *blitz*, meaning flash or lighten (as in lightning), the English words "blaze," "blond," and "blush." Ironically, via an extension of the root to **bhleg-*, meaning "to shine, flash, burn," this can also mean "black"

---

†*American Heritage Dictionary of Indo-European Roots* again.

or "blackened" (as in burnt), as well as the Latin *fulgere* and *fulmen*, "lightning" and "thunderbolt."

2. *"To blow, swell; with derivatives referring to various round objects and to the notion of tumescent masculinity."* Not surprisingly, this is the source of the English words "bowl," "ball," "bull" (via Germanic), and "phallus" (Greek). This is why phallic deities usually "have a lot of balls," literally. Then there's the Old High German *bald* meaning "bold" or brave, found in the name of the Norse God Balder (and probably also the modern English sense of "bald").

3. *"To thrive or bloom."* This is the source of words such as "foliage" and "bloom," as well as "flower" (both verb and noun). As *bhlo-to,* possibly in the sense of "to swell, gush, spurt," it gave rise (you should pardon the expression) to Germanic words meaning "blood," "bleeding," and "blessing" (consecrating with blood), as well as "blade" in both the sense of grass and weapons.

4. *"To cry out, yell."* This is the source of the English word "bell," in the sense of a sound that a stag makes, from Old English *bellan,* "to bellow, bark, or roar," as well as "bell" the musical instrument, "bellow," "bawl," and "belch."

As an exercise for the reader I will leave them to count just how many of these various meanings are appropriate to consider when studying the adventures of the omnifunctional Indo-European fire deities, especially the male ones, discussed in the following appendix.

APPENDIX F

Omnifunctional Indo-European Deities and an African Cousin

An interesting example of related Indo-European characters can be found in the myths of the Vedic Agni, Norse Thor, the Irish Dagda, the Greek Hermes,* and the Greek Heracles (Roman Hercules). The first four are fire or lightning deities and Heracles is the son of one (Zeus, the hurler of thunderbolts and guardian of the celestial fire stolen by Prometheus). The first four of them were originally omnifunctional deities, in that they exercised powers or exhibited characteristics of all of the Dumézilian functions.

Even Heracles? Yes, if we follow the classical traditions that there had been an earlier "Egyptian Heracles" who was a king, a law-bringer and engineer, a mighty warrior, and a digger of canals, then add the Greek stories of his frequent madness, which would tie him into the Outsiders, who are often considered insane.

Agni, the Dagda, and Hermes are all depicted as having been the first priest, due to their fire connection. Most of them are red-haired, have a two-ended or two-sided weapon (Thor's hammer, Hermes' caduceus, the Dagda's and Heracles' clubs), which for Thor and the Dagda at least can both kill and resurrect. Most of them are associated with snakes. Thor, the Dagda,

*I am indebted for the inclusion of Hermes into this list to Paul-Louis van Berg, whose essay "Hermes and Agni: a Fire-God in Greece?" appears in the *Proceedings of the Twelfth Annual UCLA Indo-European Conference (2000)*, JIE Monograph Series, No. 40, published by Institute for the Study of Man, 2001.

and Heracles each have an embarrassing story—at least to ma-
cho warriors—of having to dress as a woman to accomplish
some important goal (although I am reminded of cross-
dressing ordeals in college fraternities and old naval rituals involving a sailor's crossing of the equator, a liminal border, for
the first time). While Hermes was, like the others, a phallic deity, he was also depicted as bisexual. Each of these deities shows
either or both of the safe and dangerous sides of the functions
(see "The Light and the Dark" in Chapter 3). I suspect that if
I knew more about Agni, I could change "most" in the above
sentences to "all" in a few places.

What some might think of as a blow to an exclusively Indo-
European source for these particular omnifunctional characters
(one critique of Dumézil is that he actually was describing human universals, not something specifically Indo-European) can,
oddly enough, be found in Yoruba mythology! These are the
religious stories of a medieval kingdom of West Africa and the
source of much of modern Afro-Caribbean Paganism. In these
tales the red-headed Lightning and Fire God Chango has a
double-sided weapon (an axe) that can kill or cure, is associated
with snakes, and once had to cross-dress in order to escape from
an enemy.

Rather than evidence that IE-comparisons are simply human
universals, I see this as possible evidence of Indo-European influence on the Yoruba peoples. How could this have happened?
I suspect it was via the Greek, Roman, and Vandal kingdoms
that were based on the site of Carthage, but which reached all
the way to the Atlantic and the Straits of Gibraltar. These IE
cultures could have influenced the Yoruba people through the
cross-Saharan trade routes into West Africa. Other possibilities
are through trade between the Yoruba and the Greek-founded
city of Alexandria, Egypt, as well as the trade routes up and
down the Atlantic coastline from Britain all the way down to
the Niger River, which could have brought in Celtic, Germanic,
Roman, and Greek influences.

I know this suggestion will upset the Afro-Centric scholars a
bit but, you know, influences can go in both directions, includ-

ing full circle. A character in the myths of the speakers of the original African mother tongue could have been carried along through the Sudan and Egypt via the Afro-Asiatic language, to Proto-Indo-European, to Hellenic, Latin, Celtic, and Germanic speakers, then through any or all of those to the Yoruba speakers. Or one group of ancient Africans who knew the particular stories of Chango might have gone west from the Sudan instead of north into the Middle East with the other migrants, I suppose.

Why are these omnifunctional Indo-European characters (the red-haired Thunder/Fire Gods) not universal ones? Because other sub-Saharan African cultures (and most non-IE cultures) don't have nearly-identical stories to that of Chango. Significantly, Yoruba culture had the same social structure common to the Indo-European cultures, with a clergy caste equivalent to the druids, flamens, brahmins, etc. All of which is one of the reasons why I've always felt that African-Americans who want to become druids have as much right as anyone else with "pure" IE genetic or cultural ancestry. After all, most African-Americans are descended from the Yoruba or nearby peoples on one side and Celtic and Germanic peoples on the other—and welcoming them is a great way to screen out racists from your druid organizations!

I should mention that there are a few "multifunctional" characters, such as the Norse Odin, who combine the fifth function with some aspects of the first and second ones. The Irish Bridget is clearly a multifunctional, fire based one (and "daughter" of the Dagda), who is not, however, connected to the fifth function (that I know of). Jupiter Optimus Maximus in Rome and the Morrigan in Ireland, who are not fire deities, nonetheless seem to be omnifunctional ones. So as with everything else in Indo-European studies, the paradigm of the functions is a huge canvas upon which one must paint with broad strokes, not expecting every piece of it to look photographically detailed. That would require omniscience, something neither this amateur nor the many professionals in the field have yet managed to attain.

In fact, just as I was finishing this book, I stumbled over a discussion of PIE thunder/warrior gods at Axe and Oak, a Web site* dedicated to various Reconstructionist Pagan traditions. Their conversation there suggested to me that several other omnifunctional gods could be added to those mentioned in this appendix. Truly, data is infinite!

*At excoboard.com/exco/index.php?boardid=337

APPENDIX G

The Classic ADF Liturgical Design
(Summer 1991)

This is the outline of how ADF ritual was being done in the early 1990s. As was mentioned in Chapter 17, current ADF practice is still quite similar, but various parts of the ritual are merged so that it doesn't seem quite so intimidating to newcomers. Here you can see them in their full glory.

Preliminary Ritual Activity

    A. Briefing
    B. Individual meditations and prayers
    C. Lighting the Sacred Fire(s)
    D. Pouring the Sacred Waters
    E. Consecrating the Sacred Pole/Tree
    F. Consecrating the altar and tools

1st Phase: Starting the Rite and Establishing the Group Mind

CLEAR-CUT BEGINNING: CONSECRATION OF TIME

    1. Musical signal
    2. Opening prayer

CONSECRATION OF SPACE AND OF PARTICIPANTS

    3. The processional/sigil marking
    4. Purification(s) of participants

5. Purification(s) of site
6. Honoring the Earth-Mother

CENTERING, GROUNDING, MERGING

7. The grove meditation
8. Unity chant/song
9. Stating ritual purpose and historical precedent
10. Naming deity(ies) of the occasion and reasons for choice

2nd Phase: Recreating the Cosmos and Preliminary Power Raising

DESCRIBING THE VERTICAL AXIS

11. Planting the Cosmic Tree/Honoring the Sacred Pole
12. Evoking the Gatekeeper/Defining the ritual center
13. Evoking the Fire and Water deities & linking to center

GAINING ASSISTANCE AND PREVENTING INTERFERENCE

14. Invoking the bardic deity(ies) or spirit(s)
15. Acknowledgment of the Outsiders
16. Filling Out the Cosmic Picture
    Example—Triad invocation of nature spirits, ancestors, deities
    Example—Invocation of helpful beings of each world/ realm
    Example—Invocation of helpful beings by province/ function
17. The settling and focusing

3rd Phase: Major Sending of Power to Deity(ies) of the Occasion

18. Descriptive invocation of deity(ies) of the occasion

PRIMARY POWER RAISING

19. Praise offerings, dance, libations, etc.
20. The sacrifice
21. Seeking the omen of return

4th Phase: Receiving and Using the Returned Power

PREPARATION FOR THE RETURN

22. Meditation upon personal and group needs
23. Induction of receptivity
24. Consecration agreement

RECEPTION OF POWER FROM DEITY(IES) OF THE OCCASION

25. Consecration and sharing
26. Acceptance of individual blessings
27. Reinforcement of group bonding
28. *Optional*—Spell casting or rite of passage

5th Phase: Unwinding and Ending the Ceremony

UNWINDING THE ENERGY PATTERNS CREATED

29. Thanking of entities invited in reverse order
30. Thanking the Gatekeeper and closing the Gates
31. Affirmation of past/future continuity and success
32. Unmerging, regrounding and recentering: meditation
33. Draining off excess power: the restoration

CLEARCUT ENDING: DECONSECRATION OF TIME & SPACE

34. Final benediction
35. Announcement of end
36. Dissolving the sigil
37. Musical signal

Notes

A fuller explanation of the theory behind this outline, which is based on my "common worship pattern" can be found in my *Rites of Worship: A Neopagan Approach*. An old version of my "Step-by-Step through a Druid Worship Ceremony" can be found on the ADF Web site* and fuller, updated instructions will be found in a future book.

---

*At www.adf.org/rituals/explanations/stepbystep.html.

Index

Mesopaganism (Mesopagan Druids),
61–104. *See also* Reformed
Druids of North America
common beliefs, 161–65
"survivals" and revivals, 61–83
use of term, 303–4
Michell, John, viii, 295
Midsummer, 180, 186
Migrations, 14–20
Milesians, 270–71
Mishmash of Hasidic Druidism,
91–99
Misogyny, 52, 126–27, 151–53
Missionary Order of the Celtic Cross
(MOCC), 99
Mistletoe, xxi–xxii, 50, 187–88
Mists of Avalon (Bradley), 118–19
Mona Antiqua Restaurata
(Rowlands), 68
Monotheism, 51, 162–63
Monothesisism, 21–22
Monroe, Douglas, 127, 147–54
Mormonism, 143–44
Morrigan, 37
"Hymn to the Morrigan," 276–78
Mother Grove, The, 71
Mount Haemus Grove, 70
Munster, 43
Murray, Colin, 79–80
Murray, Elizabeth, 80
Musical instruments, 209
Mythological revolution, 21–24

Natural History (Pliny), xxi–xxii
Nature worship, 214–16
Nazism (Nazis), 13–14
Nemeton, 48. *See also* Sacred groves
Nemyss, 203–4
Neolithic Age, 5–11
Neopaganism (Neopagan Druids),
107–40. *See also specific groups*
Celtic Reconstructionists, 130–37
common beliefs, 170–77
FAQs about, 123–27
future of, 281–85
online resources, 137–40,
299–302
solitary druids, 128–30

use of term, 304
Nevsky, Alexander, Feast of, 194
New Celtic Review, 79–80
New Moons, 187–88
New Reformed Druids of North
America (NRDNA), 87, 88–89
rituals, 232–39
NicDhàna, Kathryn Price, 137
Nichols, Ross, viii–ix, 78–80,
180–81, 218
Noah, 15*n*
Nybor, 201

Oak Leaves, 111*n*
Oak trees, 47–48
Oberon and the Divine Musicians,
Feast of, 192
OBOD. *See* Order of Bards Ovates &
Druids
O'Dubhainn, Searles and Deborah,
138
Ogham, 150–51, 261–67
Oghma, Feast of, 194
Oimelc, 179, 183, 184–85
Olmsted, Garrett S., 187–88
Online resources, 137–40, 299–302
Ord Brighideach: A Brigidine Order
of Flamekeepers, 136, 301
Order of Bards Ovates & Druids
(OBOD), viii–ix, 78–81
ADF compared with, 113–16
Awen, 200–201
Campaign for Individual
Ecological Responsibility,
214–16
common beliefs, 165–68
contact information, 301
membership, 281
rituals, 223–31
Order of Common Worship
for Summer, 233–37
for Winter, 237–39
Order of Melchesidek, 143, 146
Order of the Mithril Star (OMS), 99,
301
Order of the Universal Bond, 71–72
Ord na Darach Gile: Order of White
Oak, 120–21, 136–37, 301

About the Author

Isaac Bonewits is North America's leading expert on ancient and modern Druidism, Witchcraft, and the rapidly growing Earth Religions movement. A practicing Neopagan priest, scholar, teacher, bard, and polytheologian for over thirty-five years, he has coined much of the vocabulary and articulated many of the issues that have shaped the rapidly growing Neopagan community, with opinions both playful and controversial.

As an author, a singer-songwriter, and a "spellbinding" speaker, he has educated, enlightened and entertained two generations of modern Goddess worshippers, nature mystics, and followers of other minority belief systems, and has explained these movements to journalists, law enforcement officers, college students, and academic researchers.

As of 2006, he lives with his wife, Phaedra, his son Arthur, and too many critters in Rockland County, New York, a reasonably safe twenty-five miles away from Manhattan.

CPSIA information can be obtained at www.ICGtesting.com
Printed in the USA
LVOW13s1805200214

374552LV00001B/106/P